Citizen Sarris, American Film Critic

Essays in Honor of Andrew Sarris

edited by Emanuel Levy

The Scarecrow Press, Inc.
Lanham, Maryland, and London
2001

SCARECROW PRESS, INC.

Published in the United States of America
by Scarecrow Press, Inc.
4720 Boston Way, Lanham, Maryland 20706
www.scarecrowpress.com

4 Pleydell Gardens, Folkestone
Kent CT20 2DN, England

British Library Cataloguing-in-Publication Information Available

Library of Congress Cataloging-in-Publication Data

Citizen Sarris, American film critic : essays in honor of Andrew Sarris / edited by
Emanuel Levy.
    p. cm.
    Includes bibliographical references.
    ISBN 0-8108-3891-5 (cloth : alk. paper)
    1. Sarris, Andrew—Criticism and interpretation. I. Sarris, Andrew. II. Levy,
Emanuel, 1947–
PN1998.3.S275 A53 2001
791.43'092—dc21   00-046382

⊗™   The paper used in this publication meets the minimum requirements of
American National Standard for Information Sciences—Permanence of
Paper for Printed Library Materials, ANSI/NISO Z39.48-1992.
Manufactured in the United States of America.

Contents

Part Five: Sarris the Provocative Critic

Part Six: Sarris the Career Maker

Part Seven: Sarris the Creator of American Movie Culture

Part Eight: Sarris's Impact Overseas

vi   *Contents*

The Fundamental Film Teacher

Martin Scorsese

I consider Andrew Sarris to be one of the most fundamental and valued teachers. His writings led me to see the genius in American movies at a time when the cinema was considered a mindless form of entertainment, worthy of serious attention only if it came from Europe or Asia. Sarris's passion, his enthusiasm, his wonderful ability to articulate for me and many others as well what we unconsciously felt about the styles of various directors played a truly pivotal role in my life. For that, I'll always be grateful.

Preface

𝒥n a 1993 meeting of the Los Angeles Film Critics Association (LAFCA), I was talking casually to my friend and colleague Mike Wilmington, who was then writing for the *Los Angeles Times,* about the state of film criticism. Andrew Sarris's name naturally came up, and we both reminisced about our first encounter with *The American Cinema* and the long-lasting effects Sarris's book has had on us. "Wouldn't it be nice to honor Andrew with a Festschrift?" I asked. "Excellent idea," Mike responded enthusiastically.

That night, in a moment of inspiration and audacity, I drafted a letter to Molly Haskell, Andrew's wife and a distinguished critic and author in her own right, whose book *From Reverence to Rape* I have read, revered, and used in several of my film classes. Rather naively I proposed to edit a "surprise" tribute volume, a collection of essays by noted filmmakers, film critics, and scholars, to celebrate Andy as the most influential critic in American film history. I say naively because I failed to realize how small and intimate the film world is; within several months, somebody spilled the beans to Andy and the Festschrift was no longer a surprise.

Also naively, I gave myself two years to bring the project to fruition, not realizing the busy schedule of the distinguished contributors I had lined up. It took much longer than I had anticipated, some of it because of my juggling two full-time careers—as a film professor and as a *Variety* critic—and some of it because of the immense challenge and scope of this book.

I would like to apologize to Andy and Molly for these delays. I also would like to apologize for sometimes being "tough" on the contributors—my military experience in the Israeli army came in handy—by incessantly calling and reminding them to write their essays. While in New York in January 1997 for the meetings of the National Society of Film Critics, Liz Weis, the Society's executive director, said to me: "You must have scared many critics; they are all working on their essays." Indeed, about half a dozen arrived into the voting meeting in person with their essays in hand. I was rewarded.

Almost every critic and professor I approached immediately responded with excitement. I began with a list of two dozen critics and half a dozen directors. Over the past five years, the list kept changing—for various reasons—and I am proud to say that the book contains essays by thirty-eight writers. I always knew that all those who said they would love to contribute meant it, even if circumstances prevented them from doing it.

There were other unanticipated issues. I decided to approach Pauline Kael and some of her devoted followers, hoping that the time for rapprochement had come. Pauline was not feeling well, and she called to explain that she was not taking any writing assignments. I had not realized that the conflict between the Paulettes and the Sarrisites was still going on, at least latently. It was certainly not my intention to reignite the infamous 1960s debate. For one thing, as far as I am concerned, the battle over auteurism was long won, with Andrew emerging as triumphant. At the same time, I was saddened that none of the Paulettes was willing to participate.

The title for the tribute, *Citizen Sarris, American Film Critic,* came easy to me, and most contributors liked it. In the reissuing of *The American Cinema,* in 1995, I described the book as the "Citizen Kane of American film criticism." I still feel that way. I can't think of another film book that has revolutionized the film world in such dramatic way.

When I mentioned to some of my former Columbia professors that I was working on a Festschrift, the reaction was "but these volumes are usually for distinguished scientists like Nobel Laureates. Besides, they are hard to get published." "There's always a first," I found myself saying, and stuck by the idea.

It was clear from the beginning that the range and style of the essays would be as diverse as Andy's own writing was over the past half a century. As Andy himself observed in 1993: "And here I am, as always, too much of an academic for the journalists, and too much of a journalist for the academics." I don't think there ever was a figure as influential as Andrew Sarris in and outside academe. Perhaps philosopher Herbert Marcuse in his Berkeley days, or Roland Barthes in Paris. The whole notion of an intellectual critic, who commands power in academe but is also respected outside the campus, has always been foreign to American arts and letters. Sadly, we see less and less of these figures—Susan Sontag was one prominent force in the 1960s.

A few words are in order about the structure of the volume. Basically, I had two alternatives. One was to arrange the essays alphabetically, with no regard to their topic. The other, which I finally opted for, was to place them according to their major theme. Neither method is completely satisfying, but I think the chosen one shows the diverse range of effects of Andy's film writings, not just *The American Cinema,* on every aspect of the film world.

What is interesting is that at least half of the contributors have met Sarris in person only once or twice and yet they all feel they have known him personally. Andy's influence has been that strong, that personal, and that lasting. And it continues through his indefatigable weekly column in the *New York Observer.*

Over the years, Andy may have mellowed but, unlike other critics, he has never become nostalgic. His observation of decades ago still describes his work: "It is through the mix of two disciplines—journalism and academe—that I seek to recapture the past without foreclosing the future."

Part One

Personal Reflections

 art one begins with Andrew Sarris's foreword to his book *Confessions of a Cultist*. At the time he began writing in *Film Culture*, Sarris was barely twenty-seven, "a dangerously advanced age," as he put it, "for a writer *manque* if not *maudit*, a dreadfully uncomfortable age for a middle-class cultural guerrilla without any base, contacts, or reliable lines of supply." Sarris had been drifting "down from Morningside Heights ever deeper into the darkness of movie houses, not so much in search of a vocation as in flight from the laborious realities of careerism."

By his own admission, Sarris was "the beneficiary as well as the victim of the intellectual vacuum that occurred in movie reviewing with the death of James Agee in 1955." Passion for film, not careerism, was—and still is—the key motivation for Sarris. As he observed: "Passion is too strong a word to apply to journalistic reviewers who would be equally happy in the Real Estate departments of their publications, or to high-brow humanists who admire the late Siegfried Kracauer's *From Caligari to Hitler* simply because they, like Kracauer, are more interested in Hitler than in Caligari." Film scholarship was in such a shambles in the early 1960s that the "risks of passion were preferable to the rigidities of professionalism."

Sarris always believed that "the subject of film is larger than any one critic or the entire corps of critics." Utterly modest, he has remained grateful to film for allowing him to focus his intellectual insights and worldviews within a manageable frame.

In her personal essay "Life With Andrew . . . and Film," Sarris's wife, Molly Haskell, a distinguished critic and author in her own right, asserts: "For as long as I have known him—over thirty years—he has happily, if a

1

little unevenly (leaning this way and that), tread the line between journalism and scholarship." Reconstructing the climate of ideas back then, she notes: "There was something wonderfully outrageous in the controversies of the sixties, with Andrew and Pauline and John Simon and Dwight MacDonald going toe to toe in passionate and personal debate, frothing at the mouth, sparks flying, diatribes flowing, at parties and in the pages of the outlets both respectable and obscure." Like Haskell, most of the contributors concur that the zeitgeist has changed, with radical effects on the work of film critics at present.

Liz Weis, a former student of Sarris at Columbia, describes in "Scenes from a Friendship" Sarris's various functions as the *Village Voice* editor, the éminence grise of the National Society of Film Critics, the teacher, the employer—and the tennis player. As a player, "Andy's not just an armchair athlete/aesthete (in his words, 'a professional voyeur watching professional exhibitionists'). He was also a damn good tennis player . . . his tennis style amazingly like his prose." Few people know that Andrew has won two club championships in West Hampton against much younger men.

Weis also discloses the "bizarre" circumstances under which she got her job at the *Village Voice*. When Andy was charged at a party, "You're no feminist. . . . You've got no women on your writing staff," he said, "Of course, I do." Further challenged, "Name one," Andy named Molly. "That doesn't count; she's your wife. Name another." After a pause, Andy said, Liz Weis, "a name that probably popped into his head because I was his projectionist at school. He called me the next day with my first assignment." At the *Voice*, Weis got mostly to review political documentaries. "Why me, when the Voice had major political writers like Jack Newfield and Nat Hentoff on the staff? Because, Andy would complain, the political columnists always wanted to review blockbusters like *The Godfather* and *Jaws!*"

Roger Ebert began reading Andrew in the *Village Voice*, where he found his voice to be "clear and energetic, free of jargon and self-importance." For Ebert, Andrew was the ideal critic, "neither particularly theoretical nor doctrinaire, but in close touch with the actual experience of seeing the movie itself." One of Andrew's distinctive qualities was his ability to see every film for what it was, or as Ebert puts it: "You could never catch Sarris praising a film because the director was in the pantheon, or disliking it because the director's previous work had not passed muster. You felt that Sarris went to every movie hoping to be delighted."

Director Budd Boetticher recalls how Sarris reinvented his career, as he observes: "I hadn't seen Andrew Sarris's review of [Sam Peckinpah's] *Ride the High Country* and had no idea of his high regard for my [Randolph]

Scott films and his inference that Sam must have seriously studied all of them to do as well as he had done with his first western." As many of the contributors note, one of Sarris's main contributions was in reevaluating the work of gifted Hollywood directors whose work was either ignored or underestimated.

David Thomson recalls how he read Sarris's book *The Films of Josef von Sternberg* and found it revelatory, "exactly the way to handle a body of work and the perilous proposition that Sternberg was some kind of genius." Placing Sarris's work in both personal and social contexts, Thomson recalls a lively argument with Andrew on the staircase at the Splendid Hotel in Cannes—"You were always good on staircases." Ending on a nostalgic note, Thomson salutes Andrew, "like one prisoner to another in *La Grande Illusion*. . . . Are we and the other writers in this book the last of a dying breed?"

Hopefully not.

Confessions of a Cultist

Andrew Sarris

$\mathscr{M}$y career as a cultist began unobtrusively, if not inadvertently, in a dingy railroad flat on New York's Lower East Side back in the unlamented Eisenhower era. It was there and then that I first met Jonas and Adolfas Mekas, the genially bohemian (actually Lithuanian) editors of a new magazine called *Film Culture,* an unfortunately pompous title that always makes me think of microbic movies under glass. I had been taking an evening course in film appreciation at Columbia between meandering through graduate English and malingering in Teachers College. The movie mentor was Roger Tilton, a filmmaker (*Jazz Dance*) himself and one of *Film Culture's* first sponsors, whatever that meant. (Among other "sponsors" listed on a back page were James Agee, Shirley Clarke, David and Francis Flaherty, Lewis Jacobs, Arthur Knight, Helen Levitt, Len Lye, Hans Richter, Willard Van Dyke and Amos Vogel). Tilton sent me to the Mekas brothers, and the rest is cult history.

The brothers Mekas were generally buried under a pile of manuscripts ranging from the illegible to the unreadable, and I am afraid I only added to the confusion. The entire operation seemed hopelessly impractical to a congenital pessimist like me. I took the satirical view that we were not poor because we were pure, but pure because we were poor, and our integrity was directly proportional to our obscurity. Still, I suppose we represented a new breed of film critic. The cultural rationale for our worthier predecessors—Agee, Ferguson, Levin, Murphy, Sherwood, et al.—was they were too good to be reviewing movies. We, on the contrary, were not considered much good for anything else. Like one-eyed lemmings, we plunged headlong into the murky depths of specialization. No back pages of literary and political pulps for us. We may have lived in a ramshackle house, but we always came in the front door.

5

Somehow, the first issue of *Film Culture*—January 1955, Volume I, Number 1—had already materialized without my assistance. I was enlisted as a reviewer and editor for Number 2. I recall that I was not enchanted by the prospect of writing and editing for no money at all. It seemed almost as demeaning as paying to be published, an act of vanity I vowed never to perform even at the cost of immortality. However, my bargaining position was not enhanced by the fact that all my previous professional writing credits added up to seven movie columns in the Fort Devens *Dispatch,* within the period of my tour of duty through the Army's movie houses during the Korean war.

At the time I started writing in *Film Culture* I was not quite twenty-seven years old, a dangerously advanced age for a writer *manque* if not *maudit,* a dreadfully uncomfortable age for a middle-class cultural guerrilla without any base, contacts, or reliable lines of supply. I was of the same generation as Norman Podhoretz, but while he had been "making it" as an undergraduate at Columbia I had drifted, like Jack Kerouac, down from Morningside Heights ever deeper into the darkness of movie houses, not so much in search of a vocation as in flight from the laborious realities of careerism. Nonetheless I agree with Podhoretz that failure is more banal and more boring than success.

Indeed, I have always been impatient as a critic with characters (like Ginger Coffey) who manage to mess up every job. The trouble with failure as a subject is that it is not instructive in any way and only contributes to an audience's false sense of superiority. Unfortunately, success stories lack "charm" unless they are leavened with audience-pleasing intimations of futility. The trick of the stand-up comic and the syndicated columnist is to ingratiate himself with his audience by groveling in his own weakness and misfortunes, real and fabricated, while withholding all the evidence of his manipulative personality.

This strategy evolves from a conspiracy of the successful to delude the unsuccessful into thinking that worldly success doesn't really matter. But as I look back upon my own failure I am appalled by my unoriginal reactions of self-hatred and mean-spirited paranoia. Every block and hang-up known to the disenfranchised intellect seemed at the time uniquely personal and chock-full of anecdotal fascination.

My biggest problem was focusing my general knowledge on a specific intellectual target. Novels, short stories, plays, screenplays, poems slithered off my typewriter in haphazard spasms of abortive creation. Far from filling up trunks, I could barely jam up a drawer, and yet if I had been knowledgeable enough to understand the fantastic odds against me, I might never have invested in a typewriter. As it was, I was not even sophisticated enough to realize what a stroke of luck my meeting with the Mekas brothers turned out to be. I was always looking beyond *Film Culture* (and later the *Village Voice*) for more lucrative opportunities elsewhere. There was never a time that I would not have given up being a cultist to be a careerist. And then one day—I don't remember exactly when—I realized that if I had not yet indeed succeeded, I had at least stopped failing. I had managed at long last to function in a role I had improvised with my left hand while my right hand was knocking at all the doors of the Establishment. I had written and published a million words under my own name, and I had made contact with thousands of people, and in the process I had managed to locate myself while mediating between my readers and the screen.

In the realm of role playing, I stopped lowering my head at the epithet "cultist" as soon as I realized that the quasi-religious connotation of the term was somewhat justified for those of us who loved movies beyond all reason. No less a cultist than the late Andre Bazin had once likened film festivals to religious revivals, and a long sojourn in Paris in 1961 reassured me that film not only demanded but deserved as much faith as did any other cultural discipline. (Cultists and buffs in other areas are generally described as scholars and specialists, but interdisciplinary intolerance seems to be the eternal reaction to the old against the new.) As I remember that fateful year in Paris, deliriously prolonged conversations at sidewalk cafes still assault my ears with what in Paris passed for profundity and in New York for peculiarity. I have never really recovered from the Parisian heresy (in New York eyes) concerning the sacred importance of the cinema. Hence I returned to New York not merely a cultist but a subversive cultist with a foreign ideology.

Thereafter I could see more clearly that the main difference between a cultist and a careerist is that the cultist does not require the justification of a career to pursue his passion, and the careerist does. Indeed, passion is too strong a word to apply to journalistic reviewers who would be equally happy in the Real Estate departments of their publications, or to high-brow humanists who admire the late Siegfried Kracauer's *From Caligari to Hitler* simply because they, like Kracauer, are more interested in Hitler than in Caligari. Of course, lacking intellectual discipline, the passion of a cultist could be perverted into mindless mysticism and infantile irrationality. (I must admit that I had qualms about the title of the book after glancing at the lucid Daily News headline shortly after the Sharon Tate murders: "Police Seek Cultist.") Still, film scholarship was in such a shambles by the early sixties that the risks of passion were preferable to the rigidities of professionalism.

As I look back on the past I have very mixed feelings about all the slights I have suffered and all the furors I have caused. People were always telling me that I was lucky to be attacked in print and that the only thing that really mattered was the correct spelling of my name. However, it has been my observation that no one enjoys being attacked in print or in person no matter what publicity may accrue from the aggression. Indeed, I have been struck by the inability of critics who love dishing out abuse to the mildest reproof in return. For myself, I can't really complain in terms of any Kantian categorical imperative. He who lives by the sword of criticism must expect counterthrusts as a matter of course. All that is required of the embattled critic as a test of his courage is that he never lose faith in his own judgment. And all the slings and arrows of outraged opponents never led me to doubt the direction I had chosen as a critic. Part of my intransigence may be attributed to the relative ignorance that my generally bookish attackers displayed in the movie medium. Not that I believe (as do the maxi-McLuhanists) that books have become culturally irrelevant. On the contrary, every aspect of culture is relevant to every other aspect, and the best criticism, like the best poetry, is that which is richest in associations. Unfortunately, too many bookish film critics have perverted the notion of ecumenical erudition by snobbishly subordinating film to every other art. Whereas the late James Agee discovered cinema through his love for movies, too many of his self-proclaimed successors chose to abuse movies in the name of Kultur.

Hence I was the beneficiary as well as the victim of the intellectual vacuum that occurred in movie reviewing with the death of Agee in 1955. For reasons that I still do not fully understand, serious film reviewing on a steady basis had fallen into cultural disrepute when I started breaking into print. My very existence was generally ignored for almost eight years, a period in which I was occasionally quoted without credit. Then in 1963 I rose from obscurity to notoriety by being quoted out of context. Even so, I was treated as a relatively unique phenomenon, however invidious to the cultural establishment. The late *New York Herald Tribune* even listed me as one of the phrase-makers of the avant-garde, a distinction that helped keep me unemployable as far as the Establishment was concerned. I didn't realize at the time that slowly but surely I was gathering professional seniority in a discipline that was about to explode. I didn't even have to maneuver or manipulate. All I had to do was stand my ground, and suddenly I would find myself in the center of the cultural landscape, returning in triumph to Columbia University, a scholar more prodigal than prodigious.

Even at the time of my most painfully polemical agonies I realized that most controversies in the intellectual world are determined by the first principle of Euclidean egometry: *Two egos cannot occupy the same position of power at the same time.* It follows that the first inkling that I had acquired a position of power came when I was attacked by other critics. Ironically, my enemies were the first to alert me to the fact that I had followers. And with followers came increased responsibilities to clarify and develop my position as a critic and historian.

Still, I shall not pretend at this date that my career as a cultist has followed a preconceived pattern. Nor shall I define the role of the film critic in self-congratulatory terms applicable only to me. My response to my role as a critic has generally been intuitive, and nothing is to be gained by institutionalizing my intuitions. Every would-be critic must seek his or her own role in terms of his or her own personality and outlook. I am grateful to film for allowing me to focus my intellectual insights and worldviews within a manageable frame. I believe the subject of film is larger than any one critic or indeed the entire corps of critics. What follows is my personal view of the films that have helped me mold my consciousness. At this climactic moment of self-revelation all I can do is commend my critical soul to your mercy and understanding.

Andrew Sarris
New York City
January 1970

Life with Andrew ... and Film

Molly Haskell

*T*he delight I felt when Emanuel Levy came to me with the idea of doing a Festschrift for Andrew has turned into a kind of dazed astonishment as the thing has actually come into being. Of all the emotions that fill my heart, the chief one is gratitude—to Emanuel Levy for initiating the project and, at great expense of time and energy, finding a publisher and pursuing busy contributors, an extraordinary lineup of illustrious writers and film professionals, to take the time to write these astonishing tributes.

Of course part of me says my darling spouse–mentor deserves every word and then some; and the other part feels almost embarrassed by this outpouring. To the extent that I identify with Andrew and speak here for him, to the extent that I too am a writer who struggles to meet deadlines and pay the bills, I murmur, how can we possibly look this gift and these givers in the face, repay such generosity, accept a labor of such love?

Just as the cinema, as Andrew has often said (quoting Chabrol), is not a wave but an ocean; not a collection of one or two or three masterpieces but a wide and endlessly churning sea of tides and tributaries, collisions, and overlappings, one film calling to, answering, and enriching another; so film criticism is not the work of a few geniuses, but an aggregate of many brilliant and joyous and contentious voices, challenging and stimulated by one another. If we take as our premise that the twentieth century has been the century of film, then it makes perfect sense that the second half of the twentieth century has been the era of great film criticism. From small or little-known publications, counterculture rags and quarterlies, to the major newspapers and periodicals, dazzling reviews, and essays, reconsideration of movies is everywhere. In the last five decades, some of the best minds and

11

most talented writers have gone into the field of reviewing, and the dialogue has consequently grown sharper, more intense, more diverse.

I would like, then, to think of Andrew almost as a pretext and the Festschrift as a book that returns the favor by displaying some of these riches, featuring these critics and film professionals engaged in the activity—belles lettres—which Andrew has always insisted, over the hoots of doubters, is what film criticism is and was meant to be.

It's very unusual, after all, for a movie critic to be honored with a Festschrift, such encomiums being generally reserved for aging scholars of venerable disciplines within the loftier reaches of academe, and Andrew, though aging (aren't we all!) does not fit the mold of the ivory tower aesthete. Nor is he quite the eager, street-swift reviewer, racing from one screening room to another in the more bruising world of showbiz reporting and up-to-the-minute deadlines, preferring the long, even lofty view. For as long as I have known him—over thirty years—he has happily, if a little unevenly (leaning this way and that), tread the line between journalism and scholarship, occupying his own niche between the jaunty pages of the *Village Voice* and subsequently the *New York Observer* on the one hand and on the other various teaching posts leading to his tenure on the faculty of the Columbia School of the Arts.

Manny Farber once called him a "semi pro journalist," which Andrew quite cheerfully accepted, taking it to mean that you did it—you scribbled, became "an ink stained wretch"—for money (a little) but weren't officially a player. I take Levy's recognition of Andrew in this magnificent form to be a way of acknowledging all writers on film who have, with the same enthusiasm and eloquence, embraced the medium as an art form as capacious, as worthy of serious discussion as music or literature; and requiring even greater resources of wit and wisdom to defend it against cinephobe superciliousness at one extreme and the stultifying jargon of sanctioned film studies at the other.

In a way, Andrew's contribution to the sixties revolution—that of illuminating the glories of American cinema in the wider context of a reappraisal of popular culture—has been so completely absorbed within the larger victory that we now live in the paradoxical climate of a sophisticated and unruffled acceptance of the raunchiest, most "debased" genres and a concomitant lessening of excitement in the debate surrounding them. There was something wonderfully outrageous in the controversies of the sixties, with Andrew and Pauline and John Simon and Dwight MacDonald going toe to toe in passionate and personal debate, frothing at the mouth, sparks flying, diatribes flowing, at parties and in the pages of outlets both respectable and obscure.

Like many others, I first encountered Andrew in the pages of the *Village Voice,* where his column "Films in Focus" was blazing the trail for auteurist criticism. He took outrageous positions: Hitchcock over Bergman, John Ford over Satyajit Ray, anyone over later Fellini. His was a passionate and truly idiosyncratic voice soaring above the hum of movie reviewing, in that era before movie reviewing had become almost as hot a career choice as moviemaking.

Not only did he rescue and validate American movies, but movies validated him. Like most movie nuts of that time, he had crawled out from under a rock for just long enough to expose his views to the world; they were polemical, perverse, idiosyncratic, often cryptic, impassioned by political engagement and personal reminiscence. He had spent hours discussing film with the late Gene Archer (later a reviewer for the *New York Times*) and other enthusiasts. Andrew and Gene had memorized all the Academy Award winners in the major categories from the first ceremony to the then present.

Andrew seemed to carry the entire history of film in his head, yet he was never merely a master of trivia or a collector of obscure dates and titles. Always there was a precocious and uncanny insight into the ways of the world—or that's how it struck me when I came to see how unworldly he really was. Even before he'd set foot on the Continent, or into matrimonial waters, or even had a long-term affair, he could write of *The Blue Angel:* "If serious criticism of the cinema were not as puritanical as it is, the experiences of Lola and the Professor would seem more pertinent to the hidden world of domestic sexuality than is now the case." He was ahead of critics then, and he said it better and more succinctly than all the later theoreticians, pro and con, when he delved with lucid empathy into the realm of cinematic desire and the eternal Sternberg theme of "man's confrontation of the myths of womanhood."

He was always attuned to the wider world, never just the parochial interests of a cultist. No one could have been more surprised than he when he became a cause celebre. He credited Pauline Kael—and the *New York Times* strike in 1965, which boosted the *Village Voice*'s circulation overnight from 25,000 to 125,000—with "making him." She put him on the map with her essay "Circles and Squares," and the threat that he was perceived to represent to the sanity of public discussion in the arts was a cause then taken up by more established eminences like MacDonald and Simon, and by anyone else who cared to trash the "auteur theory," which at that time was every screenwriter in Hollywood and many fellow critics. It was both galling and flattering, but lonely. He felt besieged—nor did the French, whose cause he had championed, come to his aid. He always felt a little betrayed that Truffaut, who was coming to know and charm the American critics, didn't utter at least a word in his defense.

Although he attracted a great many followers (and detractors: he received more mail, hate and otherwise, than anyone at the *Voice*), Andrew never set out to acquire acolytes, or form a flock of disciples to whom he would issue the party line on every film, or whose straying members he would whip back into the fold ... or excommunicate! As time went on, the sideswipes grew more numerous. Ironically, attacks on him centered on contradictory charges: he was naive, sentimental, and gullible according to one position; and, on the other, he was arrogant, dictatorial, and rigid. No article in the Arts and Leisure section appeared without some sneering reference to the "auteur theory," which was seen as responsible for the directorial megalomania then overtaking Hollywood. Auteurism was never, Andrew would point out wearily, a blank check, authorizing directors to take the money and run; it had served as a research tool, for excavating and examining (for the most part, retrospectively) the careers of directors who had been incompletely understood or undervalued.

Basically, he was opposed to ideology, to certainties; he didn't even go as far as the *Cahiers* critics (and later Pauline Kael) in auteurist partisanship. Andrew appreciated and often quoted MacDonald's witty shaft at the politique, "Homer nods, Hitchcock never," yet he did make distinctions between a director's better and lesser films. The beauty of auteur criticism was precisely its openness to discovery, its lack of a Procrustean determinism. It was somehow the perfect container for a mass medium that had been growing and spreading and flowering in diverse ways since the beginning of the century, now in need of some sort of conceptual framework that would embrace the structural, technological, and aesthetic roots and aims of the form and the personal (or political) bias of most film criticism and theory. Eisenstein and Bazin, *Cahiers* and *Sight and Sound,* Hollywood and Europe were antipodes that nevertheless belonged in the same discussion.

Auteurism was systematic, but not a System; it had preferences but no absolutes. It embraced differences as well as similarities, details as well as movements, and, as Andrew said, was as much about genres as about directors, and as much about subtexts as about texts. It has remained the most flexible, least dogmatic way of approaching film historically, and Andrew has constantly emphasized his own shifting tastes, revisions, detours, new avenues of discovery. Feminist film theory and the semioticians feed off its insights— the films under discussion in the much denigrated (but never abandoned) Hollywood classical cinema are entirely those unearthed and elucidated by the auteur critics—even as they denounce its "phallocentrism" or its emphasis on the personal over the textual. And the politique des auteurs was personal in more than one way: both in its celebration of directorial vision and in its valorization of the personal and even autobiographical response in the writing of its critics.

Andrew's writing was an idiosyncratic combination of visual analysis and psychoanalytic insight, Freud and Bazin being the twin discoveries to which auteurism led him. But Freud merely provided a conceptual framework for an uncannily intuitive mind. So attuned was Andrew to the subtextual implications of stylistic choices that in analyzing mise-en-scène he caught the drifts and eddies of a director's psyche with startling accuracy; a refreshing and very French lack of high culture (or midcult) snobbery; a depth of rapport with both American and foreign films placing him (before the advent of Pauline Kael) alone as a buffer state between the avant-garde apologists of the downtown scene and the predictably conventional tastes propagated in the mainstream press by Crowther and his ilk. Andrew sided with the French against the hierarchical Germans.

As political as were his interests, and as unwavering his democratic liberalism, Andrew was always, by his own admission, more of a Christian than a Marxist in that the epiphanies he found "in the mystical realm of mise-en-scène" were of individual redemption rather than class conflict or oppression, and the acknowledged bias in favor of characters of "Aristotelian" stature was checked or amplified by the belief that no sparrow falls without God's noticing. Like Godard, he felt that cinema is everything, and like Terence, that nothing the human mind encompasses is alien to the genuine humanist.

Andrew often expressed his conviction that there were no such things as an intellectual subject and a nonintellectual subject: there were only intellectuals and nonintellectuals. Thus he never felt that filmmakers were out to make his life miserable with bad films, and he never wrote put-upon, aggrieved reviews. He felt that they were trying to do their best and had simply failed. His prose style reflects the tastes and temperament of a critic who, as he himself has often said, quoting Adlai Stevenson, "would rather light a candle than curse the darkness." That is, no matter how bleak the movie situation looks, no matter how unspeakable a given film, and no matter how much rhetorical mileage he might get out of lashing out or dismissing with withering scorn, he rarely exploits the situation. If a film was trash—a word he never used—it was not a violation of art but an insufficiency of art. Kitsch, another word he never used—wasn't an enemy, out to displace art.

The confusion arose, he felt, because most people are deficient in appreciation. Nevertheless, unlike those intellectuals who, while embracing the poor and downtrodden or the glamorously funky, despise the middle class, Andrew believed you didn't abandon people simply because they lacked the capacity to appreciate art. Rather, you showed the chain of connection, you linked the beautiful and sublime with the rest of life and left the door open, inviting everyone to the party, abandoning no one.

It's hard for me to separate Andrew the film critic from Andrew the husband, so much has our life together revolved around films and so much have movies fed his inexhaustible curiosity and charm as a conversationalist. It is that charm and interest that have kept our marriage merrily afloat, but in truth, as with most of our sharpest movie critics, his interests range far beyond movies. His model has, by his own admission, always been Graham Greene's "mass observer," and one reason he responded to Jean-Luc Godard was that he recognized in the Swiss Parisian a similarly omnivorous and eclectic sensibility.

He and I discovered not only that we loved Paris, but that we'd been there the same year; though I'm sure that Paris in 1961 wasn't yet the right moment for the consummation of our—to use a favorite expression of Andrew's—elective affinities. I was studying at the Sorbonne and going to French movies while he was looking at films at the Cinematheque and debating *Cahiers* versus MacMahon with Gene, Patrick Bauchau, and other members of the brotherhood. It was there and with them that he found his spiritual home. In Paris, said Patrick, there was a place for appreciators, "les amateurs." Andrew was a talker even more than a writer, and Paris was not just the city of light or the city of love, it was the city of talk and of amateurs.

In sidewalk cafés, where foreigners never felt like outsiders, Andrew could participate in that celebration of conversation not tied to immediate gain, not interrupted by the feverish rush to deadlines, not vitiated by the insidious competition to get ahead nor choked off by its failure. It was a moment of epiphany, he wrote much later, when he realized that auteurism had been an unconscious means to an end, "that end being the common experience some of us shared in Paris, London, New York and other cosmopolitan centers, of being on the outside looking in, victims of failed career seeking to justify the hours and hours of addictive gazing at the screen for some shred of insight into the human condition." This love of talk informs his entire sensibility; it is what he absorbed growing up with articulate and voluble Greek parents; it is what joined us together.

I was an English graduate at a time when colleges were beginning to admit the occasional art film into their curriculum, but it would never have occurred to me that one could think and write about American films with the same erudition or intensity as one brought to art films or literature or music, or that writing on movies could aspire to such eloquence.

Film Culture, the magazine that Andrew first wrote for, might have been, in retrospect, the rubric for the sixties and early seventies. It was the moment in film comparable to what must have occurred in the wake of the explosion of the nineteenth-century novel, when that popular art form first began to receive the serious thematic and formal attention of critics, when a certain self-consciousness inevitably set in, but with it a deeper appreciation of the form. Andrew's column, his approach, gave license to take what one loved seriously, and thus oneself, one's instincts. I had spent a year in Paris, much of it going to films, but had been only dimly aware of *Cahiers du cinema* until Andrew made it available in English.

I was working at the French Film Office at the time, and we met when Andrew came to pick up material for an article he was doing for GQ on Jean Paul Belmondo. He arrived fresh (so to speak) from the IND and Queens in something less than sartorial splendor, briefcase bulging with the seven daily newspapers he was then accustomed to reading. He greeted me in an elaborately courtly manner, out of breath, scattered as he was between one post (or berth as he described them) and another.

Along with the weekly column for the *Voice,* he put out an issue of *Cahiers* in English when enough translated material had accumulated, was a member of the selection committee for the New York Film Festival, did a weekly extemporaneous radio broadcast on WBAI, and had just gotten a teaching job at the School for Visual Arts; and in that year of our meeting— 1966—the Museum of Modern Art published his first book, *The Films of Josef Von Sternberg,* in my opinion still one of the best film books ever written. Nevertheless it wasn't a living wage (WBAI actually paid nothing), but it was just enough for him to (at my urging) come into the city and take a small apartment in the Village. Certainly it had never occurred to him, as he lay year upon insolvent (inactive) year on his mother's sofa in Queens, drifting between conscious and unconscious reverie, that one day he would get paid or publicly attended to for thinking and writing (and above all talking) about films.

Even now, the Oblomovian habit of lying recumbent on a sofa being second nature to him, it is not easy to tell whether he is, as a cartoon given to him by a friend once had it, "a' settin' and a' thinkin' or just a' settin'."

With Andrew, the two are not easily separated as his unconscious seems always on the simmer, prompting the remarkable connections that seem to come out of nowhere. He has a streaky mind: he takes off from a point of departure, surging forward; he picks up steam and ideas as he goes along, hands moving, head bobbling the original theme becoming encrusted with thoughts and associations. His lectures, when he's on a roll, are a dazzling performance. He would rather think and talk about movies than anything; writing is an arduous second.

He has that block, common to some writers, of being unable to put pen to paper or finger to keyboard until his back is to the wall, and the deadline is passing into history. When he can delay no longer, he makes his way over to his portable Smith Corona (c. 1955) and, the column having more or less formed itself in his head, types it out, finished copy, making only a few changes on the manuscript. The revisions that the rest of us make on computers he has already made in his mind, perhaps even in his sleep.

A couple of years ago, the Directors Guild held a panel at Lincoln Center to celebrate thirty years of auteur criticism. In his opening remarks, Andrew paid tribute to all the critics who'd influenced him: not just Agee, Ferguson, Farber, and Warshow, but also Meyer Levin and Gilbert Seldes of *Esquire.* Then he told the assembled cinephiles of his first film memory. It was a movie called *Mysterious Island* (he wasn't quite sure of the title, or that it had even been his very first movie), whose action took place on an island under the sea. All the inhabitants moved along the ocean floor in that half-swimming, half-walking slow-motion way. This image, to a toddler of three or four, had been overwhelming. "The liquidity of the scene and of film," Andrew said, "was truly magic, especially to someone not many years out of the womb himself."

That leap backward in time, the linking of womb and film, of the magic of cinema as something both already known and utterly unfamiliar, the metaphor and the imaginative way of pulling it all together, of *seeing* in a way entirely personal yet universal—all seem to sum up Andrew, his sensibility, his poetry, his insight, his amazing ability to turn his love of film into something that illuminates life and the art of film simultaneously, and that plumbs the deepest emotions of his audience and readers. And just what he couldn't do in the world of people, or even in the water—two mastoid operations prevented him from ever learning to swim—he could do in movies: let himself go, unafraid of the amorphousness of the medium, able to negotiate it without the reassuring markers, divisions, and boundaries that others found necessary.

It was a mellow evening: he talked of the present; he reflected that he and Pauline Kael had more in common than in uncommon. As a young person, he had picked up some of the snobberies that surrounded him, but he had discarded them as he went along. "Now," he said to them or to me, "I have less and less shame about anything. I develop my hypotheses as I go along." He said that night that he felt his role was to celebrate and affirm, to be open to any source of art and artists in the future.

"I'm not and have never been a prophet or seer," he said, and then told the story of the time Richard Goldstein, arts editor of the *Voice,* was preparing a special film issue and asked Andrew to find and perhaps interview the "future Martin Scorsese." Andrew laughed. He has known Martin Scorsese in the early days; they had shared an office in the sixties, when Marty was

ous dames and heartthrobs: the sunshiney all-American June Allyson, the delicious croak and spunk of Jean Arthur (he could never forgive Billy Wilder, in *A Foreign Affair,* for turning Arthur into a prudish American officer, a portrait made nastier by its pointed comparison with the glamorously worldly Dietrich). The luscious Ava Gardner over the two-dimensional Marilyn Monroe, the glorious combination of sophistication and warmth in Danielle Darrieux. . . . It always comes back to emotion and intensity. He intuited intention through style, and whether the transaction between actress and director was one of affection and desire, or contempt. He agreed with Astruc that "what is seen is less important than the way of seeing." Warmth coupled with dispassionate analysis; he himself possesses the combination—so essential to a critic—of detachment and feeling. His love of film takes precedence over his own ego. He has less sense of embarrassment than most people and would rather be outrageous than insipid.

Andrew could write panegyrics about ostensibly lost causes—*Lola Montes*—until they weren't lost anymore. Dietrich was never one of his favorites, yet no one has written more eloquently about her complex persona in the films of Sternberg, "the equation of sexual magnetism with political power." In *Morocco,* she "is in the process of discovering herself, and the awakening of self awareness visibly delights her." Others might laugh and deride the ending and cry "camp!" but Andrew wouldn't retreat in his view that "the complaint that a woman in high heels would not walk off into the desert is . . . meaningless. A dream does not require endurance, only the will to act." A manifesto on behalf of dreams, the guiding principle of a life's work that has remarkably endured.

At Telluride, a couple of years ago, he was invited by guest curator Phillip Lopate to introduce and lead discussions of the retrospective films of Frank Borzage. Borzage was someone Andrew had "discovered" apart from Cahiers, since he was never in the canon of French taste. After a screening of *Man's Castle,* Andrew stepped down to the mike and began speaking to a small band of eager listeners. I stayed for a while, then ran out to do an errand—it was our last of three days in that glorious mountain movie town—and when I returned some ten minutes later, Andrew had barely taken a breath. As far as I could gather, he was still in the same paragraph, his listeners spellbound, a festival official waving frantically, trying to get his attention in order to clear the theater for the next show. That was Andrew: simultaneously lost in film and found—in film he allowed himself to sink and swim. I think of *Reap the Wild Wind,* the movie in which John Wayne wrestles an octopus undersea: Andrew grappling with the slippery liquidity of film and the sink or swim challenge of words, finally dropping a plum line of insight, moving the reader as he was moved.

I recently took a seminar of *The Iliad,* and another on Greek Tragedy, and was astonished to find echoes of Andrew reverberating through descriptions and details of the ancient Greeks. Platitudes: the chorus, whose lines scholars have analyzed down through the ages, are for the most part simply providing a kind of ambient noise, respite from the sturm and drang, by expressing the most familiar of truisms. "It is better to be alive than to be dead." "He whose grasp exceeds his grip will meet with misfortune." At last! Andrew's penchant for the obvious, his absolute comfort in the uttering of familiar banalities, had historical roots and literary lineage.

Then there was the Greeks' indifference to the pleasures of suspense. The same old play, over and over again, knowing how it would come out: Andrew shared this too. He wanted to know the ending in advance—whether of a movie or a tennis match—the better to enjoy the intricacies of the game, without the distractions of suspense. And finally: tears. The Greeks cried at the drop of a hat; in *The Odyssey,* heroes and warriors sob and lament at frequent intervals. Far from being considered unmanly, not to cry would be a sign of lack of feeling.

Andrew cried even more easily at movies than I did. When I was working on *From Reverence to Rape,* he would occasionally recount the plot of some woman's film I hadn't seen and wasn't likely to in those pre–VCR and cassette days. I remember on one occasion his telling me the story of *When Tomorrow Comes,* in which Irene Dunne's union activist and Charles Boyer's married musician fall in love, but, after a night in which they are stranded by a flood and think they will die, the waters subside and they must part. In the concluding scene they meet for a last meal, she wearing a new dress for which she has spent all her hard-earned wages. As Andrew began to describe Irene Dunne telling Charles Boyer about her dress, he choked up, tried to continue and couldn't. We sat there feeling ridiculous, laughing and crying together. I myself have always been a sucker for noble renunciation, that staple of thirties and forties movies and the novels of James and Wharton.

No doubt our chemical attractants (or "elective affinities") brought us together, recognizing similar patterns of desire or Oedipal guilt, the unrequited yearning for that first unobtainable love, and the immense pleasure in its numerous surrogates. Luckily we were able to have our cake (each other) and movies too: renunciation and gratification at twenty-four frames a second.

Scenes from a Friendship

Elisabeth Weis

*W*hat can I say about Andy's profound influence on not just film criticism and scholarship but perhaps the course of film history that won't be said more eloquently by the illustrious disciples and friends who are contributing to this volume? They will explain how he brought his prodigious insight, passion, and erudition to his writings and ennobled the art of film criticism.

Instead I will talk about Andy the person, about the habits of mind and quirks of personality that make him such an original thinker and endearing friend. I have known Andy since 1970, as my teacher, my editor at the *Village Voice,* my employer, a tennis opponent, and a Chair of the National Society of Film Critics (NSFC). Let me reminisce and hope I can suggest with a few vignettes about each of these Andys the delightful idiosyncrasies as well as powerful influence that is Andrew Sarris.

ANDY THE VILLAGE VOICE EDITOR

In 1972, there was no higher aspiration in film criticism, no better place to be published, than in the *Village Voice.* Andy's writing stable included Stuart Byron, Mike McKegney, William Paul, George Morris, Richard Corliss, Jim Stoller, and Stephen Gottlieb. All of these critics had seen many more films and had much more fully developed opinions about film than I did. So how did I end up writing there for two years?

Tom Allen—classmate, *Voice* writer, and lay priest with a great astuteness about horror films—told me many years later how I got the job. Tom was chatting at a party with Andy, when a third man walked up to Andy with smug belligerence and said, "Andy, you're no feminist!" "What do you mean," gulped Andy, taken aback. The guy went on: "You've got no women on your writing staff." "Of course, I do," retorted Andy. The guy: "Name one." Andy named Molly. "That doesn't count; she's your wife. Name another." Andy paused a few seconds and said "Liz Weis," a name that probably popped into his head because I was his projectionist at school. He called me the next day with my first assignment.

Just to be clear, Andy is a true feminist; it just comes naturally that he doesn't distinguish intellectual qualities or abilities by gender. I suspect he was a feminist before the word was coined.

Andy gave me assignments about once a month on the *Voice,* which is as much as I could have handled. As often as not, he asked me to cover documentaries about politics. Why me, when the *Voice* had major political writers like Jack Newfield and Nat Hentoff on the staff? Because, Andy would complain, the political columnists always wanted to review the blockbusters like *The Godfather* and *Jaws!*

ANDY AS ÉMINENCE GRISE OF THE NATIONAL SOCIETY OF FILM CRITICS

Enough said.

ANDY THE TEACHER

When I entered the masters program in film at Columbia, in 1970, Andy had only been there a short time, but his Film History class was already legend. The department had to shift classrooms to find one big enough, from the auditorium of Butler Library to the cavernous theater of Dodge Hall. Andy would start off by lecturing on the masterpiece that had been screened for the day.

His lectures seemed impromptu and rambling at the time, but the notebooks I keep to this day belie that casualness. When, as a college professor of twenty-seven years' experience, I want to freshen my lectures or rethink the canon, I can do no better than to take out my lecture notes from his classes. What I see now is not Andy's passion for movies (which would have skipped my writing hand and gone directly to the heart), but his extraordinary clarity—his ability to get right to the nugget of what was most important about a film. Andy always came up with an insight more trenchant than anything available in books at the time.

As a scholar I have always thought that the mark of genius is simplicity. Surrounded as I am now by the obfuscation and jargon that characterize academic writing (I wonder how many words it would take the current theorists to say $e=mc^2$), I appreciate all the more the lucidity and precision with which Andy expressed his ideas. And Andy wasn't just brilliant on favorite auteurs like Ford, Hawks, Ophuls, or Hitchcock; those notebooks show me how good he was at differentiating Eisenstein from Pudovkin, Mizoguchi from Ozu.

Andy was the most revered critic among college students at the time. We all knew the rankings in his *American Cinema* by heart. (More than one of us had a secret dream of making such a persuasive case for an underappreciated auteur that the director would be added to the "More than Meets the Eye" category.) So when Professor Sarris opened the lecture floor to questions, they were less likely to be on the topic of the day than on a current release—the class was dying to know Andy's opinion about the latest film before it hit the press.

In those days, Andy had a morning class, an afternoon class, and an evening class, all on the same day: Wednesday. His deadline at the *Voice* was Fridays, and he would spend Thursdays writing his reviews. So those of us who attended all three classes got to watch a great mind at work. On Wednesdays, Andy could be heard working out his ideas of the next day's column as the day progressed; the rough ideas of the morning became more developed by afternoon and quite refined by the evening class—so that on Thursdays Andy could polish it for print.

Jump ahead to 1977 and another scene of Andy talking: my doctoral defense on "Hitchcock's Aural Style." (I was such a confirmed auteur that I trusted, without first checking the films, that Hitchcock's use of sound would be as distinctive and controlled as his use of visuals. It was.) Only one person had defended a dissertation on film at Columbia before my turn, and that hadn't gone well. Since there was no one with a doctorate in film to serve on my committee, I had chosen Leo Braudy from the English Department as an advisor, with Andy as my second reader. I also had to defend in front of a philosopher, a musicologist, the theater chairman, and a comp lit professor, none of whom knew a thing about Hitchcock's use of sound.

It was anybody's guess what my inquisitors would ask. Andy took care of that problem by becoming my gallant knight. Whenever possible, he talked and talked, taking up so much time that it minimized the questions for me. The committee got annoyed with Andy, but I only had to change one sentence! There have been interviews since where I wished I had an Andy to deflect the tough questions.

ANDY THE EMPLOYER

In my second year at Columbia, Andy hired me to replace Tom Allen as his secretary/researcher. My most enjoyable assignment was gathering information on Little People to help Andy prepare for an interview with Herve Villechaize. The most tedious was amassing the complete credits of films as they came out in the *New York Times*. But mostly I typed Andy's mail, to which he dictated replies.

It's rather appalling that readers considered Andy to be public property. There were glowing tributes and cranky complaints in his mail, as well as lots of requests from young people asking how to become a critic. Andy answered them all. Granted, he did so only two to three times a year, but he did eventually respond to every letter. I imagine he still does. Occasionally, I am asked as executive director of the NSFC by some illiterate teenager how to become a critic. I feel like writing back "get a life—or at least a dictionary." I don't always answer, and if I do, it's only a sentence or two. But Andy was unfailingly gracious, even when receiving a letter from a man in prison who needed money for ointment to cure his contagious skin disease. (We loved picking up that letter.) I hope I'm not giving anything away when I recall that Andy's answer always included the wise advice to "find your own voice."

Because Andy and Molly had a small apartment, his office was a studio on Ninth Street, in Greenwich Village, which had been his bachelor's pad before he met Molly. I remember a Greek mother who visited occasionally, and books overflowing the bookcases and stacked on planks suspended between pieces of furniture. But mostly I remember incessant basketball games, because Andy always had the NBA game going while he dictated. Given that he is deaf in one ear, conversation was quite a challenge.

He had TV basketball on, too, when I visited him in the Rusk rehabilitation hospital. That was after the catastrophic illness, due to some long-undiagnosed cytomegalovirus, which Molly wrote about in *Love and Other Infectious Diseases*. It was a shock seeing Andy. We all knew he had almost died. But I did not expect how changed he would look: the rings were gone!

At Columbia, there had been a huge poster of a panda in the film department. It had escaped no one's notice that our Andy–Panda had the same enormous dark circles around his eyes, which we had always surmised were caused by too much movie going. Somehow the hospital stay erased the rings, and they are gone to this day. The doctors could never explain why the virus had ravaged Andy. Nor could they explain what had taken away the rings.

ANDY THE TENNIS PLAYER

Andy's not just an armchair athlete/aesthete (in his words, "a professional voyeur watching professional exhibitionists"). He was also a damn good tennis player till his illness cramped his style. His tennis style was amazingly like his prose. Wearing a white sailor's hat with a narrow brim that concealed his eyes, he would just stand there seeming barely awake. But somehow, he always got to the ball and returned it with remarkable finesse, never using more energy than was needed nor less. He won two club championships in West Hampton against men much younger than he.

I sometimes played doubles against Molly and Andrew with a pal who had a secret crush on Molly. One winter evening, my friend suggested we play at Randall's Island, which is only ten minutes by cab from the Sarris apartment. As my friend had predicted, it was easy getting a court even on Saturday night because so few people knew this court had a bubble in winter.

We had the place to ourselves and had a great game. The attendant departed before we finished and told us the door would lock automatically behind us when we left. For half an hour after the match we tried phoning for a taxi, but the shows were letting out on Broadway and most of the lines were busy. The few cab dispatchers who did answer would not come so far. So we decided to go hunting for a ride. We walked outside to find ourselves locked out in a swirling snowstorm that had not begun when we arrived. Molly and I were in sneakers and tennis dresses. No problem; we'd walk up the ramp to the Triborough Bridge tollbooths. It was too blinding to see them, but we knew we had driven through them to get there. We trudged up a ramp and got within a hundred feet of the booths. Unfortunately, we were on a different ramp and no one could see or hear us. We came upon a sign reading: "Pedestrian walking; Queens, three miles." We walked back down the ramp.

Randall's Island has no (legal) residents. It looked pretty much like the isolated location where they filmed those huge bridge piers in *The French Connection*. I thought we ought to take our chances and flag down a ride. Andy suggested quite reasonably that anyone driving about on this island at midnight was up to no good. I flagged down a car. It slowed. Andy-the-knight-protector waved it on by, shouting: "Never mind, our car is right around the corner." I stopped another. Andy saved us again from God knows what fate. Finally, I saw a station wagon big enough to hold the four of us in addition to its tough-looking passengers. Over Andy's protests I begged for a ride. He was right. They did have guns; they were off-duty cops and drove us over to relative safety in Harlem.

Not long after this adventure, Andy and Molly were indeed mugged—while on vacation in Palm Springs.

ANDY AND ACADEME

Speaking of bridges, Andy has written about his youthful ambition as the son of poor immigrants to make it over the bridge to Manhattan. But unlike some arrivistes, he never ignored his roots. Once, while Molly was giving a guest lecture at Brooklyn College, where I teach, Andy came along (not snobs, they forewent the free car service and took the subway) to show her where he lived as a youngster. Andy has no trouble playing second banana to Molly; while she was being wined and dined, Andy took me for a nostalgic walk around the neighborhood, showing me his old haunts; the junction where he lived as a child at Flatbush and Nostrand, which he said had trolley tracks then, the grade school he had attended. The field that had become Brooklyn College's main quad, he told me, had once been the storage grounds of a circus. In all my years at the school, no one else has mentioned our distinguished predecessor.

Of course, Andy himself was very popular on the college lecture circuit. He was an enchanting raconteur who could segue easily from art to politics, who could entertain the masses while enlightening the academics. It is hard to explain to today's undergraduates why Andy's ideas seemed so radical in the 1960s. Film history has so much absorbed auteurism that students can't imagine a world where Hitchcock wasn't considered a major artist. Remember that Andy's first review for the *Voice* was of *Psycho* and that he was the only major critic to give it a rave (many critics revised their initial opinions later that year). Andrew Sarris, more than any other American critic, gave film academics respectability. He showed us that genre films could be as profound as the films of Bergman and Antonioni. He and his pal Vincent Canby also encouraged us to discover the glories of foreign masters like Fassbinder and Mizoguchi.

But almost as soon as film studies had achieved status as a legitimate academic discipline, the field evolved. Today film scholars consider movies as "texts" to be plumbed for their inherent political inequalities. And I've attended academic conferences where no one has mentioned a movie. An entire generation of graduate students has become credentialed without seeing or loving movies. They think a movie is only valuable if it agrees with their politics. Andy—a self-described "knee-jerk liberal"—loves to talk politics as much as he loves to discuss film. But he doesn't dismiss all art created by reactionaries. He recognizes the inherent difficulties of reconciling politics and art. Andrew Sarris ought to be required reading today for anyone who wants to teach film.

Two of Andy's favorite—okay, overused—words of the 1970s were *frisson* and *epiphany* to describe moments or films that affected him profoundly. These words could also describe Andrew Sarris's effect on those exposed to his ideas.

The Original, or Maybe the Third Guy Who Has Seen Every Movie of Any Consequence

Roger Ebert

It was, if memory serves, Manny Farber who once described auteurists as a bunch of guys standing around trying to catch some director shoving art up into the crevices of dreck. When I was appointed film critic of the *Chicago Sun-Times,* I had met only one of them in the flesh, a solemn, pre-occupied man named Ron Szoke who wrote about films for the *Daily Illini,* the student newspaper at the University of Illinois. I was the editor from 1963 to 64 and asked him to write the column because he had apparently found time in the first twenty-one years of life to see every movie of any consequence. He wrote about Otto Preminger and Anthony Mann with the same seriousness I had learned to apply to Bergman and Antonioni, and I listened awestruck as he found the meaning in Preminger's dislike of over-the-shoulder shots.

Two years later I was a graduate student at the University of Chicago, hotbed of Doc Films, a film society that seemed to consist of rooms full of Szoke clones. Where did they find the time to see so many hundreds or thousands of films, in those days before home video, and how did they remember them all? I had a part-time job on the *Sun-Times,* writing Sunday magazine pieces about snake charmers and mineral water magnates. A few months later, in April 1967, Eleanor Keen retired and I was given the job, no doubt because I was the youngest member of the features staff and had written a piece about the underground film programs on Monday nights at Second City.

I loved films and had written about them as an undergraduate. But I had never taken a film course—none were offered at Illinois—and I felt a great lack of preparation for the job. I bought copies of Arthur Knight's

The Liveliest Art and Pauline Kael's *I Lost It at the Movies* and read them in my $110-a-month furnished apartment in the attic of the Dudak's house on North Burling. In December of that year I was invited to attend the world premiere of Bo Widerberg's *Elvira Madigan* in Stockholm, and on that trip I read every word of Andrew Sarris's *Interviews with Film Directors*. I underlined at least a quarter of the book and put a star in the margin next to Sarris's observation, in the introduction, that "even art films have to make money and even commercial films have to make some statement. To put it another way, more and more critics are demanding that there should be more fun in art, and more art in fun. . . . In the process . . . it has become possible to speak of Alfred Hitchcock and Michelangelo Antonioni in the same breath and with the same critical terminology."

This, to me, was a signpost pointing the direction that a daily newspaper film critic might choose. One might also remember that for a nickel, then the price of the paper, the reader might reasonably expect to be entertained, since 95 percent of the readers would not go to 95 percent of the movies and yet might read the review.

I began to read Sarris regularly in the *Village Voice* and found his voice to be clear and energetic, free of jargon and self-importance. Although he was famous as the leader of the auteurist critical school in America, he was not particularly theoretical or doctrinaire and seemed in close touch with the actual experience of seeing the movie itself. "A man goes to the movies," Robert Warshow had written, "and the critic must be honest enough to admit he is that man." You could never catch Sarris praising a film because the director was in the pantheon, or disliking it because the director's previous work had not passed muster. You felt that Sarris went to every movie hoping to be delighted.

This was the time when I was learning, on the job, how to be a movie critic. There were few critics' screenings in those days (although Balaban & Katz and Universal both had Chicago screening rooms). I got up from my desk at the *Sun-Times,* walked across the river to the Loop, went into a theater, sat down, and watched the show. There was no pressure to review everything on opening day; reviews appeared as space allowed. At nights I went to O'Rourke's Pub on North Avenue, then the watering hole of Chicago authors and journalists (Algren and Royko were regulars) and met a crowd of characters who took on the task of my film education.

There was John West, thin and balding, who lived in a flat around the corner with dozens or hundreds of 16mm prints and had persuaded the owners of a burlesque theater to allow him to book it as the Town Underground. There he scheduled Welles's *Chimes at Midnight,* Bunuel's *The Ex-*

terminating Angel, and Adolfas Mekas's *Hallelujah the Hills* before the owner decreed that the strippers should return. West carried on awhile doing publicity for the strippers because he needed the money. The same girls danced every week, but he decided the show would seem fresher if they had different names. We thought them up at O'Rourke's: Bonnie Ann Clyde and Her Blazing 45s, Miss Abba E. Bond and Her Gaza Strip, Miss Rowana Martin and Her Bath-In.

West was friendly with Jay Robert Nash, one of the truly legendary Chicagoans of the last thirty years, who was then publishing the *Chicago Literary Times* ("Founded by Ben Hecht; edited by Jay Robert Nash"—with no mention of a lapse of several decades between). Nash, like West, had seen every film of any consequence ever made. They began to shame me with quizzes about Hawks and Ford, and even Hitchcock, whose earliest works I had never seen.

They sent me, or took me, to the Clark Theater, which in those days was a shabby Loop palace with a daily change of double feature and an irresistible package deal: for $2.95, you could have a ticket to the show, free parking, and a three-course meal in the Chinese restaurant next door. The Clark operated twenty-two hours a day and advertised its films in a monthly mimeographed bulletin that had a rhyming couplet for every feature ("Rosebud the bane/Of Citizen Kane"). The Clark was run by a gentle, confiding man named Bruce Trinz, who fought a tireless war against those who considered his theater their residence. Soon I met Jim Agnew, his night manager, a fresh-faced son of Irish immigrants, who had also seen every movie of any consequence ever made and knew all of the Clark's customers by sight: those who came to see Fritz Lang and those who came to stay warm. It was Agnew, I believe, who suggested a solution to the problem of strange men sidling up to unaccompanied women: between the Clark's main floor and its balcony was a sort of sub-balcony of forty seats, which he named "The Little Gallery for Gals Only." Here women could watch the show unmolested my men. "You can't win," Agnew confided in me one evening. "Now they complain they're being propositioned by women."

At the Clark I saw titles by Hitchcock, von Sternberg, Huston, Minnelli, and Hawks. Weeks of films from Italy and Sweden. Festivals of gangster films (Did the Clark use the word *noir* then? I can't remember. Not much rhymed with it.). Musicals. Tributes to RKO and Republic. W. C. Fields. The works of Bogart, Garbo, Mitchum, and Original Pancake House. Once during a screening of *A Hard Day's Night,* a patron in the balcony shouted out, "I'm coming, John!" and threw himself over the edge.

Jim Agnew and Jay Robert Nash eventually met (through me? I can't remember), and their circle grew to include Alex Ameripoor, an Iranian who had been the cinematographer for several of Herschell Gordon Lewis's gorefests. We all met at Lewis's apartment on Sheridan Road, where he threaded a 16mm projector on his dining room table and screened *The Treasure of the Sierra Madre,* while everyone in the room performed a simultaneous commentary.

Lewis, who is remembered for making some of the sleaziest films of all time ("10,000 Maniacs," "The Gore-Gore Girls") had a deep love of film, but it was nothing compared to Ameripoor's. The plump, shiny-faced Persian believed that John Ford was the greatest of all directors, and from Ford and Wayne he formed his idea of America, his adopted country. Together, in 1967, we attended Ford's personal appearance at Doc Films, gloomy because of the old man's truculence at finding that the print of *The Long Voyage Home* had been edited to remove the framing scenes. When Ford died, Ameripoor and Agnew drove all the way cross-country to his graveside to stand and sing "Shall We Gather at the River?"

Agnew lived in his family's boarding house in Uptown, where the tenants included such characters as Self-Destruct Prescott, a student revolutionary so described because he dressed in battle gear and claimed to carry grenades with which he could kill himself if captured by fascist agents. In the living room there one night, Nash and Agnew showed me *Yankee Doodle Dandy* and scenes from other Cagney pictures and explained why Cagney was the greatest of all American actors.

In those days before video cassettes, revival houses and film societies were the best ways to see old films (the Late Show on TV was too unpredictable and cut up by commercials). But fanatic film lovers such as these had their own collections of 16mm prints. Where did they obtain them? Don't tell, don't ask. One night I told West I had been assigned by *Esquire* to interview Kirk Douglas, and he admitted me to his quadruple-locked apartment and showed me *Out of the Past, Young Man with a Horn,* and *Lust for Life.*

At about this time I became aware of an emerging generation of still younger filmgoers who had also, of course, seen every film of any consequence. I was asked to lunch one day by four students at Evanston High School, two of whom were Charles Flynn and Todd McCarthy. Within a few years they would coedit the famous anthology *Kings of the Bs.* I had by then been a full-time movie critic for two or three years and had benefited from the Clark, Doc Films and many evenings of 16mm, yet still I had not seen a fraction of the films they'd already seen—in high school. Flynn went on to the University of Chicago, where he met his future wife, Barbara Bernstein, who had also seen every film of any consequence. One night at the Chicago

Film Festival (I think he was by then film critic of the *Chicago Maroon*), Flynn introduced Howard Hawks with such elegance that even Hawks smiled: "Howard Hawks had made films about cowboys. He has made films about gangsters. He has made films about auto racers. He has made films about pyramid builders. He has made films about test pilots. He has made films about newspaper reporters. He has made films about big-game hunters. Ladies and gentlemen—Howard Hawks!"

Flynn went into the law; McCarthy became a film critic for *Variety*. At about this time the first issues of the *Chicago Reader* appeared—a thin, free weekly with uncompromisingly auteurist reviews by Terry Curtis Fox and Myron Meisel, also Doc Films types who had seen every film of any consequence. They began a *Reader* tradition of contrarian film criticism, which later embraced Dave Kehr and Jonathan Rosenbaum.

It was John West who suggested to me one day that since I had not seen every film of any consequence, I could at least look at selected films in greater depth. This was the favored approach in the University of Chicago's English department, which preferred deep textual analysis of a few works to a survey of many. "Football coaches use a special kind of 16mm projector which allows them to analyze the films of their games," John told me. "Why can't you use the same approach with a movie?"

I was teaching a night school class at the University of Chicago, and I experimented with *Citizen Kane*. Sitting next to the projector, I could freeze a frame, back up, proceed at silent speed, and in general trek through the film a shot at a time. What I learned was astonishing. During the past twenty-eight years, more recently using laser discs, I have taken the same approach every year at the University of Colorado and at several film festivals. A sort of democracy forms in the dark: anyone can shout out "Stop!" and then we discuss whatever caught the eye.

Of course many of the insights we've discovered in this way may be fanciful. There is no way to say exactly what a director or an actor had in mind at any particular moment. Often you may know, or sense, that you are looking at a special effect and yet have no idea how it was achieved. (That famous shot in *Vertigo*, for example—does Hitchcock track in while zooming out, or zoom in while tracking out? Even Robert Harris and James Katz, who restored it, are not sure. And what Hitchcock told Truffaut is of course always suspect.)

The shot-by-shot classes have been a consolation. If I have not, and never will, see every film of any consequence, at least I have seen fifty or sixty films in great detail, some of them twenty or thirty times. It's not important to be right or wrong about a given shot; what's important is to develop the mind-set in which composition and technique are as visible as story and acting.

In the mid-1970s I went to the Cannes Film Festival and met the original man who had seen every film of any consequence, Andrew Sarris. (Well, perhaps William K. Everson and Henri Langlois were the first two guys, and Sarris was third.) Andrew and Molly Haskell were staying at the Hotel Splendid, which was then at the unfashionable end of town (although the new Palais was later built across the street). We'd met before, at the New York Film Festival, but now Andy and Molly and I became friends, sitting late at night in the American Bar of the Hotel Majestic in a crowd that included the few other American critics who were then regularly at Cannes: Rex Reed, Charles Chaplin, Richard Corliss, Jack Kroll, Kathleen Carroll, Gene Moskowits. Andy was already a legend, but a jolly one, who found festivals infinitely amusing and a great deal of fun. I cannot call up in my mind a picture of him discussing a film without smiling. One year *Apocalypse Now* was being premiered at Cannes, and Pierre Rissient gathered a boatload of American critics to visit Francis Coppola on his yacht. That was the night Coppola told us he considered Cannes his "out-of-town try-out," and Sarris asked, "Where's town?"

In those years the Majestic Bar was ruled by Billy (Silver Dollar) Baxter, a New Yorker of great presence who called all the waiters "Irving," picked up all the tabs, and never, so far as I can remember, went to a single movie. One year Baxter threw a party for his pals at the Voile d'Or, the hotel on Cap d'Antibe that had once been owned by Michael Powell's father. We sat in the sun and ate strawberries and looked over the sea toward Monte Carlo, and I remember Andrew and Molly playing tennis, and being struck with how often they laughed, and what utter disregard they had for the score. It was that year, I believe, that the Sarrises went on to Italy and Andy contracted the infection that almost cost his life. The absence of the Sarrises from Cannes was like the end of Jay Gatsby's parties; the season was over, and there would not be another like it.

I will never see every film of any consequence. Today I can say I have seen most of the consequential films of the past thirty years, and a good many others. That is the best I can do. But I have been pointed in the right way to countless films I would not have seen, because of Andrew Sarris. His *The American Cinema* remains an invaluable volume, not because it is right or wrong in its list of the pantheon but because it is there—because someone had the balls to make and defend a list so others could fight over it. Now he is seventy-one and I am fifty-six, and that means that when I first met him, at the New York Film Festival, he was fifteen years younger than I am right now. And had already seen every film of any consequence.

The Critic Who Reinvented My Career

Budd Boetticher

$\mathcal{D}$ear Emanuel Levy:

I was delighted to receive your letter inviting me to contribute a few words for your book on Andrew Sarris. Mr. Sarris wrote a glowing article about me and my career way before I was even certain how to spell *Boetticher*. When I returned from my seven-year exile in Mexico while filming *Arruza,* my prime requisite was to make a personal visit to the Sarrises in New York to say "thank you." Following that impromptu meeting I felt that I could now refer to my gracious hosts as Molly and Andy, and there is no other couple in our industry I would rather help honor.

Going over your list of film critics and discovering the names of my close friends Michael Wilmington, Dave Kehr, and Richard Pena, I'm certain you couldn't have improved your choices. These fine gentlemen took over my career after Andy set them up, and through thick and thin, they have been loyal "aficionados" who have been patiently awaiting my return to my craft. Fortunately, I can now report that I will begin directing my screenplay *A Horse for Mister Barnum* in the south of Spain.

Now, reading your wonderful list of directors, all of whom I heartily admire, I would rather make my contribution a personal note to you. I'm certain Martin Scorsese and my pal, Peter Bogdanovich, will write sensational essays on the brilliance of Andrew Sarris and motion picture criticism in general. I would rather relate, with a sense of humor, how even critics whom you dearly love can, on occasion, truly foul up or vastly improve your personal life.

While in Mexico, I was given the script of *Major Dundee* to read. It seemed that Sam Peckinpah wanted Elsa Cardenas, the lovely Mexican star, to play a small part in his film. I looked it over; I realized that it would be a fine picture starring Charlton Heston, but that young Mr. Peckinpah didn't understand ladies any better than I, so Elsa turned it down. Sam immediately sent a limousine to my dirt-floored adobe but in Tlalpan, where I was busy waiting for Carlos Arruza to return from a prima donna pouting session in Spain and, to pass the time, I was also fooling around with a screenplay I called *Two Mules for Sister Sara*. It was a Sunday afternoon and when I was ushered into Sam's suite at The Del Prado Hotel, I was confronted by numerous cast members of past pictures and nearly all of my personal film crew. I had heard great things about Sam Peckinpah from my dear, dear pal Lucien Ballard, and I was looking forward to a delightful visit. But I hadn't seen Andrew Sarris's review of *Ride the High Country* and had no idea of his high regard for my Scott films and his inference that Sam must have seriously studied all of them to do as well as he had done with his first western. In other words, I was completely naive and unarmed. My gracious host walked toward me, Bloody Mary in hand, and opened with: "Budd, I just want you to know I've seen *Bullfighter and the Lady* ten times." Naturally, I was charmed. Then I accidentally blew it.

How do you like my westerns? I asked. It just seemed like a natural question, and I would have been interested in his opinion However, Sam's eyes turned gunslinger gray. "I have never seen a one of them!" the now-villain answered. And that was the end of that. I wasn't at all sure that I was even going to get the chauffeur and limousine to drive me home. And, when I finally returned to Hollywood, no matter how hard Lucien tried, Sam and I never got around to being friends. The honest shame is that I truly admired Sam Peckinpah. But, damn, I must admit, when I did get the opportunity to read Andy's article, I loved every word of it!

A more unusual, and completely unexpected, example of critic's power occurred shortly after I learned that Sergio Leone was the head of the judges of the Italian Salsomaggiore Film Festival, where they were also honoring me. I had, by this time, read many articles comparing my Randolph Scott pictures with Leones's distinctive "Spaghetti Westerns." To me, this was absurd, as there was absolutely nothing in either series that looked or sounded alike. But critics wrote that they did and referred to me as Mr. Leone's "Maestro." So I was sure that he, also, hated my guts. I warned my beautiful Mary that, if she saw him first, to warn me and I would try to promptly disappear into the shadows. Well, following the bellboys into the hotel elevator we ran smack-dab into dear, wonderful, funny Sergio Leone, who immediately threw his arms around me and literally shouted: "Buddye, darling I stole *everything* from you!" Of course we became great pals and spent every possible moment together throughout the festival. We decided that, as soon as he completed his movie in Russia, he, *personally,* would produce *A Horse for Mister Barnum.* "Just think of that!" he would exclaim. "Us *together!* Even people who don't like us will go see our picture." I really loved the guy. We did have dinner *together* every evening, but he did agree on one part of our deal. He would stay off the set. I think that comes under my idea of any director–producer relationship.

So, *Arruza* was released and didn't make a penny, but Roger Greenspan's review in the *New York Times* ended: "For all of this, and for the genuine complexities revealed in its spare and lovely style, Boetticher's *Arruza* may belong among the last great examples of classical filmmaking." What director–writer could ask for more than that? And my book, *When, In Disgrace,* based on the making of *Arruza,* got better reviews from my "aficionados" than most of what they claimed were my finest films and will directly follow *A Horse for Mister Barnun* onto the screen. However, since I have been fortunate enough to have made all the mistakes an ambitious fellow can make throughout my youth, middle age, and up to the time, twenty-three years ago, when Mary and I were married, may I please submit a list of things NOT to do, rather than exert the pomposity of how things should be done? The following may read as facetious or funny but Andrew Sarris, above all others, will realize I'm deadly serious.

Thank you again for this invitation. I am extremely proud to have been allowed to become a small part of what you are doing. And, as we say in the "plaza," "Muy buena suerte, y dos orejas y un rabo!"

Always my best,
Budd Boetticher

ONE DOZEN "NEVERS" FOR YOUNG ASPIRING DIRECTORS

1. NEVER say your movie "could have been better." The honest re-action will always be: "What the hell happened to you?"
2. NEVER tell your leading man that you would rather have had his role than direct. He'll be glad to trade you.
3. NEVER spend too much social time with your producer because he'll end up snowing you into believing he's your friend.
4. NEVER, ever, under any circumstances, agree to casting the producer's girlfriend—or boyfriend—as your star, although circumventing this major problem can be dangerous. I nearly got myself executed by outmaneuvering the president of Mexico's mistress.

5. NEVER be discouraged by the "Reader's Report." D. W. Griffith knew that readers can't read.
6. NEVER give your editor too much film. They all have great ideas, and you may not recognize your picture at the premiere.
7. NEVER contact an agent until you have exhausted every possible effort to get in touch with your desired actor *personally.* If forced to, try disguises: makeup, wigs, costumes—go to their homes as a nun. If it works, it will have been well worth the effort.
8. NEVER feel discouraged when your brilliant cameraman looks at you as if you've lost your mind. Squeeze his arm gently (because he's probably right), and say: "You really don't understand what I'm trying to do." Then walk away—hurriedly.
9. NEVER call your boss by his first name until he asks you to. This respect may be out of style but, as you grow older and smarter, you will discover how annoying that can be.
10. NEVER hold your leading lady's hand in the darkened projection room. That perfect girl up there on the screen is what you have helped create. The one sitting next to you isn't like that at all.
11. NEVER trust a major studio. Try to get your artistic control on paper. The real tycoons who could make decisions—the Cohns, Zanucks, Goldwyns, and Warners—are all dead, and the new executive committees might just sneak-preview your *Citizen Kane* into a rock musical.
12. NEVER go to bed with your leading lady until the last night of the picture, or you may soon discover you have two directors on your set.

Leaving Las Vegas?

David Thomson

$\mathcal{D}$ear Andy,

I wonder, have you spent time in Las Vegas? Or do you reel with mock horror at the suggestion? I am writing from there, from a splendid room in the Mirage Hotel. Not that this place lays claim to accommodations that are less than luxe or inspiring. To be here is to sign up to be transported, or changed. It's so like the pitch for old movies.

My plan was to say something on how your essay on von Sternberg looks today, in the light of Maria Riva's book on her mother and Steven Bach's *Marlene Dietrich,* to say nothing of the passing on of Marlene herself, and the helpless slip of time.

I remember coming upon *The Films of Josef von Sternberg* in London, just a year or two after Richard Roud had run the pictures—or all he could get—at the National Film Theatre, and at the same time as I was reading (and deciding how much to laugh at, or with) *Fun in a Chinese Laundry.* Your essay seemed then like a revelation—exactly the way to handle a body of work and the perilous proposition that Sternberg was some kind of genius. Looking at it again, it's hard to imagine a more stimulating guide to seeing the films. But isn't there something confounding in that now, thirty years after your book, there's maybe more need (and less call) for it than there was in 1966? By which I mean to say that our young educated class today probably knows less about Sternberg than the same age-group did in 1966, which was still the exciting up slope of film education, encouraged by the rhythm of new waves. Certainly, today, you'd have a harder time persuading young people to watch black-and-white films or accept the stylization, the tongue-in-cheek, the elusive irony of Sternberg.

41

In 1966, you wrote, with absolute correctness, that "the last ten minutes [of *Shanghai Express*] are as emotionally profound as anything Sternberg has ever attempted. . . . Once the issues of the melodrama have been resolved, he [Clive Brook] waits for Dietrich to make some gesture of explanation or expiation. She makes none. Her face merely taunts him in a myriad of mirrors until he surrenders to the illusion she represents, but on her terms rather than his."

That moves me still; it makes me want to see the film's fraught silences again; and it is a tribute to wry, intimate art emerging from unlikely circumstances—the factory system, where movies were meant for the largest crowd, for all of us, or them. (Which was it?) Today, I suspect, it would be hard to present *Shanghai Express* to the young—even the best of them—without having them ridicule the project, because the work is what they would call camp. Of course, it always was. To quote you again: "There is conscious humor in the director's awareness of his own absurdity though some spectators still imagine they are laughing at Sternberg when they are actually laughing *with* him. The colorful costumes, the dazzling decors, the marble-pillared palaces merely underscore by ironic contrast the painfully acquired wisdom of the all too human prisoners of grandiose illusions." (You *had* been to the Mirage, decades before it was built!)

In other words, in offering von Sternberg, then and now, one has to ask an audience to see that within the trappings of self-parody and voluptuous artifice there is a bright white bone of true feeling, all the more adult in that it observes the bittersweet comedy of its own vanity and frustration. This is not anything the movies of the last couple of decades have trained our young to notice.

However, there is one significant point not voiced in your essay, one that Riva and Bach help us see. The greatness of von Sternberg cannot be dealt with without assessing the ambiguous phenomenon of Dietrich. You say that Sternberg made films before and after Dietrich—from *Underworld* to *Anatahan*—and they are plainly films by the same man, intrigued by the same themes, moods, and methods. But I have to doubt that they are equal to the Paramount work. It's not just that in Dietrich Sternberg found his best player or carrier; he also fell into his subject and the completeness of large feeling. In no other works do we feel the torment of the ridiculous fellow feeling of Jo and Marlene.

Between them, Riva and Bach help us see authorship in a larger context. For just as Sternberg "discovered" Marlene, so very soon her eminence protected him. He wouldn't have lasted as long at Paramount without her; yet he might not have behaved as self-destructively but for her fatalistic influence. She was much more than the right face in his light, the face he chose to regard as lost or stranded once he passed on. Dietrich knew how to be photographed that was not just knowing where the lights should be, it was a way of treating the camera as if it were Menjou. Jo taught her, but the education was done through love and bitter experience, and her refusal to be committed to him. The special knowledge in the films depends on solitude. She was too career-minded, too selfish, too fickle, and too addicted to being elusive. Too much a woman—is that it? Or was she exactly the creature his lofty masochism required—without being able to rationalize the transaction? It is easier now to see how many of Sternberg's stricken heroes (most of them with the scar of mustache) resemble their director—something, I suppose, only he "got" at the time.

As you said, *The Devil Is A Woman* was "a . . . gallant gesture to one's once beloved"—and a shrewd guess that neither of them would be the same again. For just as *Shanghai Gesture, Jet Pilot,* and *Anatahan* are not as piercing as his best work, so I can't see anything Dietrich ever did later matching the subtlety or the exquisite balance of pain and pleasure in her Sternberg films. Authorship, in other words, has to explore their interaction, just as it should refer to both the hostility and the facilities of the Paramount where they worked.

And Paramount, I suggest, the archetypal movie studio, has passed into our culture more thoroughly than the genius of Sternberg or the beauty of Dietrich. The medium is stronger than its best messages. And Paramount prepared us for the environmental campiness most fully realized in this Las Vegas where I am writing.

That is not meant to endorse the vies of Las Vegas as a gangsters' creation or a place where vulgarity is spread out like liquid neon and an all-you-can-eat buffet. There's truth in such charges. An honorable person coming to Las Vegas for the first time will be depressed by the lowliness of human nature and the blindness to regular nature. For Vegas is a riveting fabrication set down with its back to a beautiful and vast desert.

I have mixed feelings about Las Vegas, but I am here at the Mirage to assist the writing of a book about Nevada. Have I given up the movies? No more than they have given up me. I am eager to write about more than just movies, and that's part of some feeling that what we do is a threatened venture. It's also because Nevada and Vegas have much in common with the excitement and ghostliness of the movies.

Before I pursue that, let's ask what it is we have been doing. "We" here is not just Sarris and Thomson but that band of brothers and sisters (the contributors to this book?) who try to write about movies in the way our best teachers taught us to think of literature.

Many of us came out of English classes—your wisest and most moderate espousal of auteurism had things in common with F. R. Leavis's recognition of a "great tradition" in novel writing. We have believed in fine work and the people who made it—and in the set of forces that opposed good work. Most of us have done some teaching as well as writing in which we sought to identify the pantheon from the lightly likable. In academia and in print, we have done our best to defend this attitude against semiotics, Hollywood gossip, and the blunt accounting of the box office.

From early in the 1960s until around 1980, the wave of film education came up and helped us feel we understood the ocean. In academia, film studies was hot. People read you and Pauline to keep up—and it was a pretty good time for movies what with the French, the Germans, the Italians, the English even, late Bunuel, and maybe the last golden moment in America. But not many of us now are less than fifty, and if we don't yet hear the chimes at midnight still we guess our moment has passed.

No need to get morbid. We had a good time (I hope) when the wave was ours. We were lucky enough to be kids when the entertainment movie was as vivid and innocent as Lew Hoad before his back went. And didn't we both marry shining students? Like Rick and Ilse, we'll have some things for keeps—Lubitsch's Paris, and Godard's, and even *Paris, Texas,* over which I recall a lively argument with you on the staircase at the Splendid in Cannes. (You were always good on staircases.)

As I look out of the hotel window here, the setting sun has picked up the amber facade of the Mirage so that the light falls back on the world like gold. I have not been in Vegas for a few years, not since driving the Corlisses to the Telluride Film Festival, when we stayed at the Flamingo out of deference to Bugsy Siegel, not that the Flamingo of the 1990s much resembles his new studio.

The old Flamingo was a hotel and a casino. For its time, it ventured into luxury, flash, and drop-dead ostentation, as well as the allure of wickedness (Bugsy's death was a boost to business). But those old places were just rows of rooms stacked on top of the casino floor, restaurants, a pool, and a showtime theater. Across from the Mirage now is what remains of the Sands, a classic establishment, blown up just a few days ago. The marquee still stands with its message: thank you for forty-four years (it opened in December 1952). And on the other side of the dead neon display is the slogan of the Sands—A Place in the Sun—which must have implied Clift and Taylor then and the killing dream of the good life.

The Sands is swept away by progress, to be replaced with one of the new "theme" hotels. The turning point in Las Vegas style was Caesar's Palace, which opened in 1966, built on Roman lines. That entailed a legion of statues, pastiche Roman architecture, and waitresses dressed as slaves. (You have to behold the physical splendor and the dead faces of many women in Vegas to know how much vitality there is in, say, Marlene's "mask.") The masquerade was kitsch and laughable until Caesar's added a Forum of shops constructed as a winding Italian street that passed a replica of a Bernini fountain.

The shops have come to the Forum over the years—high fashion outlets in the main—but the real coup is that the entire street is beneath a canopy roof, a painted sky, that changes its lighting schemes so that you feel the passage from dawn to sunset. This is artificial, theatrical light, and not a mediating of the ample Nevadan light outside.

The Forum is neither kitsch nor comic. It is an uncanny version of an Italian environment (though air conditioning saves you from the real heat—it may be 110 degrees F outside). The streets are cobbled. There are "open-air" restaurants (Spago, for one). The fountains play. There are buskers, clowns, and brass bands. The passing crowd—as always in Vegas—is Felliniesque. And the magic (or whatever) is something managed by those generations of designers, lighting people, and show makers who moved from Hollywood to Vegas.

There was a lull while the town digested this effect, and then the revolution began. Much prompted by a gambler's son, Steve Wynn, who stands over the new Vegas as Selznick stood over *Gone With the Wind,* Vegas has developed a series of theme hotels. The Mirage is based on the tropical rain forest; the Luxor is ancient Egypt; the Exacalibur is Arthurian; the MGM Grand has an enormous lion outside—in Vegas you can still believe in MGM; Treasure Island stages a daily battle between pirates and the British navy—the pirates win, for in Vegas winning itself is antiestablishment; Circus Circus (you can guess); and New York, New York, with a surreal gathering of New York landmarks.

So the Strip is now one great complex of sets. It is the closest you will find today to that world described by Tod Hackett at the start of *The Day of the Locust* as he moves through a studio back lot. No Hollywood lot is like that now. The kicker to Vegas is that these sets, or dream worlds, are not just decor for photoplays, but places where we can move, live, and interact.

And Vegas is booming again. The blunt business of gambling faltered in the late 1970s and early 1980s. People could gamble elsewhere, or on Wall Street, and most had tried Vegas, felt its limits, and its rather hangdog sleaziness. The theme business altered that and made Vegas a place for children. Originally, the town had flirted with the idea of its own "sinister sophistication." But now the worlds there, as they say, are made for the child in all of us. Families come to Las Vegas, and people of all ages play with the fantasy of having escaped their duller lives.

We've heard that before, haven't we, as the happy social contract in moviegoing. It was part of the romance of Paramount, say, that we were transported to Morocco, Shanghai, or old Russia. So I thought I would pass this resemblance on for historical consideration. But I wasn't sure how much weight to put on it, or how much it was worth stressing the possibility that narrative and vicarious involvement in it was being replaced by interaction with an imaginary, yet accessible, world.

Then this happened. You've met our son, Nicholas, who is ten now. When he was younger he loved to watch and re-watch movies on the VCR. As a dutiful parent I guided him through the pantheon (and the lightly likable). He acquired a detailed knowledge of *Red River, El Cid, Meet Me in St. Louis, The Black Stallion, Winchester 73,* Olivier's *Henry V, Bambi,* and so on.

But school taught him that the television set could be used for other things. In a matter of weeks, he fell in love with cartoons and nearly everything on the Nickelodeon channel. His favorite show is *Steven Spielberg's Tiny Toon Adventures,* produced, by the way, by one of the best students I knew at Dartmouth. Nicholas now exults in the action of animated shows and that in turn has led him to the movies of Schwarzenegger et cetera. His preferred movie of all time today is *Independence Day.*

He is only ten, and much can change, but it's clear that he responds to effects and action more than to what we would call narrative. Well, at the homes of friends he had encountered the kind of interactive computer games that are available, many of which are violent combat duels. As parents, Lucy and I deplore such things. We don't have the equipment that can play the games.

The Mirage has what is called a Video Arcade. It is a room really, crammed with kids, eager to play the games. Nicholas found the Arcade and begged most appealingly for a chance to play there in return for being polite about Hoover Dam (another story). He played the games and was nearly radioactive with excitement (a metaphor that comes easily in Nevada). At dinner that night I asked him whether he preferred movies or video games. He considered the matter carefully and said, "Video games." And then he said, "You should try them, Dad."

I tried them. And I am altered. The combat games do not move me, but I don't go for Jackie Chan, either. There is another game, however, Indianapolis 500, in which you sit in a padded driver's seat. You have a brake pedal and an accelerator and a small steering wheel like a hair trigger. You put in your four quarters and the screen in front of you becomes the Indy track, the Brickyard itself, as seen from the driver's seat. There's a countdown and you're off. Other cars appear on the screen, passing you or there to be passed. The track has containing walls. As you nudge or collide with them you are slowed. A wipeout loses you five seconds. But what you can do, once you get the hang of it, is truly race, at speeds close to 200 miles per hour. As you accelerate, the machine gives you the snarl of the engine. I realized after a while that I was leaning over to compensate as I took curves, just as if I were in a real car on a dangerous track.

That is what "interactive" means, and it is one of the most exhilarating experiences I have ever had—with a screen. No, it's not Mizoguchi or Renoir or Sternberg, but it is astonishing, giddy, and instantly habit-forming.

And this *is* a sort of movie, surely the kind of thrill our new "screenagers" want. Why am I telling you this? Well, for one thing because I think you could have a good time in a video arcade. But I know this essay is meant for a book of serious essays, and my real point is to say that, whether you and I or the members of our band like it, this is where moviegoing is. And it leaves me wondering whether the medium hasn't always been more dynamic than its auteurs, and whether we haven't always been flattering a sly, lovely theft of reality. If I had confined my piece to Dietrich and Sternberg, I was going to try to argue that neither one of them was ever as potent as just the dark, the light, and the fantasy of their presence.

In general, I hate the new movies—especially the American ones—but I cannot help seeing how far they are derived from that lesson or how much they resemble the illusion that lets you drive the Indy 500. Above all, I see the history of movie (or film) as an attempt to defy, supplant, or ignore reality that has always been more pressing than the expression of artists.

History won't stop. Our old world may come back. But it won't be quite the same without us to notice it. Meanwhile, like one prisoner to another in *La Grande Illusion,* I salute you. Are we and the other writers in this book the last of a dying breed?

Part Two

Sarris's Magnum Opus

Part two examines the tremendous influence of Sarris's magnum opus, *The American Cinema,* on a whole generation of film scholars and critics.

Director John Sayles, whose movie *Passion Fish* was chosen by Sarris as one of 1992's best films, recalls how as a college student in the late 1960s, "there were about five books in the library about movies." Though Sayles didn't always agree with Sarris's evaluations and rankings, "the very idea that a director might put a stamp on a film and be held accountable for it was a new one." For him, Sarris "found a way of looking at movies, not the only one, but obviously a very powerful one."

Oscar-winning director Curtis Hanson (*L.A. Confidential*) reconstructs in his piece how as a teenage movie fan, struggling to make sense out of what he liked and why, he had the great good fortune to read several pieces of film criticism by Andrew Sarris. Then came the "mother lode," *The American Cinema,* purchased by Hanson for $2.95 from Larry Edmunds Bookstore on Hollywood Boulevard, across the street from Musso and Franks. Hanson recalls: "The day I bought the book I went directly across the street, ordered lunch, and started to read. I loved everything about Andrew Sarris's book, from the table of contents with the witty, aggressive chapter headings ("Pantheon Directors," "Less Than Meets the Eye," "Strained Seriousness") to the directorial index at the back."

Sarris introduced Hanson to a few directors and prompted him to reevaluate others: "When I agreed with him about a filmmaker, my own opinion was reinforced, supported by additional evidence. When I disagreed, I found my own opinion to be stronger for having been challenged. A pattern began to emerge. We seldom disagreed about directors he praised.

When we parted company, it was usually because I liked someone's work more than he. Often, the bigger the name, the bigger the disagreement"— Billy Wilder, John Huston, Kazan. Hanson realized that Sarris enjoyed "calling attention to worthy filmmakers who had a tough going commercially and critically." Especially valuable in the book were the filmographies that accompanied the comments on each director—they were a road map to movies: "It's hard to imagine now, but those were the first comprehensive chronological lists of the movies." For Hanson, *The American Cinema* still represents "the best $2.95 I ever spent."

Phillip Lopate ("The Gallant Andrew Sarris") situates *The American Cinema* among a handful of books that have transformed our understanding of a whole field, such as Walter Benjamin's *Illuminations* in criticism or Jane Jacobs's *The Death and Life of Great American Cities* in the field of urbanism. He observes that "though Sarris never used an explicitly psychoanalytic vocabulary, the Freudian in him . . . emerges everywhere between the lines, in the simultaneous recognition of the price repression extracts and the necessity to maintain the discipline of civilization and decency in the face of discontent." Like the other writers, Lopate is "amazed that Sarris can continue to write intelligently and open-mindedly about movies year after year in his *New York Observer* column." And he concludes: "Clearly Andrew Sarris's criticism has meant the world to me. If it no longer affects me as deeply, that is partly because I have become my own man through cannibalizing him. Isn't that what *Festschrift* is meant to demonstrate?"

In "The Critic Who Helped Teach Me to Think about Movies," critic and author Leonard Maltin recalls how he discovered a magazine he had never seen before, *Film Culture,* at the new New Yorker movie bookstore. As he notes: "Who will forget the provocative cover of that issue." Certainly not Maltin: "I bought it on the spot. (Having half-naked Busby Berkeley chorus girls on the cover was . . . an amusing nod to salesmanship." At that time, Maltin was a kid, immersed in the Marx brothers and W. C. Fields, but hadn't yet encountered Sam Fuller or Budd Boetticher. As he puts it, "To this young and impressionable film buff, Sarris's writing—and his polemicizing—had a profound effect. It urged me to form my own counteropinions and to find a way to express them."

L.A. Times critic Kenneth Turan has a special passion for books, including film books. As he observes in the aptly titled piece "Ruined by a Book": "If I had to select one [film book] as the most influential, the choice would be clear, *The American Cinema.*" Turan, like most writers, still has his own old copy, "inevitably worn and marked by fingerprints, its spine faded, its classic Milton Glaser–designed cover cracked and marred." For Turan, the year of *The American Cinema*'s publication, 1968, was coincidentally also the year that he "first seriously entertained thoughts of becoming a film critic." Several years ago, while watching Anthony Mann's *Man of the West,* Turan wondered what Sarris had thought of the director and consulted his book. Sarris talked about Mann's "psychological intensity," and how his films were interesting "for their insights into the uneasy relationships between men and women in a world of violence and action." Turan realized that Sarris was "on the money again, after all these years."

In "The American Cinema and the Critic Who Guided Me through It," film professor Peter Lehman claims that he owes his career to three people: Blake Edwards, Andrew Sarris, and Laura Mulvey. The three figures are, not surprisingly, connected. Lehman owes to Edwards and Sarris "the passionate love of films and film criticism that led to my career." To this day, Lehman remembers the first time he picked up a copy of *The American Cinema* and how he immediately looked for an entry on Blake Edwards. As he observes, "If *The Pink Panther* and *A Shot in the Dark* had taught me to love the American genre cinema, Sarris taught me that substantive observations could be made about that cinema and its directors." No one would dispute Lehman's claim that "it is impossible to overestimate how important it was at that point in time that there was someone in the United States of Sarris's stature and visibility who legitimized the artistic worth of American genre-entertainment directors."

In my essay "The Legacy of Auteurism," I contextualize the French and American versions of auteurism, suggesting that the auteur policy was formulated as a response to the potential opposition between directors and studio heads or producers. In many ways, auteurism was a political imperative, a strategy used by French film critics who wanted to become directors and knew that the fastest way to achieve that was to repudiate and destroy the old system. That the French battle of the late 1950s had ideological and aesthetic, along with political, implications was all for the better. That it had immense influence on a whole generation of filmmakers—Spielberg, Scorsese, De Palma, to name a few—is also for the better.

The test of any theory is the degree to which it produces new knowledge and new understanding of reality. Auteurism has proved its pervasive impact with a number of theoretical and practical results that evolved out of its revolutionary ideas. Auteurism introduced new ways of seeing films; it abolished the distinction between art and entertainment; it elevated film studies to a legitimate area of scholarly concern; it legitimized the status of film as an art form (Sarris once observed that book editors don't remove chapters from novels without the writer's consent, but in Hollywood, final cut is usually done at the producer's discretion). Auteurism led to the rediscovery and revival of obscure American films in museums and art houses across the country, it resulted in new rankings of individual films within directorial careers, and it influenced what's considered to be the American film canon. Finally, in the New Hollywood, auteurism has become a marketing tool; movies are no longer described in terms of their stars, but in terms of their directors: a Scorsese film, a Spielberg film.

A New Powerful Way
of Looking at Movies

John Sayles

*W*hen I was a college student in the late 1960s, there were about five books in the library about movies. One of them was *The American Cinema* by Andrew Sarris. Somehow I had managed to see many of the films he was talking about, and although I didn't always agree with his evaluations or rankings, the very idea that a director might put a stamp on a film and be held accountable for it was a new one to me.

Now there are five thousand books about movies, and even first-time directors shooting 16mm on their mom's credit cards take a possessory credit. Sarris found a way of looking at movies, not the only one, but obviously a very powerful one. If the people who direct episodic TV get hold of that book, there could be big trouble.

The Best $2.95 Investment in the World

Curtis Hanson

*A*s a teenage movie fan struggling to make sense out of what I liked and why, I had the great good fortune to run across a couple of pieces of film criticism by Andrew Sarris. I was stimulated, intrigued, provoked. I wanted more. I began seeking out his byline, reading his reviews and his commentary. Sometimes I agreed with him; sometimes I didn't. It didn't matter. I was in love with the movies, I wanted to talk about them, to think about them, and I felt I had begun a dialogue with someone who loved them, too, someone who knew more than I did, could articulate it better, and had a unique point of view.

And then came the mother lode: his book *The American Cinema*. Purchased for $2.95 from Larry Edmunds Bookstore on Hollywood Boulevard, across the street from Musso and Franks. I mention all that because it was the best $2.95 I ever spent and the day I bought the book I went directly across the street, ordered lunch, and started to read.

I loved everything about Andrew Sarris's book, from the table of contents with the witty, aggressive chapter headings ("Pantheon Directors," "Less Than Meets the Eye," "Strained Seriousness," etc.) to the directorial index at the back. On the pages in between, some of what was there was familiar, but it was said with such clarity and such conviction that I felt I was hearing it for the first time.

Other ideas were startlingly new. He introduced me to a few directors and prompted me to reevaluate others. When I agreed with him about a filmmaker, my own opinion was reinforced, supported by additional evidence. When I disagreed, and continued to do so after considering his argument, I found my own opinion to be stronger for having been challenged. A pattern began to emerge. We seldom disagreed about directors he praised.

When we parted company, it was usually because I liked someone's work more than he. Often, the bigger the name, the bigger the disagreement. Billy Wilder and John Huston, in particular, I felt he underestimated. Kazan, too. Did Sarris have a bias against some of the bigger names? And did his bias affect his critical judgment? I thought so, and as his bias became clear, I began to feel personal affection for him, the way one does for a gambler who bets his heart and not his head or a criminal who does the wrong thing for the right reason. These filmmakers have been praised enough, I felt he was saying, overpraised, perhaps. Let's take a look at those whose work has been overlooked, undervalued, or forgotten.

This, I felt, was what Sarris enjoyed most—calling attention to worthy filmmakers who had a tough going commercially and critically, and if he appeared to do so at the expense of some who had won every conceivable award, then so be it. Sarris always was something of a provocateur and, besides, I like to root for the underdog, too.

Especially valuable were the filmographies that accompanied the comments on each director. Hard to imagine now in this era of apparently limitless information, but those were the first comprehensive chronological lists of the movies of many of those directors that I had seen. They were a road map to movies seen and others only heard about. Poring over those lists, one could call upon memory and discern thematic and stylistic continuity.

Sarris italicized his favorites. With bold efficiency, he turned a listing of titles into a discussion and, of course, offered up a guide or wish list at the same time. The better known titles might appear on the schedule of one of the half-dozen revival houses that existed in Los Angeles at the time. The others, in those prevideo days, could often be found on commercial television. L.A. had seven stations back then. It doesn't sound like much, but all of them had feature film libraries. Any given week might include Joseph Losey's *The Prowler,* Andre de Toth's *Slattery's Hurricane,* Vincent Sherman's *The Damned Don't Cry,* and Nicholas Ray's *Born to Be Bad.* Not the best way to see them, to be sure, and often they were in the middle of the night, but today one is hard-pressed to find those movies at all.

I still have that beat-up $2.95 paperback, and I still feel about movies the way I did when I first bought it. It's clear from his reviews in the *New York Observer* that Andrew Sarris still loves them, too. I had the opportunity a few years ago to meet Andrew Sarris face-to-face for the first time, when he presented me the Best Picture Award for *L.A. Confidential* on behalf of the New York Film Critics Circle. He was, of course, at a distinct disadvantage. How could it be otherwise with him unaware, as he was, that we had been having a dialogue for three decades?

The Gallant Andrew Sarris

Phillip Lopate

*A*mong the books that have most influenced me, transforming forever my understanding of a whole field—alongside, say, Jane Jacobs's *The Death and Life of Great American Cities* in urbanism or Walter Benjamin's *Illuminations* in criticism—must be counted Andrew Sarris's *The American Cinema*. Actually, it was the first magazine incarnation of this text, rather than its book form, that changed my life, falling into my hands in 1963, when I was nineteen; and my copy of *Film Culture* #28, with its cover still of six chained maidens, their nudity chastely covered with flaxen tresses like a sorority of Lady Godivas, remains in my collection of treasured publications. One reason it is so dog-eared is that I was then running a film club at college, and I eagerly underlined all possible booking suggestions (Abe Polonsky's *Force of Evil,* Edger G. Ulmer's *Daughter of Dr. Jekyll*). Under Robert Parrish's entry was the madly tempting comment, "The Purple Plain stands out in the above list like a pearl among swine. What burst of Buddhist contemplation was responsible for such a haunting exception to such an exceptionable career?"

Part of what captivated me was Sarris's allusive, alliterative, epigrammatic wordplay ("exception-exceptionable"). That combination of authoritative judgment and space restriction exerted such compressive force on his prose. Has anyone ever noticed what an irresistible subgenre of film criticism is this Wise potato chips approach? (See also Pauline Kael's short-shorts in *5001 Nights at the Movies* and David Thomson's often-revised *A Biographical Dictionary of Film*.) Who knows how many hours I have spent hopping from entry to entry, whole afternoons wasted or at least consumed in the decoding of these three's koans? But Sarris got to me first and shaped my tastes the most: initially it was because he provided a map, a system (essential to the young novitiate), but later, I realized, it was because I subscribed more closely to the value system, the humanist romanticism, beneath his judgments. Long after I had ceased caring whether Sarris was wrong for not placing William Wyler or John Huston in the pantheon, I continued to resonate to the waltzing fatalism of those directors he cherished most: Ophuls, Mizoguchi, Renoir, Murnau. You might say that I had that same regretful, oxymoronic music in my soul that he was always alluding to when he wrote, say, "But ultimately there is no dramatic conflict between Boudu and his benefactors. They are all part of Renoir, part of his joyful sadness, part of the feeling he expresses so lyrically about the irreconcilability of life's choices." That ole irreconcilability, yes! The same critic who once confessed in the *Village Voice,* to my shock of recognition, that he would have a hard time getting laid in Stockholm, went on to allude in myriad sentences to the gap between libido and duty. He seemed to cherish movies because they spoke to one's half-buried desires, but then cherished most those with an "adult" (one of Sarris's favorite words) perspective, which acknowledged the necessity for sacrifice, whether gallant or otherwise. This applies not only to old films he praised in the past, such as Ophuls's *The Earrings of Madame De* or McCarey's *Love Affair,* but even recent movies he had admired, such as *Flirting with Disaster* or *My Best Friend's Wedding* (speaking of reluctant sacrifice).

Though Sarris never used an explicitly psychoanalytic vocabulary, the Freudian in him—the late Freud of heroic restraint—emerges everywhere between the lines, in the simultaneous recognition of the price repression extracts and the necessity to maintain the discipline of civilization and decency in the face of discontent. Some of this I have gleaned from a patient reading of Sarris over decades; some was confirmed to me when, years later, I came to know him socially—and went to the Sarrises' parties, which were always divided evenly between film people and psychotherapists. Andrew and his wife, Molly, make no secret of the fact that they have been analysands forever.

Sarris's reviews tend to move from the specificity of proper noun, character, and plot, to some large sweeping statement about the human condition, as grasped from a viewpoint of tolerance for people's need to reach for happiness and the inevitable suffering when they don't get it. I would call this the "wisdom" perspective. He is always trying to move the reader to a more adult—by which I mean disenchanted but self-aware and, therefore, hopeful again—grasp of the patterns under human behavior. (*Behavioral,* another Sarris word!) At his best, he is able to show how a film's technique, its story, and the larger sociopolitical themes it touches upon all converge to create a certain aesthetic experience.

If *The America Cinema* had the most impact on me, my favorite book by Sarris has become *Confessions of a Cultist,* partly because in these reviews he seems most relaxed, most in tune with the films that were being released, and most able to keep all these factors of visual formalism and sociology in balance. Take, at random, this excerpt from his piece on Resnais's *La Guerre Est Finie:*

> If *La Guerre Est Finie* is in some ways the most satisfying movie Resnais has made, credit is due largely to the lucidity and integrity of Yves Montand's characterization of Diago, a revolutionary engulfed by fears, fantasies, and futilities. However fragmented the director's feelings may be, Montand remains a rock of commitment, and with Montand's solidity as an actor serving as an anchor of style, a sea of images can be unified into a mental characterization. Whereas the awesome majesty of the late Nikolai Cherassov obliterated montage in the late Sergi Eisenstein's *Ivan the Terrible,* the humanity of Montand domesticates montage in *La Guerre Est Finie.* We are no longer concerned with the pretentious counterpoint of love and the Bomb, past and present, illusion and reality, society and individual, and so on. We are obsessed instead with the doubts and the fantasies of Diego. Through his mind passes what we know and feel about the heritage of the Old Left, that last, desperate camaraderie commemorated in kitchens and cemeteries as old comrades grapple with the old rhetoric they are doomed never to forget and the new reality they are doomed never to understand.
>
> For Resnais it is enough to celebrate remembrance and mourn forgetfulness as fragments of personality and politics disintegrate in the void of time. Civilization is the process of trying to remember, and Resnais once did a documentary on the Bibliotheque Nationale as the supreme ornament of civilization. Cinema, however, is more than remembering and forgetting. It is also acting, doing, resolving, indeed being. Cinema, like life, is a process of creating memories for the future. Resnais has always drawn on the past without paying for the future. His cinema has been hauntingly beautiful if dramatically improvident in its ghostliness. His characters have been paralyzed by the sheer pastness of their sensibilities.
>
> Montand's Diego is no exception, but a marvelous thing has happened. Montand's dignity and bearing have broken through the formal shell of Resnais' art to dramatize the doubts and hesitations of the director. Diego has become a hero of prudence and inaction. He has shown what it is to be a man without the obvious flourishes of virility so fashionable today. (Even the stately explicitness of the lovemaking is a measure of the hero's stature.) To be a man it is above all necessary to be patient as one's life dribbles away on the back streets, blind alleys, and dead ends of political impotence. The at times agonizing slowness of *La Guerre Est Finie*

achieves the pathos of patience by expressing a devotion to detail common to both Diego and Resnais.

It has always seemed that Resnais was more suited to documentary than fiction because of preoccupations with facts rather than truths. The parts in Resnais always seem superior to the whole, and if *La Guerre Est Finie* is an exception, it is because the integral behaviorism of a performer has buttressed the analytical style of a director. It is as if Resnais were dropping things all over the screen, and Montand were walking around picking them up. That *La Guerre Est Finie* finally makes us weep is a tribute to Montand's tenacity.

This is careful, cultivated, highly perceptive prose, much more serene and poised than one expects to find in a weekly column; and it reminds us what a fine writer Sarris can be, when he takes the trouble. I would single out for attention: (1) Sarris's deep grasp of film history (Eisenstein, Resnais's entire oeuvre), which helps place this particular picture in context; (2) his shying away from unpacking the Ideas in a film (as he says about Pierrot le Fou, in what could be a credo: "But the point is still to see what is felt rather than to figure out what is meant"); (3) the flexibility of his auteurism stance, as evidenced by his willingness to credit Montand with the much of the film's tone; (4) his stoicism and generalized wisdom teaching: civilization is remembering; to be a man requires patience "as one's life dribbles away"; and (5) the formal analysis of montage and mise-en-scène, here given especially witty expression in the image of Montand picking up what Resnais has scattered.

I am more partial to Sarris's reviews from this period than to his polemics. The problem with the polemics (see *The Primal Screen*) is not so much that they seem dated as that they raise the spectacle of an insufficiently acknowledged hostility in a critic whose strong suit is fair-minded balance. No regular critic of the arts can be entirely free of aggressive hostility; some of the best (such as Pauline Kael or John Simon) know how to dramatize their malice in an entertaining way. But Sarris has always been slow to anger, a reluctant counterpuncher, so that when he takes after an opponent he does so in a conflicted way, backtracking, qualifying, and so on, and when he lands a direct punch its mean-spiritedness seems out of character.

The gleefully provoking Kael is perhaps the only female opponent who could have elicited from Sarris an ungentlemanly surliness. Since the closing of the "auteurist wars," what has become more and more noticeable in Sarris is the consolidation of his gallantry. He seems to go out of his way to endorse any movie with a strong woman character who is treated respectfully or emerges triumphantly (which sometimes results in overpraising flawed films like *Chasing Amy* or *Beyond Rangoon*). He has compiled lists of the years' best performances by actresses, however small the role or unsung the picture, dispensing what seems like a big, gushing valentine to what used to be called "the fairer sex."

He will rush to the defense of a maligned actress, as when he denounces "all the gleeful gossip about the commercial demise of Ms. Roberts. She has never been lovelier or spunkier or more intelligently womanly." Formerly I was tempted to see his wife's feminist hand in all this, but the more I came to know Molly Haskell, the more I realized that she tends to be both more tough-minded and less sentimental about women. No, Sarris's chivalry toward women is his own likably quaint feature, marking him as a man from a bygone generation.

I am amazed that Sarris can continue to write intelligently and open-mindedly about movies year after year in his *New York Observer* column. What I miss, to be honest, is his visual analysis; whole columns may go by without his saying a word about camera placement, mise-en-scène, surface textures. In its place is a great deal of social commentary—attempts to spar with the zeitgeist—which frankly interests me less. Sarris has metamorphosed his persona into a somewhat grumpy, still liberal old geezer commenting on matters of race or economics or gender.

I noticed the same thing happening to Kael in her last years at the *New Yorker:* an increasingly irritable attempt to monitor the zeitgeist, while withdrawing a certain emotional energy from caring about movies themselves. The current Sarris will often use a film as a jumping-off point for a disquisition on some social phenomenon or a chance to walk down memory lane (sometimes by quoting himself from an earlier review). He will also often announce a prejudice—such as indifference to a genre or to a certain performer—and disqualify himself in advance as the ideal reviewer for the movie in question, even as he grapples with a few issues it raises. Sometimes it is clearly a matter of passion spent and loyalty to one's youth, as when he announces his refusal to take the up-and-coming French filmmaker Oliver Assayas as seriously as the old New Wave directors. (As Lloyd Bentsen would put it: I knew Francois Truffaut, Mr. Assayas, and you're no Francois Truffaut.)

So essentially what Sarris's weekly column offers is the opportunity to watch him shifting through the celluloid sand of time, pronouncing on the day's headlines and sharing his enthusiasms for some aspect of a new movie. It is a column, more than an actual review, and, as such, a basket for digressions. What is curious is that this onetime systematizer has lost the appetite to put the cinematic present in order. He likes movies, always has, and will respond with pleasure, if given half a chance, to the latest release. Gone is the hierarchical itch, however. I miss the old lawgiver: it's a bit like watching one's once-terrifying father sink into a mild, fond embrace of the moment. But enough of the Oedipal subplot. Clearly Andrew Sarris's criticism has meant the world to me. If it no longer affects me as deeply, that is partly because I have become my own man through cannibalizing him. Isn't that what *Festschrift* is meant to demonstrate?

The Critic Who Helped
Teach Me to Think about Movies

Leonard Maltin

*A*ndrew Sarris helped teach me to think about movies . . . but he didn't do it in an easy way.

I had gotten the movie bug quite young, and by the time I was twelve I was traveling from my home in New Jersey to the New Yorker Theatre on Broadway and 88th Street in Manhattan on a regular basis. The New Yorker was a haven for movie buffs, and a godsend for a budding one like myself, because it programmed an endless series of great double features from the vast reaches of film history. Upper West Siders like Peter Bogdanovich and William K. Everson helped theater owner Dan Talbot with ideas and program notes. This was the mid- to late 1960s, and it was a great period for this quintessential revival theater.

One day I read that someone was opening a movie bookstore around the corner to be called the New Yorker Bookshop. I wandered in on its opening weekend, and there discovered a magazine I'd never seen before: *Film Culture*. It was, in fact, the issue in which Sarris's manifesto on American cinema was first published. I bought it on the spot. (Having half-naked Busby Berkeley chorus girls on the cover was, I thought, an amusing nod to salesmanship.)

As I started to read the issue, I became confused and angry. Why was Billy Wilder—already a hero of mine—relegated to a section called "Less Than Meets the Eye"? Why was Lewis Milestone a lesser director because he made both a great antiwar movie *(All Quiet on the Western Front)* and a probing look at war itself *(A Walk in the Sun)*? And why was Sarris so enthusiastic about filmmakers whose names I barely knew? How could they rate more enthusiasm and approval than, say, Otto Preminger?

Please understand: I was a kid. I was just feeling my way. I was immersed in the Marx Brothers and W. C. Fields and hadn't yet encountered Sam Fuller or Budd Boetticher. The first director I ever encountered in person (when I was about sixteen) was Rouben Mamoulian. My awareness of filmmaking up to then was superficial. I was so enamored of stars, especially stars of the "golden age," that I seldom thought about writers or directors. Mamoulian changed all that, during a weeklong visit to the then–Huntington Hartford Museum, when the notorious Raymond Rohauer presented a retrospective of his work. Mamoulian cut a very impressive figure, especially to my youthful gaze. He had an imperial bearing and was irresistibly eloquent. (When Rohauer presented him with an award in the form of a bronze sculpture, depicting a sticklike human figure, Mamoulian thanked him for "this emaciated Oscar.") Suddenly, hearing this man talk about the many creative decisions—and mundane problems—involved in making *Becky Sharp,* or *Dr. Jekyll and Mr. Hyde,* or *Queen Christina,* or even *High, Wide and Handsome,* I became aware of the power of that man behind the camera and how completely he fashioned the finished product onscreen.

And now, I had to contend with Sarris and his argumentative evaluations. (Mamoulian, incidentally, was not exactly dismissed, but pigeonholed with the eccentrics.) To this young and impressionable film buff, Sarris's writing—and his polemicizing—had a profound effect. It urged me to form my own counteropinions and to find a way to express them.

Then, a few short years later, I had occasion to meet Sarris. By this time, I was editing my own film-buff magazine, though still in my teens. We were both scheduled to speak before a conference of schoolteachers in New Jersey, and I did my presentation first, which had something to do with vintage Hollywood short subjects. I can't remember much about it except that I showed a very funny Joe McDoakes comedy from the 1950s called *So You Want to Go to a Nightclub.*

What I will never forget is the way Andy picked up on my presentation and wove it into his extemporaneous talk. He cited scenes from the comedy short—bringing up points I hadn't thought of, naturally—and talked most pointedly about the difference between real life and real-life-as-seen-in-movies. He used as a dramatic example an incident everyone in that auditorium knew far too well: the shooting of Lee Harvey Oswald by Jack Ruby. At that time, closer to the events of 1963, everyone had committed that television coverage to memory.

But it took Sarris to point out, to this lay audience, that if a movie director had staged the same event, he would have had "coverage." There would have been shots of Ruby approaching the area, close-ups of Dallas cops reacting, shrieking faces in the crowd, and so on. All this may sound obvious, but to us sitting there that day, it wasn't; it was a perfect way to lead us into a deeper discussion of how a director manipulates "reality."

I never had the opportunity to sit in on any of Sarris's classes at Columbia, and I regret that. I have a feeling that he must be a wonderful teacher. He certainly taught me, not only by example, but by prodding me to think on my own, to reach for ideas I otherwise might not have formulated. For that I'll always be grateful. And I suspect I am not the only one who was affected that way by his groundbreaking critical work and directorial research.

What's more, he was right about Fuller and Boetticher . . . and he's long since apologized in print to Billy Wilder and elevated him to his pantheon of great directors. How can we not admire, respect, and pay homage to this most influential of critics?

Ruined by a Book

Kenneth Turan

*W*hile admitting it is something of an embarrassment for a film critic, in many ways it is books that are my true passion. It is books that I treasure and collect the way my colleagues acquire videos and laser discs, books that I find myself turning to for solace and enlightenment.

Film books, not surprisingly, are a special interest, and of all the increasing thousands that continue to pass through my hands, if I had to select one as the most influential, the choice would be clear: *The American Cinema: Directors and Directions, 1929–1968,* by Andrew Sarris.

As I write this, my original 1968 Dutton paperback copy of Sarris's book sits next to me, its pages inevitably worn and marked by fingerprints, its spine faded, its classic Milton Glaser–designed cover cracked and marred. Also nearby is the less frequently seen hardback edition, as well as the spring 1963 issue of *Film Culture* (America's Independent Motion Picture Magazine) with that boggling still of chained maidens from "Roman Scandals" on the cover, the first place Sarris's study appeared.

But it's that paperback that holds the strongest memories because looking at it recalls the excitement I felt when I first discovered the book, brings me back to where I was at the time, and reminds me why Sarris's thoughts had such a strong effect.

The year of *The American Cinema*'s publication, 1968, was, coincidentally, also the year I first seriously entertained thoughts of becoming a film critic. As a graduate student of journalism at Columbia University in New York, I signed up for a seminar in reviewing from Judith Crist and was intrigued at the possibility of combining my twin enthusiasms for writing and film. In those prevideo days, I was spending much of my life taking subways between the Bleeker Street, the New Yorker, and the Thalia theaters, filling in gaps in my moviegoing experience. Naturally, I was looking to books for the same kind of sustenance, and when I came across *The American Cinema* I got more serious assistance than I was prepared for.

Since (to paraphrase Cocteau on both Abel Gance and Picasso) there was American film criticism before Sarris and film criticism after it, since so much of what he brought to the table is now taken for granted, it is difficult to go back and pinpoint the elements that made his book such a potent experience when first encountered. But picking up that rugged Dutton paperback and flipping through its pages helps highlight several factors. For instance: startling comprehensiveness. For someone who would've had trouble naming more than a few dozen American directors, the fact that Sarris not only knew some two hundred but also found specific things of note to say about each of them was a situation I found as personally daunting as the book's "alphabetical list of over 6,000 films with the year of release and director included." Clearly, if I was to become a critic, I had a lot of catching up to do, a process that is still going on.

Acuity of judgment conveyed in an elegant style. Like many of my friends, one of whom took to ironically calling Sarris's book "Bible," I did not so much read it cover to cover as bit by bit, consulting and digesting the sections on particular directors when appropriate.

For years afterward, for instance, after making the extended acquaintance of a particular filmmaker's work, I'd reach for *The American Cinema* and see how my thought about it compared to Sarris's. And invariably I'd be impressed by how well he'd extracted each filmmaker's essence. I still, for instance, can't see anything by Sam Fuller, a director I'd been fascinated with since childhood, without thinking of Sarris's dictum: "Fuller is an authentic American primitive whose works have to be seen to be understood. Seen, not heard or synopsized."

Though it's been a while since that Sarris impulse struck me, I recently caught up with Anthony Mann's little-seen *Man of the West,* starring Gary Cooper, and wondered what Sarris had thought of the director. There he was, talking about Mann's "psychological intensity" and how his films are especially interesting "for their insights into the uneasy relationships between men and women in a world of violence and action." On the money again, after all these years.

The nerve of judgmentally dividing up all of American filmmakers into eleven categories, ranging from "Pantheon Directors" and "The Far Side of Paradise" through "Expressive Esoterica," "Lightly Likable," and "Strained Seriousness." Though I'd quibble with some of his choices today, few of them are seriously off the mark (though putting Sam Peckinpah in "Oddities, One Shots and Newcomers" is a jolt, given what he accomplished post-1968), and besides, the subjective notion of accuracy is far from the point. The very act of division encouraged the kind of serious discussion about Hollywood that was ultimately more important than who was placed where.

Insistence on the importance of some directors I had not yet given much thought to. Douglas Sirk and, yes, even pantheonist Howard Hawks were little more than vaguely familiar names to me at the time. Sarris did more than make an investigation of their work seem imperative; in a broader sense he taught me not to be narrowminded, to look at as wide a spectrum of film as possible before reaching decisions as to who was important and who was not.

I've saved what was unquestionably Sarris's biggest and most obvious impact for last: his championing of the auteur theory. Though we are now living in an age of child cineastes, who presumably are exposed to Sarris in the cradle, there were none in my Brooklyn neighborhood, where I was such a faithful viewer of WOR-TV's Million Dollar Movie that it shocked me to learn that the program had borrowed its theme music from *Gone With The Wind* and not the other way around.

I'd never heard of the *politique des auteurs,* and I was used to thinking about films one at a time without giving much thought to what if anything anyone except the actors had done previously. The auteur theory's championing of the director as a man of consistent vision gave me a way to examine films, to better understand them, that had frankly never occurred to me.

Like many young critics, I had a tendency, especially at first, to overdo things, to overapply Sarris's thoughtful lessons. The director was Ahab to me, out there alone, the captain of a film's destiny. It rarely seemed necessary to worry about the other people involved, the rest of the *Pequod*'s crew so to speak.

Living and working in Los Angeles for many years has not surprisingly tempered much of my classically youthful zealotry. For one thing, the role of the writer is at times as overlooked now as the director's ever was, if not more so. For another, I began to realize that, especially in the American system of filmmaking, any number of individuals, from the cinematographer, editor, and producer to the production designer, composer, art director, set decorator, and so on down the line, can all have their own strong influences on the shape of a film. In fact, to accurately assign either praise or blame on any given picture, you have to be on the set yourself or risk being easily misled.

Looking at all this now, I've come to realize that Sarris's influence was somewhat different than I'd initially imagined. It's not so much his passion for the director that has been lasting, but his intelligent passion for film itself. Reading *The American Cinema* convinced me, almost without my knowing it, that the movies were a subject that could handle serious thought, that could be written about lucidly and intelligently. I still think that's true, and whenever I manage a successful stab in that direction, I feel myself in Sarris's debt.

The American Cinema and the Critic Who Guided Me Through It

Peter Lehman

$\mathscr{I}$have often thought that I owe my career to three people: Blake Edwards, Andrew Sarris, and Laura Mulvey—and the three are, not surprisingly, connected. I owe to Edwards and Sarris the passionate love of films and film criticism that led to my career, and to Mulvey the central place that gender studies would hold throughout my career. To pay tribute to Sarris, I must touch on the other two.

I started college at the University of Wisconsin-Madison in the fall of 1963. Throughout my entire undergraduate education there was, to the best of my knowledge, not one film course offered at the university. In one of my classes, a very short unit on cinema was devoted to Arthur Knight's *The Liveliest Art*. In 1964, like many of my peers, I went to see *The Pink Panther* and, later the same year, *A Shot in the Dark*. Also like many of my peers, I loved both films. I presumed that what delighted me was Peter Sellers's now legendary performance as Inspector Clouseau. Indeed, I liked both films so much that I returned to see them numerous times, the first time in my life that I had returned to a theater repeatedly to see the same film. I memorized not just lines but entire scenes.

In the process, I discovered that what made me laugh was not just the story, not just the acting, not just the dialogue but rather where the camera was, how it moved or didn't, the editing, and the composition (especially screen space and offscreen space). And so, with what many considered and still consider trifling slapstick visual humor, the concept of cinema was born in my mind. Who, I wondered, was responsible for creating this entire complex whole, deciding where to put the camera and how to stage the action? I had discovered the concept of the film director.

71

During the summer of 1968, I moved to New York City, where I spent the next three years. The entire New York cinema scene had an extraordinary impact upon me—the revival houses showing classic Hollywood films, the European art cinema, and, perhaps most of all, the silent cinema with retrospectives of Griffith, Chaplin, and Keaton. I grew up in a small town in southern Wisconsin, and I had never even seen a silent film. Yet in many ways the most important thing for me in the midst of all this was Andrew Sarris, who became my guide through the bewildering maze.

Before coming to New York, I had never heard of Sarris, nor for that matter the *Village Voice*. To this day, however, I remember the first time I picked up a copy of *The American Cinema: Directors and Directions 1929–1968*. Thumbing through it, I immediately looked for an entry for Blake Edwards. If *The Pink Panther* and *A Shot in the Dark* had taught me to love the American genre cinema, Sarris taught me that substantive observations could be made about that cinema and its directors. Even more importantly, standing in a New York bookstore, I felt vindicated. It is impossible to overestimate how important it was, at that point in time, that there was someone in the United States of Sarris's stature and visibility who legitimized the artistic worth of American genre-entertainment directors. He didn't read what the films told us about the country at the time they were made, or any other such important-sounding thing; he valued the films for what they were—art, and sometimes great art. He talked about the director's vision, worldview, and style, and he talked about these things like they really mattered.

The combination of coming to New York with my discovery of Edwards's Clouseau films and picking up Sarris's book in 1968 primed me for the 1969 release of Edwards's *Darling Lili*. It was the first film I ever went to with an auteurist frame of mind, and my delight in it sealed the deal.

When I returned to the University of Wisconsin in 1971 to finish an M.A. degree in English, I discovered that a new department of communication arts with a film studies area had been formed. I immediately changed majors and received my M.A. and Ph.D. in film studies. When it came time to write my M.A. thesis, I proposed one on Blake Edwards and was told that he wasn't worthy. It is important to remember that aside from Sarris and his students, such as William Paul at the *Village Voice*, virtually no one in the United States was taking Edwards seriously at that time. Influenced in my next choice by Sarris's *The American Cinema,* I was able to make a case for John Ford due to the long-standing recognition his work had received, and so began another major thread of my career. To this day, my research on John Ford and that coauthored with William Luhr on Blake Edwards remains central for me.

Looking back upon Sarris's entries on Ford and Edwards in *The American Cinema* today, I am still struck by beautifully written passages of startling clarity and insight. For example, Sarris boldly links Ford's *How Green Was My Valley* with Orson Welles's *Citizen Kane,* noting that, though made respectively by a middle-aged man and a young man, they are both really the work of old men, inaugurating a new cinema of memory. Summarizing Ford's career by decade, Sarris economically delineates Ford's work from the thirties through the fifties in regards to drama, the epic, and symbolic forms.

In some regards his entry on Edwards is even more remarkable for two reasons. Sarris quotes from a 1963 piece in which he perceived Edwards as a significant auteur even prior to *The Pink Panther* and *A Shot in the Dark.* Whereas Ford's career was over by 1968, Edwards was entering his middle period. But this didn't stop Sarris from getting to the heart of central issues. He characterizes the importance of the manner in which Edwards's style is built upon a blatant disregard for such slapstick conventions as the fact that there should be a probable premise for a slapstick gag and that no one should get hurt.

Sarris's version of auteurism has not fared well in academia, nor for that matter has any version. This is not the place to rehearse the by now well-known sequence of events that included revisions of the auteur theory by Peter Wollen; the rejection of it by 1970s Marxist/feminist/psychoanalytic ideological criticism mounted in such journals as *Screen;* the famous "death of the author" pronouncements by such influential figures as Roland Barthes and Michel Foucault; and the more recent cultural studies and reception studies approaches that have studied the culture at large and the audiences for popular films. Since I have been influenced to varying degrees by all of those critical schools of thought, however, it helps me pay tribute to Sarris by considering just why he remains of such central importance to me more than thirty years after he wrote *The American Cinema* and after so many years of theoretical and critical water over the dam. What precisely is his lasting importance? Why do I care so much about Sarris that thirty years after I discovered him, I jumped at the opportunity to be part of Emanuel Levy's tribute volume, rearranging my schedule and rushing to meet a tight deadline during the holiday season? This essay means as much if not more to me than anything I have published. Why?

Sarris, of course, has had a long varied career and like any such career there are many phases to it. The publication of *The American Cinema* in 1968 is certainly only one small part of Sarris's contribution and one that, on balance, may frequently be overemphasized. But this essay doesn't pretend to possess such balance. I only met Sarris once briefly when he spoke in Tucson during the 1980s, and he himself, as I recall, tried to minimize the era of his notorious auteurism. But writers do not control what part of their work has lasting influence, and for me the publication of *The American Cinema* had great influence, and it is to that work that I devote this essay.

The profoundest tribute that I can pay to Sarris is not to say that I followed him; I am in no sense a disciple. My dissertation, *John Ford and the Auteur Theory*, is clear in demarcating my methodological differences from Sarris's version of auteurism. Young scholars are typically driven to define and validate their own methods and style by, in part, revolting against established figures, and I was no exception. Indeed, I suspect one could read my dissertation as being highly critical of Sarris, though, from my perspective, that would be a misreading.

At that point in my life, long, detailed, formal analyses of individual films with much attention to visual style and motifs were one major characteristic of my work that contrasted quite sharply with Sarris's brief emphasis on entire career overviews and worldviews. In my later work on Ford and my coauthored work on Blake Edwards, I added feminist and psychoanalytical models to the formalism. Anyone familiar with Sarris's *The American Cinema* as well as his other writings would hardly characterize them as formalist, feminist, and psychoanalytic in approach.

To me, the highest form of tribute to pay someone is to acknowledge the manner in which his or her work enabled one's own. This became clear to me years ago when Chris Straayer, currently a film studies professor at New York University, told me, in a remarkably generous moment, that my work on masculinity and the male body gave her the courage to do her work. If there is a grain of truth in that remark, it is for me the highest compliment I can imagine because Straayer's work is of such importance. At the time that she made the observation, I was surprised that the work of a heterosexual man on the male body would be of such importance to a lesbian feminist. And it is here that I want to turn to Mulvey for a moment.

While in graduate school in the early 1970s, I met Laura Mulvey. Once again, Blake Edwards's films played a role; we quickly discovered we shared a love of them. When Mulvey published "Visual Pleasure and the Narrative Cinema," in 1975, it had an immediate, profound impact upon me. My interest in Mulvey's work gradually led me to an area her essay not only overlooks but also virtually denies: the sexual representation of the male body in cinema as an object of the gaze. Yet, without Mulvey's opening the door, it is unimaginable to me that I could have ever done that work.

It is only figures of the greatest importance that open such doors for a multitude of scholars. Most of us are thrilled if we can do so for one or two people. Similarly, once the door has been opened, it only makes sense that those who walk through will pursue different paths. Imitation is not the highest form of flattery; originality and departure is. Those who follow and imitate are usually condemned to be pale copies of their masters. In Sarris's case, woe unto him or her who would attempt to copy. He wittily gets to the point in a manner that many academics never do. He once remarked to the effect that John Simon was the greatest film critic of the nineteenth century, that a Buster Keaton retrospective was one of the greatest artistic events of this or any other century, and that James Aubrey while head of Paramount was always judged guilty until proven guiltier. I can no longer recall the exact quotations and may very well be misremembering them, much like we so often misremember favorite moments in movies—they become the moments we want them to be, but they do so because the force of the writing or the imagery grabs us and becomes part of us in some way.

Sarris is a somewhat unique figure within American film culture, straddling the lines between academia and the culture at large. As this tribute volume demonstrates, he reached so many different kinds of people ranging from those within the film industry to the academy to countless filmgoers who never pick up an academic film journal or book. And yet his teaching at Columbia University has left a rich legacy within academia, with former students such as William Paul and Emanuel Levy assuming positions of prominence.

Sarris's fate within academia itself is indicative of a central component of film studies: its notion of progress. Throughout most of the United States, film studies as we know it today began around the time that Sarris published *The American Cinema*. Before then, there were only a handful of isolated programs; now nearly every college and university curriculum includes film studies. Yet during this approximately thirty-year history, what strikes me is how quickly a succession of competing methodologies and schools of thought have been taken up and abandoned. Many academics pride themselves on how what they are doing at the moment cuts through the errors and limitations of previous methods, marking a clear progress over them.

At its best, this spirit has pushed film studies into new directions, and at its worst it has led to simple arrogance, dismissiveness, and condescension. On balance, however, what strikes me is how quickly scholars and their methods are forgotten. I chose the word *abandoned* above very carefully since my point is not, of course, that we shouldn't move onward. I do believe, however, that we should not simply abandon and forget what came before nor should we construct simple narratives of progress of how we got from there to here. We have to have a rich historical appreciation of why certain key figures like Sarris spoke with such impact to his audience when he did, and not just view his work as wrong or limited, as if the march of history discovered the truth and broke the limitations. There are lasting insights in Sarris's analysis of the American cinema and its directors.

Authorship studies, not surprisingly, have come back in film studies, and all the different models of the director as author are, in part, indebted to Sarris's critical heritage. Just as certainly as no one can fully grasp montage without Sergei Eisenstein, or long takes with depth of field and moving camera without Andre Bazin, no one can fully grasp authorship without Sarris. Within the context of a tribute to Sarris, it is fitting to address the inadequate notion of progress in much of film studies with reference to a film by one of his pantheon auteur directors—John Ford's *The Man Who Shot Liberty Valance*. In it, Ford presents a justly celebrated, complexly ambiguous account of progress in the Old West. The settling and taming of the West and the transformation of the desert into the garden is not just represented as a simple good; something valuable and vital is lost as well.

And so it is with film studies and Sarris. Sarris helped ignite a passionate love of films and the directors who made them. Aesthetics mattered, as well they should. I for one miss that passionate love of films and filmmakers in the current academic climate. To this day, when I discover a new filmmaker who I think is really good or even when I begrudgingly want to compliment a filmmaker whom I don't like, I'll often simply remark in shorthand that he or she is a real "auteur," by which I mean a filmmaker of substance who shapes and forms films with careful thought and attention to style, not just as window dressing but as integral to storytelling. For whatever cultural significance films may have, the single most important question for me when I go to a movie remains, "Who directed it?" I pursued a career teaching and writing about movies because of my love of them and the people who made them. I owe that love in part to Andrew Sarris, and I thank him for it.

The Legacy of Auteurism

Emanuel Levy

"I believe a work is good to the degree that it expresses the man who created it."

Orson Welles

"Auteurism is the single most productive concept in film history over the past quarter century."

Thomas Schatz, film historian

$\mathcal{O}$ver the past three decades, auteurism has influenced the very way we perceive, think, and write about movies. In this essay, I wish to contextualize auteurism, both its French and American versions, and to show its pervasive effects on every aspect of the film world.

FRENCH ORIGINS

In the late 1940s, French critic Alexandre Astruc drafted the auteur theory around the metaphor of the camera-stylo, the camera as fountain pen. Astruc suggested that film should be read as a text, and that a good film is one in which the director is the main creative force. Accordingly, the entire production crew should be subsumed under the director's leadership for his self-expression. The Paris-based journal *Cahiers du Cinema,* founded by Andre Bazin and Jacques Doniol-Valcroze in 1951, was extremely important in propagating auteurism in the film world.

The approach was formalized by a group of critics writing for the magazine, who fashioned the "auteur policy" as an alternative to the then-prevalent sociological method of content analysis. Francois Truffaut first postulated auteurism in his 1954 article, "Une certaine tendance du cinema francaise," in *Cahiers du Cinema*. In this seminal piece, Truffaut developed the concept of "la politique des auteurs," in which he argued that a single person, the director, should assume aesthetic responsibility for the film's overall look. Truffaut's target was the "Tradition of Quality" ("la tradition de la qualite"), manifest in French postwar films that were adapted from novels and were heavily dependent on plot. Truffaut attacked the "psychologically realistic" films of Claude Autant-Lara, Jean Delannay, Rene Clement, and others, because they were more of a writer's than a director's movies.

La politique des auteurs assumed immediate and specific meanings. First, it called for a strong stance in favor of some directors and against some others. Auteurists elevated the stature of French filmmakers Jean Renoir, Robert Bresson, and Jean Cocteau, and of American directors Howard Hawks, John Ford, and British-born Hitchcock. Second, auteurism called for the reevaluation of Hollywood directors who had to overcome many more obstacles than their European counterparts. During the studio system, directors were assigned scripts over which they had little control and had to deal with domineering studio moguls and powerful movie stars.

Searching for thematic and stylistic consistencies among the various films of individual directors, the auteurists elevated identifiable personal signature to a standard of value. Auteur directors were defined as the creators of a personal world vision and a distinctive cinematic style. The *Cahiers'* critics perceived Hollywood as the most extreme contrast to the "refined" French cinema of the 1950s, which they wanted to destroy. It was when the *Cahiers'* critics applied the auteur theory to the apparently complacent functionaries of the Hollywood factory system that controversy erupted. The feeling was, as Dave Kehr has observed, that Hawks and Hitchcock, who engaged in the commercial exploitation of "juvenile" genres, such as westerns and thrillers, couldn't possibly be elaborating a personal vision of the world stamped with their own marks as artists. In pointing out how deeply the supposedly uncaring craftsmen were involved in their movies, the auteurists succeeded in unearthing numerous personal—and by their definition good—Hollywood films.

AMERICAN AUTEURISM

In 1962, the magazine *Film Culture* published two articles by Andrew Sarris that revolutionized American film criticism. In the first, "Notes on the Auteur Theory," Sarris Americanized Truffaut's "la politique des auteurs," suggesting the director as the author of a film and visual style as the key to assessing a director's standing as auteur. In the second piece, Sarris evaluated 106 American and 7 foreign directors, placing them in categories that ranged from "the Pantheon" to "Oddities and One Shots."

The immediate reaction to Sarris's essay was violent, particularly Pauline Kael's outrageous piece "Circles and Squares." To this day, more people have read Kael's rebuttal than Sarris's original essay. But the effect went beyond Sarris and Kael—the entire critical establishment was shaken up. Dwight MacDonald reportedly resigned his column in *Film Quarterly* when Sarris was invited to contribute, and Richard Dyer MacCann conspicuously omitted Sarris from his anthology *Film: A Montage of Theories,* although he included Kael's piece. Serving as the catalyst for discovery, auteurism was part of a general ferment, a shake-up that ultimately did a lot of good.

Auteurism and genre criticism dominated film studies until the late 1970s, when new perspectives, mostly European, began to leave their mark. Genre criticism treated established cinematic forms, such as the western and the screwball comedy, whereas auteurism, in both its French and American versions, celebrated certain filmmakers who worked effectively within those forms. These critical approaches, which complemented one another, reflected sensitivity to mainstream filmmaking in addressing themselves to practices that had already prevailed within the industry.

The notion that the director is—and should be—the controlling creative force was a logical step in film criticism. As Thomas Schatz has noted, anyone who discussed the "Lubitsch touch" in the 1930s or talked about the next "Hitchcock thriller" in the 1940s was in fact practicing auteurism. Hitchcock once said that he was "less interested in stories than in the manner of telling them." In many ways, auteur analysis was a formalized response to this particular conception of filmmaking.

It took several years for Sarris's work to exert its influence on critics and scholars. Sarris was then writing for the *Village Voice,* a popular publication among young intellectuals. His challenge to the near-monopoly of the social-realist critics was gladly adopted by younger critics, who found it refreshing to examine films as the creation of individual artists rather than abstract social forces.

In 1968, Sarris expanded his theory to book length with *The American Cinema,* often called "the Bible of Auteurism." The book is devoted to the ranking of Hollywood directors according to aesthetic criteria, starting "at the top with the bundles of movies credited to the most important directors, and work[ing] downward, director by director, movie by movie, year by year, toward a survey of what was best in American sound movies between 1929 and 1966."

Sarris's goal was to restructure American film history in terms of the careers of individual directors, starting with the greatest and working down to those of lesser interest. He looked for thematic and stylistic continuities, focusing on the totality of a director's work along dimensions of coherent/incoherent and personal/impersonal work. Sarris claimed that, because so much of the American cinema is commissioned, Hollywood directors are often forced to express their personalities through the visual treatment of the material rather than its literary content.

In *The American Cinema,* the number of directors totals about two hundred, placed in eleven categories. Fourteen names appear under the heading of "Pantheon Directors": Charlie Chaplin, Robert Flaherty, John Ford, D. W. Griffith, Howard Hawks, Alfred Hitchcock, Buster Keaton, Fritz Lang, Ernst Lubitsch, F. W. Murnau, Max Ophuls, Jean Renoir, Josef von Sternberg, and Orson Welles. The Pantheon group is defined as "directors who have transcended their technical problems with a personal vision of the world. To speak any of their names is to evoke a self-contained world with its own laws and landscapes. They were also fortunate enough to find the proper conditions and collaborators for the full expression of their talent."

Auteurists never ignored the fact that movies are a collaborative art. However, drawing an analogy with architecture, they claimed that though many craftsmen may contribute to the building of a cathedral, not every team member is equally responsible for its overall design. Similarly, for a movie to be interesting and coherent, a single personality—the director's—must come to the fore and exert its influence.

From the beginning, auteurism was more of a policy or strategy than a precise theory. Four tenets of auteurism caused the greatest dispute:

1. The director as the film's author, which meant that attention should be focused on the director, and that a film should be explored as an essentially visual medium.
2. Directorial careers, their total outputs, are more important that individual films made by filmmakers.
3. Certain Hollywood directors, when subjected to such examination, are proven to be as cinematically interesting, as emotionally rich, and as philosophically complex as European directors of "art films."
4. Mise-en-scène became the single most important idea that Sarris contributed to American film criticism. Sarris defined mise-en-scène as all those variables of a movie that remain once the screenplay has been subtracted—camera placement, duration of shots, lighting, movement of actors—variables that should be placed under the director's immediate personal control.

Shifting the emphasis from the verbal to the visual, Sarris opened a new field of exploration in his insistence that mise-en-scène was a vital element of style and of meaning. He wrote: "The auteur critic is obsessed with the wholeness of art. He looks at a film as a whole, a director as a whole. The parts, however entertaining individually, must cohere meaningfully." For Sarris, meaningful style "unifies the what and the how into a personal statement." Hence, a good film is "unified by a central idea" in which the director's personality triumphs.

On the occasion of auteurism's twenty-fifth anniversary, Sarris corrected some misunderstandings. He claimed that, from the beginning, "auteurism was more pragmatic than Platonic," and that "all we young revisionist critics knew was that there were a great many good movies from the past in danger of being dumped in the dustbin of film history by an assortment of 'realist' and 'Marxist' historians." Thus, "when we found a cluster of good movies linked by the same director, a hypothetical auteur was postulated, and the search began for an individual theme and style."

But critics need not make an "irrevocable choice" between cinema of directors, cinema of actors, cinema of genres, and cinema of social themes. "Ultimately, the auteur theory is not so much a theory as an attitude, a table of values that converts film history into directorial autobiography." The auteurist's work proceeds "bit by bit, thousands of films and thousands of conversations. Auteurism is truly a life's work."

USES AND APPLICATIONS OF AUTEURISM

A whole tradition of film scholarship, juxtaposing genre and auteur criticism, emerged. Scholars began to examine the influence of individual filmmakers, such as Ford, Hawks, and Anthony Mann, on an established genre like the western. They explored the possibility of individual vision in the context of the collective–corporate nature of film production. Any importance attached to individuals who influenced a film was weighed against the notion of film as a creation of artists, technicians, and businessmen. This did not dispute the auteur theory of attributing the film's style and meaning to its director. Nor did it deny qualitative differences that distinguish art from mediocrity. Rather, it suggested social meanings that transcended any one filmmaker. Ford and Hawks developed a distinctive point of view and personal style, but they also dealt with issues inherent in the western genre, reflected in the westerns made by other directors.

Other scholars, such as Tad Gallagher, have classified major Hollywood directors into different types of auteurs:

1. The director as an author who dominates his films completely, such as Orson Welles and Josef Von Sternberg.
2. The director as an architect who reigns, such as John Ford and Jean Renoir.
3. The director as a collaborator who keeps a low profile, such as George Cukor.

SCREENWRITERS AS AUTEURS

Critics of auteurism claimed that, by elevating only the director, other crafts were neglected, such as screenwriting. Writers create or adapt (from other sources) the film's plot, characters, dialogue, and themes. If the director is an interpretive artist, should not the screenwriter be considered the real creative force? Richard Corliss, who was a student of Sarris's, wrote the book *Talking Pictures* (1974), in which he proposed that, unless he writes the screenplay, the Hollywood director is an interpretive artist, steering the script, actors, and camera in the right direction. According to this conception, the director is less an architect than a foreman, less a painter than an illustrator, less a composer than a conductor. For Corliss, the solution to the scenarist-versus-director problem will be resolved when the same individual writes and directs a picture.

Tracing thematic patterns and consistencies in the work of major screenwriters, *Talking Pictures* was meant to challenge and "correct" Sarris's notion of auteurism. Corliss felt that auteur critics were relinquishing the original intent of analyzing visual style as the key to directorial temperament, settling instead on the analysis of thematic structures, which, he argued, was the writer's, not the director's, domain. He proposed that writers who imposed their ideas on a diverse variety of directors should be valued as central creative forces, calling for a more detailed consideration of film as a collaborative art. Ideally, film criticism should consist of painstaking efforts in assessing the relative contribution of the producer, director, writer, actors, cinematographer, designer, and actors.

As interesting as Corliss's proposition is, it is impossible to accomplish until and unless critics are present on the set as participant observants of the filmmaking process. Year after year, the Los Angeles Film Critics Association debates whether to establish a new award category for editing, and the counterargument is that critics never really know the particular contribution of the editor vis-à-vis the director on the final cut.

Opponents of auteurism have charged that they place greater value on the director than on the film itself. There was fear that a fashionable acceptance of some directors would reach the point where criticism ceases to ask questions and lapses into a celebration of excellence. There was also the danger that a worthy film would be rejected because its creator has not made good films up until then. Andre Bazin, who was not an auteurist in the way that his disciples were, had pointed out that mediocre directors can make good films and geniuses can make bad ones. Bazin felt that auteurism needed to be "supplemented" by other theoretical approaches.

Sarris stressed the importance of combining thematic and stylistic explorations, but there was a risk that auteurists would favor thematic over stylistic analysis. Indeed, if one classified directors just by the themes of their movies, Nicholas Ray and Elia Kazan are similar (in *Rebel Without a Cause* and *Splendor in the Grass*), though their work is vastly different stylistically. Still, at the very least, auteurism raised the issue of relative and specific contribution (who did what) and suggested that responsibility and credit should be allocated more precisely. For example, several crucial speeches in John Ford's *Grapes of Wrath* were written by its producer, Daryl Zanuck, who didn't get any writing credit.

Guilty of hero-worshipping, early writings by auteurists imagined directors as autonomous geniuses who transcended the genres and the economic conditions under which they worked. Auteurism implied a certain autonomy to specific directors; a director's work was analyzed for the common elements that reflect his distinctive "worldview." But neo-Marxist critics pointed out that directors were only one variable in the total institution called cinema, that they were implicated in the system financially and ideologically, and that their worldview expressed these factors. These critics questioned the validity of auteurism because of the special ways in which cinema works as an ideological apparatus.

There was also fear that auteur critics would not respond adequately to new films. It soon became clear that auteurist criticism was of greater value in judging new films by veteran directors than in judging new films by young directors who have not established yet consistent themes or styles. One of the interesting empirical questions became, At what point of his career is a particular director justifiably declared an auteur? The problem today is that young filmmakers, such as Jim Jarmusch and Hal Hartley, are perceived as auteurs after making only one or two movies, which was never Sarris's intention.

The claim that the text expresses the feelings and personality of the author, as Richard Dyer noted, presupposes a transparency between an author and his text. For Dyer, the text could express the author's unconscious and artistic personality as something distinct from his personality in other areas of life. Since expression is only possible through codes, and codes tend to be shared, he proposed a new direction in auteurist studies that should analyze the specific way of working with codes as a way to identify a film as a typical Hawks or Hitchcock work.

Other critics pointed out that the auteurists' aim to uncover the "deep structure" (the director's personality) in order to interpret the film's "surface structure" should take into account the director's manipulation of industrial, political, technical, stylistic, and narrative variables that influence the film's final shape. Society's dominant culture and the genre's established conventions might determine the director's specific approach (in terms of formal and thematic codes) much more than the director's own personality.

MOVIE STARS AS AUTEURS

Auteurism also led to a series of studies of actors—stars as auteurs. Richard Dyer proposed a classification of movie stars along the following dimensions:

1. Actors who totally controlled their image, such as Fred Astaire or Joan Crawford.
2. Actors who contributed actively to their persona, such as Marlene Dietrich and Robert Mitchum.
3. Actors who were just one disparate voice among others in their image construction, such as Marilyn Monroe.
4. Actors who were totally the product of the studio machine, such as Lana Turner.

The extent of power movie stars possess and how they exercise their power can be determined by deconstructing them as auteurs of their films. Some stars—such as Charlie Chaplin, Buster Keaton, Mae West, Jerry Lewis, John Wayne, and Clint Eastwood—scripted or directed themselves in films. However, stars serving as just one force in their film have been more common, since that voice is not limited to matters of performance and costume but may also affect other aspects of filmmaking.

In his book *James Cagney, The Actor as Auteur,* Patrick McGilligan wishes to demonstrate that Cagney was the author of his films. According to McGilligan, under certain circumstances, an actor may influence a film as much as a writer, director, or producer. Some actors are more influential than others, and there are few performers whose acting capabilities and screen personas are so powerful that they embody and define the very essence of their films. If actors are responsible only for acting but are not involved in other artistic decisions, then they are passive icons, manipulated by writers and directors. But actors who influence artistic decisions (casting, writing, directing) and demand certain limitations on the basis of their screen personas may be regarded as "auteurs." When actors become so important to a film production as to change lines, shift meaning, influence the narrative, and signify something clear-cut to audiences, despite the intent of writers and directors, then they assume the force of an auteur.

For McGilligan, Cagney's films made with Lloyd Bacon, William Keighley, and Roy Del Ruth are all similar to one another, and more like Cagney's other films, than films by those directors with different stars. But McGilligan doesn't provide the specific aspects of Cagney's performance or character and his statements are vague. He singles out one quality of these directors' films, such as "spontaneity" (a characteristic of Bacon), "a polished emphasis on action and dialogue" (Keighley), and "urbanity" (Del Ruth).

In *Sex In The Movies,* Alexander Walker examines the various forces in the production of Greta Garbo, arguing for a model of which Garbo was only one out of many factors. Garbo had certain given features: her appearance (feminine face, masculine body), spiritual face, and pessimistic temper. But there were collaborators in the total effect, particularly Mauritz Stiller, who gave her the name *Garbo* (meaning "wood nymph" in Swedish), and William Daniels. Stiller discovered Garbo in Stockholm and shaped her performance style in line with his own idea of her. And Daniels was Garbo's lighting cameraman on all but two of her sound films. Finally, the construction of Garbo's image took place within the elaborate but specific system of the MGM studio, where Garbo had huge battles over the quality of her scripts.

In my book *John Wayne: Prophet of and the American Way of Life,* I showed that Wayne was a powerful creative influence on most of his movies after John Ford's *Stagecoach,* and particularly after Howard Hawks's *Red River.* Wayne's carefully planned theatrical entrance sets the tone for the entire movie, and his distinctive voice and delivery, cold eyes, and ironic smile shaped the meaning of his films as much as the written scripts. In the last two decades of his career, Wayne became the auteur of his films, which expressed his own vision of life rather than that of the screenwriter or director he worked with.

Since Hollywood has always emphasized "movie stars" above other elements—especially in the 1930s and 1940s, during the Golden Age of the studio system—for Dyer, the study of movie stars as authors belongs to the study of the Hollywood production system itself. For him, it is possible to establish continuities and transformations either in the totality of a star's image or in discrete elements, such as acting style, screen roles, and iconography. But continuity in stars' public images does not necessarily prove that they are responsible for them. Who is responsible, and to what extent they are responsible, for the continuities in Marilyn Monroe's screen image? The star herself, or the studio's publicity machine, trying to satisfy the public's expectations of her as a sex symbol and performer.

EFFECTS OF AUTEURISM

The test of any theory is the degree to which it produces new knowledge and new understanding of reality. Auteurism has proved its validity and pervasive impact with a number of theoretical and practical results that evolved out of its revolutionary ideas.

New Ways of Seeing Films

Auteurism marked an important intervention in film criticism—its polemics challenged the prevalent view of Hollywood as a monolithic system. Classifying films by directors represented a new way of organizing film knowledge and of ordering a new experiencing of cinema. Critic Claire Johnson noted that Sarris altered irreversibly the way movies were seen, revealing dimensions that traditional literary-based criticism had ignored. By treating movies as movies, not as poor relations or extensions of books and plays, Sarris introduced a new method of criticism. Auteurism raised the issue of whether a film should be judged as an individual work unto itself or with reference to the director's other films, both those that preceded and those that followed that work.

The *New York Times* adopted auteurism as a guiding principle when Vincent Canby, formerly writing for *Variety,* was appointed chief film critic in 1968. Implicitly or explicitly, most contemporary critics, even those who do not define themselves as auteurists, pay a greater attention while reviewing a particular film by a particular director to what that director has done before or to the specific place of that film in the director's overall career.

Art Versus Entertainment

Auteurists noted that because of the industrial–commercial nature of Hollywood, serious film artists often come through the back door. Hence, the Hollywood industry underwent a major reevaluation. The reputations of directors like Hitchcock and Minnelli, who had been dismissed by critics because they worked in such "lowbrow" forms as the suspense thriller and musical, were reconsidered. Directors who somehow had escaped the attention of American critics (such as Hawks) were recognized as major filmmakers, along with other gifted stylists who had directed low-budget "B" productions, such as Sam Fuller or Anthony Mann.

Auteur criticism pointed to the possible tension between the director's vision and the conditions and constraints for realizing this vision: studio pressures, genre conventions, star demands, and story requirements. However, for some, these constraints proved to be a source of strength, imposing discipline on their wildly eccentric instincts. As Thomas Schatz pointed out, the most celebrated American auteurs did their most expressive and significant work within conventionalized genres and within the studio system.

While acknowledging the commercial–industrial constraints placed on filmmakers, auteurists rejected the artificial distinction between art and entertainment, signaling a new way of thinking about movies. Auteurists noted that a presumably "serious social drama" by Fred Zinnemann might be less serious, less social, and less dramatic than the presumably "escapist entertainment" of a Ford western, a Minnelli musical, or a Hitchcock thriller. This notion stemmed directly from Sarris's pioneering and audacious ranking of directors, claiming that "Orson Welles makes many more mistakes than Fred Zinnemann ever could, and yet I wouldn't trade one shot from *Chimes of Midnight* for the entire oeuvre of Zinnemann."

Auteurism and Film Studies

Auteurism elevated film studies to a legitimate area of scholarly concern. In the 1960s and 1970s, there was a growing number of film courses devoted to a single director: Renoir, Hitchcock, Ford, Hawks. Auteurism also led to a new focus in film scholarship, with a flood of books on individual directors, both monographs of their work and critical biographies of their lives. The new trend began with Sarris's own monographs—*The Films of Josef von Sternberg* (1966), *The Films of Max Ophuls* (1973, unpublished), and *The John Ford Movie Mystery* (1975)—in which he examined the oeuvre of these directors as a totality rather than as a series of unrelated films. It also included *Who the Hell Is Hawks?*, Robin Wood's seminal volume on *Hitchcock,* and many other books.

Auteurism and the Legitimacy of Film

Sarris once observed that book editors don't remove chapters from novels without the writers' consent, but in Hollywood, final cut is usually done not by the director but at the producer's discretion. When a subliteray work is brought to the screen, the critic may ignore the original, but when a classic novel (say, Theodor Dreiser's *An American Tragedy*) is concerned, comparisons are inevitable. Nonetheless, no matter what the source material is, for the auteurists, final judgment of aesthetics and meanings must be based on the film qua film.

Auteurism and Film History

Up until Sarris, film criticism had been dominated by "forest critics," who described Hollywood as a factory run by capitalists and philistines and who focused on what pictures have in common rather than on individual differences. Sarris argued against Hollywood's cultural inferiority complex: "Film by film, director by director, year by year, Hollywood has been superior to that of the rest of the world," hence demanding—and according—higher status to American movies. Sarris allowed that if Hollywood yields at the very summit—it has not produced many Fellinis, Bergmans, Antonionis, Kurosawas, and Truffauts—it completely dominates the middle ranges, particularly in the realm of good–bad movies.

The auteur policy was useful not only in treating foreign directors who had control over their films, but in reconsidering those Hollywood directors who, despite the constraints of the studio system, were able to instill a personal style into their work. Sarris's work led to a systematic revaluation of film art, based on his belief that American movies deserved to be judged by the same artistic standards applied to European films: not all foreign films are good, and not all Hollywood films are bad.

As a result, the American cinema changed gears from being an industry totally despised to one that's respected. Conferring respectability on previously underappreciated Hollywood directors, Sarris claimed that undiscriminating champions of foreign movies against Hollywood movies might profitably inspect the crisp authority of Samuel Fuller's *Merrill's Marauders* or Don Siegel's *Hell Is for Heroes*.

(Re)Discovery of American Films

Auteurism led to the rediscovery and revival of obscure American films in museums and art houses across the country. Sarris was the first to suggest that a director who works within the studio system and succeeds in imposing his personality on material written by others should be elevated. As a consequence, film societies mounted ambitious and complete retrospectives of Hollywood directors. Sarris was also influential in reranking filmmakers previously stigmatized as B-movie directors, such as Samuel Fuller. In *The American Cinema,* Fuller and nineteen other directors are placed in a category called "The Far Side of Paradise." These are directors "who fall short of the Pantheon either because of a fragmentation of their personal vision or because of disruptive career problems." Included among them are Robert Aldrich, Frank Capra, George Cukor, Cecil B. De Mille, Leo McCarey, Vincent Minnelli, and Nicholas Ray.

Cukor, Minnelli, and George Stevens were all A-directors nominated for and winning Oscars during their careers, but Aldrich or Ray benefited from Sarris's reevaluation. "It is the artistic force with which his ideas are expressed that makes his career so fascinating," Sarris observed about Fuller. "It's time the cinema followed the other arts in honoring its primitives. Fuller belongs to the cinema, and not to literature and sociology."

In the 1990s, the Los Angeles Film Critics Association has conferred its prestigious Career Achievement Award on such directors as Don Siegel, Budd Boetticher, Joseph H. Lewis, and Abraham Polonsky. It's doubtful that the association would have done so without Sarris's pioneering work.

Ranking Individual Films within Careers

Sarris reacted against the conventional Hollywood thinking that directors made more "mature" films after the Second World War than before or during. In George Stevens's case, he noted: "I wouldn't trade one *Swing Time* for ten equivalents of *The Diary of Anne Frank,* or one *Penny Serenade* for ten *Giants.*" Even the esteem of widely heralded directors, such as Ford, whose reputation had long been established, underwent a critical revaluation that reflected a basic reconsideration of Hollywood filmmaking. Auteur critics argued that Ford's genre films—war films like *They Were Expendable* and westerns like *The Searchers* or *The Man Who Shot Liberty Valance*—showed stylistic richness and thematic ambiguity that made them superior to the calculated artistry and social consciousness of Ford's "serious" works, such as his "Oscar caliber" movies *The Informer* and *The Grapes of Wrath.*

Auteurism and the Film Canon

The scholar Virginia Wexman pointed out that, though critics often consider themselves disinterested observers, their activities are shaped by concrete historical contexts. This explains why certain films, such as *Vertigo,* are continuously chosen for critical discussion and reevaluation. Film scholarship, with its fluid and shifting canon, lends itself well to this kind of sociologically oriented inquiry. Changes in *Sight and Sound*'s ranking of the "Ten Greatest Films of All Time" show that the values held by contemporary critics are certainly historically shifting. Four new films appeared on the 1982 list, compared with the 1972 one: *Singin' in the Rain, Seven Samurai, The Searchers,* and *Vertigo.* The appearance of three American films in 1982 is at least partly accounted for by the continuing vitality of auteurism.

Auteurism and Movie Marketing

In the New Hollywood, auteurism has become a marketing tool. Movies are no longer described in terms of their stars, but in terms of their directors: a Scorsese film, a Spielberg film. This trend has been explored in essays by Donald A. Cook, "Auteur Cinema and the Film Generation in 1970s Hollywood," and by Timothy Corrigan, "Auteur and the New Hollywood." In this volume, Sundance Festival's Geoffrey Gilmore and Good Machine's James Schamus address themselves to auteurism as a marketing hook in the independent film milieu. For example, Fine Line Features has produced several offbeat hits, such as Robert Altman's *The Player* and *Short Cuts* and Gus Van Sant's *My Own Private Idaho.* Fine Line's approach, defined by its founding president, Ira Deutchman, favored director-driven projects: "We feel strongly that the director ultimately has the responsibility for whether what we're reading in a screenplay is going to turn up on a screen."

In conclusion, those claiming that "auteurism is dead" may actually mean that, as a critical method, it is so absorbed in our consciousness and so integral to our movie culture, that there is no need anymore to fight for it.

The battle over auteurism is long over. And the winner is . . . Andrew Sarris.

Part Three

Sarris and His Contemporaries

$\mathscr{D}$irector (and former film critic) Peter Bogdanovich (Oscar-nominated for *The Last Picture Show*) reaffirms Andrew Sarris's status as "an extremely influential film historian . . . essentially altering perceptions in this country about our own movie heritage . . . with his insightful and eloquently expressive articles about directors, actors, and films."

Daniel Talbot, head of the *New Yorker* who has known Andrew Sarris for forty years, singles out what was special about his criticism: "In his writing he does not exactly 'review' a film. He brings to the table a cornucopia of opinions on the prevailing ideas, cliches, and social styles of whatever is current in politics, sports, romantic love, the headlines, rendered in his elegant Jamesian manner." Another unique quality of Andrew is that "he cares about what he says and hopes to have some imprint on the success of a film he likes. He is a partner in this complex enterprise, a link between the high walls of distributor, exhibitor, newsprint, a fickle public."

Oscar-winning filmmaker Robert Benton (*Kramer vs. Kramer*) discusses in "Andrew Sarris and the New American Filmmakers" Andrew's impact on America's reception of the French New Wave in the early 1960s. The era in which Sarris came to prominence as a critic was when film criticism in general came to prominence. As Benton observes: "It was Andrew's writing that really gave focus and order to [the New Wave] for me. He was the only person writing about films in the same way that the New Wave directors were making films. He brought the Hollywood movies from my childhood and the art cinema of my adulthood together for me. He was speaking a language I could read, and he became the steady friendly voice."

According to Benton, Sarris is not given credit for introducing the contextual approach to film, which was implied in auteurism. For Benton, the novelty in Sarris's approach was that he "talked about the work of directors the way we had learned to talk about the work of writers or painters. He talked about movies in relationship to the body of the artist's work as opposed to talking about a movie as if it was an entity that existed in a vacuum, or as opposed to simply talking about whether you liked or disliked the work. . . . It was mostly about directors, but . . . [Sarris's] criticism also placed movies in a number of contexts."

In "Advantage, Andy," Richard Schickel states: "When Andy Sarris played tennis . . . he would usually take up a position a few feet in from the baseline, not generally regarded as an ideal place, strategically speaking, to cover the court." Schickel sees an analogy "between Sarris the tennis player and Sarris the film critic. His stance on the court was not entirely unlike his stance as our leading practitioner of auteurism: firmly committed to a carefully chosen position, which he defended with a nice blend of passion, good nature, and individuality. . . . Tennis and criticism are both games that test and reveal the character of those who play them, tennis probably more clearly than reviewing, since it offers no opportunity to cover your mistakes or perception and judgment with a nice diversionary phrase."

It was as a controversialist that Schickel first heard of Andrew. Sarris had written "Notes on the Auteur Theory in 1962" in *Film Culture,* a magazine unknown to Schickel: "Like a lot of people . . . what I knew of it was Pauline Kael's famous assault on it, which was written in 1963 but which caught up with me in 1965, when she included it in her first collection of essays, which for my sins I reviewed favorably in the *New York Times Book Review.* She was even then a devastating polemicist, with a special gift for making anyone who disagreed with her look not just wrong but foolish. The portrait of Andy that emerged from her piece was of a sort of idiot savant desperately hammering together a theoretical structure."

Charles Champlin fondly recalls that in the grand days, when he used to attend the Cannes Festival, one of the great rewards was that Andrew was often there, along with Molly Haskell, Rex Reed, and Roger Ebert. "Andrew Sarris was, to no one's surprise, indefatigable in his attendance upon the festival's bill of fare. He retained the true moviegoer's indoor pallor, untainted even by the occasional need to walk from hotel to cinema and cinema to cinema." Champlin was in awe in Sarris's presence—described as "this sturdy indoorsman, pale and hollow-eyed, with dark circles that you could fantasize had been burnt there by the reflected light from a thousand screens. The awe was . . . predominantly because of the literally thousands of films I knew he had watched, thought about, analyzed and *had opinions on.*" Andy's opinions were given "as irrefutable judgments, papal bulls issued *ex cathedra,* Supreme Court decisions from which there is no appeal, no stay of execution." What was beyond doubt was Sarris's "transcendent" love for movies that "embraces the best of what was and is open to whatever comes next (and will place the new in the context of what has been, sorting out innovation from limitation with an unerring eye . . .)." Sarris has become "part of every critic's . . . education, or the education is necessarily incomplete."

The Influential Film Historian

Peter Bogdanovich

$\mathscr{A}$ndrew Sarris has been an extremely influential film historian and critic since the mid-1950s, when he was writing for the *Village Voice* and *Film Culture* and essentially altering perceptions in this country about our own movie heritage. For forty-five years, his insightful and eloquently expressive articles about directors, actors, and films have been in the vanguard of thought on this subject. To me personally, Andy was often tremendously instructive and generous with his time at a particularly important moment in my development around the movies. For this, he has my lasting gratitude, something countless others, in and out of the business, owe him for his deeply thoughtful illumination of film art and film artists of the twentieth century.

Andrew

Daniel Talbot

$\int$hortly after cranking up the New Yorker Theater on Broadway and 89th Street in New York City, in March of 1960, I met Andrew Sarris. He had been, since 1955, a contributing editor and writer for Jonas Mekas's magazine, *Film Culture.* A handsome fellow, tall, sweaty, with eyes that poked into your soul, he talked rapidly and brilliantly, as he still does almost fifty years later, his brain a Niagara Falls of ideas and information. He lived with his mother in Kew Gardens. Like many young people, stretching backward to the Depression, he lived at home because he had no regular job. Andrew was not suited to work in an office or engage in blue-collar work. He was too busy going to the movies, too busy thinking about them in a serious way. When he wasn't watching movies he spoke and wrote about them in his uniquely circular way, a philosopher of the screen, an encyclopedist who spread the excitements of cinema. A voracious reader of many newspapers and magazines, Andrew always enjoyed talking about sports and politics, the day's headlines, ready to take on those with pretentious notions about how our society works. He could spot a four dollar bill in two seconds. His principal target has always been ideological cant, be it radical chic or skin-deep fads. Andrew would have been a big number in Parisian salons inhabited by the likes of Voltaire, Diderot, and Beaumarchais.

Andrew, when I first met him, was a close friend of Eugene Archer, the second film critic of the *New York Times.* The influence of Andre Bazin on these two was already apparent. Their idols were Hitchcock, John Ford, Howard Hawks, Max Ophuls, Ernst Lubitsch, and Luis Bunuel. With the help of my assistant, Peter Bogdanovich, I began a Monday Night Screening of film classics at the theater. We invited Andrew and Eugene, along with

Jack Gelber, Robert Brustein, Jack Kerouac, Jonas Mekas, Harold Humes, and others to write program notes for the films in the series (*Shors, Dead Of Night, The Last Laugh, Sabotage, Nosferatu, Foolish Wives,* among others). My notion was to educate audiences into thinking more seriously about film, without the intervention of publicity hype. During this period, Andrew wrote program notes for *Man of Aran, Louisiana Story, The Thirty-Nine Steps, Foreign Correspondent,* and *Oliver Twist.*

In 1960, Andrew, Eugene Archer, and I came up with the idea of publishing a large encyclopedia of film. Andrew and Eugene would write many entries while inviting other critics to make contributions. My role was to coordinate all the activity, including the search for a publisher. In 1959, Simon and Schuster had published my film anthology, so I brought our project to them. It would have been the first scholarly film encyclopedia. For whatever reason, it was turned down. I tried other publishers, to no avail. Years later, Richard Roud published a two-volume film encyclopedia. Other large tomes came along, by Ephraim Katz, Leslie Halliwell, David Thomson.

In 1960, Andrew became the chief film critic of the *Village Voice,* where he wrote weekly until 1989. His reviews were widely read and discussed. In recent years he has been writing the weekly film column for the *New York Observer.* In his writing he does not exactly "review" a film. He brings to the table a cornucopia of opinions on the prevailing ideas, clichés, and social styles of whatever is current in politics, sports, romantic love, the headlines, rendered in his elegant Jamesian manner. There were a number of serious film critics before Andrew. In America, Otis Ferguson, James Agee, and Manny Farber had reviewing posts for magazines like the *Nation,* the *New Republic,* and the *New Leader.* Pauline Kael was already publishing in various places, including the *Partisan Review.*

From 1927 to 1933, serious film critics had a platform in *Close Up,* a magazine published in Territit, Switzerland. Ernest Betts, Kenneth MacPherson, Herman G. Weinberg, and Harry Alan Potamkin (the first hard-core Marxist critic) wrote for this magazine. Others who wrote for the magazine, famous writers, included Gertrude Stein, Osbert Sitwell, Havelock Ellis, Bryher, André Gide, and Dorothy Richardson. I cite all these names, lest it be thought that since movies are a popular art, film reviewing has some obligation to meet the mass reader halfway. Nothing could be further from this condescension when it comes to Andrew Sarris. He is interested in educating film taste, in examining what's going on below the surface of things, in enlarging our view of the world.

In the heyday of the *Voice* days, Andrew and I maintained our close, familial relationship. As a film distributor who feeds critics with press books and who has expectations of good reviews, I have no hesitation in talking intimately with critics about my films. Critics are not godlike. They are human. If they are at all any good, they will express their humanity and their intelligent insights in their work. The better critics are simply not taste arbiters alone (heirs of the Matthew Arnold tradition of selecting The Best). They are commentators and if they approach the exalted level of a George Orwell, so much the better. I think that Andrew has all these traits in his writing.

In 1973, I picked up the U.S. distribution rights to Rainer Werner Fassbinder's *The Merchant of Four Seasons*. The bells in my head rang when I first saw this film at the New York Film Festival. I ran into Andrew in the elevator of the building where *Merchant* had just been screened for the press. He was ecstatic about the film. He told me that he was going to write a rave review in the next issue of the *Village Voice*. When you open a film without stars or vast publicity hype, timing is crucial. You have to open with a bushel full of articles and review. An independent distributor does not have the deep pockets that allow a really good film to sit in a theater until significantly large audiences catch up with it. One wag I know has estimated that you need eight thousand spectators of a film before word-of-mouth kicks in. Don't ask how this number came about. I accept it.

In any case, I was waiting for Andrew's piece to appear on Wednesday. When I picked up the *Voice* at a newsstand and did not see a review of the film, I called Andrew from a corner pay phone and raised hell with him. My feelings about Andrew were sufficiently familial that I had no hesitation in calling him on the carpet. But like any normal sibling, he began screaming at me, telling me that he wasn't going to take this crap from a film distributor and that he had been paying his dues for a long time. A week later Andrew's rave review of the film appeared. He and I were back on square one, as if no serious confrontation had taken place.

Over the years I have followed his writing like a hawk. It matters to me what he says about a film. Although I am not a dyed-in-the-wool auteurist, I am influenced by his thoughts on film, even if occasionally we disagree. After forty years as a critic, Andrew is still concerned about what his friends think of his opinion. This is the mark of a good critic. In other words, somebody who cares about what he says and who hopes to have some imprint on the success of a film he likes. He is a partner in this complex enterprise, a link between the high walls of distributor, exhibitor, newsprint, a fickle public. He knows that a film will not change your life, but on the other hand isn't life transiently pleasanter when in the embrace of a good hunk of film? Andrew still loves good films. He's very upset about the junk that has been rolling out of Hollywood these past ten years or so, even if upon occasion he praises that rare good work.

Most Hollywood films are industrial machines that mug the brain. Bad enough to have to sit through all that dreck, but then to have to think about them and write at least a thousand words about them has to be harsh punishment for an educated adult. I know any number of brilliant people who adore this junk. It's a schlockmeister mentality that reads symbolism into these films, a confirmation of the mindlessness of the spectator, a mass-man. I'm convinced that the reason that many French critics in past years placed Jerry Lewis high in their pantheon of auteurs was because he symbolized the American common man. Enough said about this piece of arrogance. Andrew has never played this game. For him the stakes are too high. He has put his brain on the line for over forty years, and we have had the good fortune to be instructed by him.

Andrew Sarris and the New American Filmmakers: An Interview with Robert Benton

Christian Keathley

Question: The period when Andrew Sarris came to prominence as a critic was, in a sense, when film criticism in general came to prominence. What was it that made you respond to Sarris above anyone else?

BENTON: I'd have to go back, not only to when I first read him, but to before that, when I was a child, to the initial connection I made with the movies. When I was growing up I would go to the movies at least two or three times a week. And I was never particularly discriminating about what I saw. I would see movies because I had crushes on movie stars. I think I had the largest collection of photographs of Gloria DeHaven that ever existed.

And obviously I wasn't seeing art cinema in Waxahachie, Texas. I was seeing Hollywood movies. The first art movies I saw were when I was in high school, when the first art house opened in Dallas. I saw *Henry V, The Red Shoes, Children of Paradise,* and *Symphony Pastorale.* I remember when I was a freshman in college going to see *Rashomon,* and it was as though I stepped off the earth. I had loved other movies before, but I'd never had a movie devastate me the way that did.

When I came to New York in 1953, I began to see more international cinema, and I also got to re-see a lot of Hollywood films from my childhood that I only half remembered. There were a lot of art and revival houses in those days, which were wonderful places. There was the Symphony, and the Museum of Modern Art, which in the old days was a truly spectacular theater. So even before the New Wave, there was an Ur–New Wave: it was this mixture of movies that were playing in New York all the time. Among my friends most of the talk was about movies, and there was an intense kind of energy was created by it all, but it was one that really had no focus.

101

Criticism at the time wasn't very helpful. James Agee may have been a great critic, but I didn't know it until way after the fact. Bosley Crowther was at the *New York Times,* but he wasn't a particularly interesting critic for me, and Pauline Kael was not yet at *The New Yorker.* Andrew talks about Eugene Archer, who was the third string critic at the *Times,* as one of the people that he owes a real debt to, but I don't really remember reading him. And then the New Wave arrived, and that did a lot, but it was Andrew's writing that really gave focus and order to all of it for me. He was the only person writing about films in the same way that the New Wave directors were making films. He brought the Hollywood movies from my childhood and the art cinema of my adulthood together for me. He was speaking a language I could read, and he became the steady friendly voice. My overly melodramatic analogy was that it must have been what it was like to be living in occupied Europe and hear the voice of Free France.

Q: I wonder if your background in painting and the other arts helped make auteurism particularly appealing.

BENTON: I suppose because Sarris talked about the work of directors the way we had learned to talk about the work of writers or painters. He talked about movies in relationship to the body of the artist's work as opposed to talking about a movie as if it was an entity that existed in a vacuum, or as opposed to simply talking about whether you liked or disliked the work. There was always the other movie Andrew was seeing and that movie's relationship to the subject, and to the world around it. It was mostly about directors, but it wasn't only about directors. So his criticism placed the movie in a number of contexts.

Q: It's always struck me how, in addition to this contextualization, the reviews seem to me intensely personal at least in the sense that I always seemed to have a clear sense of the person writing.

BENTON: I have for years tried to get Andrew to write his autobiography, and the last time I brought it up he said that he had really written it already in all the pieces he's done in his life. And I suspect that's true.

Q: Although Sarris and Pauline Kael are generally regarded as antagonists, it's striking, in retrospect, how much their tastes were alike. In a recent essay in the *New York Review of Books,* Louis Menand, writing about Kael's latest collection of work, cataloged her taste: she disliked Bergman and Fellini; she loved Renoir, Neo Realism, the New Wave and Hollywood cinema of the thirties. Sarris loved all these things as well. And so their differences had less to do with their taste in movies than their taste in criticism.

BENTON: That may be true, but from my point of view, the differences between them are differences of character, and as a result, their critical points of view were diametrically opposed. For one thing, as Menand says, Pauline loves movies because of the writing, and Andrew loves movies because of something more invisible—the spaces in between the writing. The writing is less important to Andrew than certain formal values, or than simply being able to watch an actor. Pauline would get carried away over actors all the time; Andrew gets enthusiastic but he never gushes.

For example, I recently read a review in which Andrew provides a very intelligent discussion about the differences between Debra Winger and Meg Ryan, attempting to place each of them in her particular historical tradition. And that, for me, is a very serious discussion. Now, maybe that's because, in my adolescence, I fell in love with Gloria DeHaven in a movie called *Two Girls and a Sailor,* and all my friends fell for the other lead, June Allyson. And I spent an inordinate amount of time trying to figure out the differences between them. Therefore I will always buy into those kinds of discussions. But Andrew does not do what Pauline would do, which is tell you that Debra Winger was the greatest actor that ever lived and trash Meg Ryan, or vice versa. He will spend a great deal of time and thought analyzing each actor in relation to a larger context.

It's not that Andrew is not opinionated. *The American Cinema* is a book-length version of a top ten list, but it's a top ten list in an historical context. And that's why his first rankings of American directors in *Film Culture* in 1962 had such a profound influence on me. I don't know, for example, that I would have known about someone like Anthony Mann, whose work I love, had I not read Andrew writing about him. I don't know that I would have gone back and reexamined many of the filmmakers that I had earlier dismissed if it hadn't been for Andrew.

The first time I saw *Rio Bravo,* which is absolutely one of my favorite movies, I walked out at the point where Dean Martin and Ricky Nelson sing "My Rifle, My Pony and Me." And then when I saw it again after reading Andrew, I began to weep in that scene. I cannot look at the scene where Angie Dickinson gets mad at John Wayne about "wearing this outfit for anybody else" or where she gets drunk after throwing the flowerpot without being extraordinarily moved by it. And Andrew is responsible for opening my eyes to that.

Q: Part of what you're referring to here is the fact that, in contrast to other critics of the time, like John Simon or Stanley Kauffman, Sarris was part of a cultural project that was rethinking the distinction between high and low art.

BENTON: Yes, he really helped a lot of us to shake off the notion of a high–low definition of culture and to treat a lot of films more seriously than had been done before. The New Wave directors understood that, and there were references to the movies of Hawks or Sam Fuller or whoever in their own films, but that's all they could do—make references, show the influence of, and, in effect, quote. The writings of Truffaut and Rohmer and the other *Cahiers* critics weren't available in English at the time, and so it was Andrew, as far as we were concerned, who put together this large, complicated set of ideas that came to be called the auteur theory.

This change in how we saw movies as a result of Andrew's writing re-ordered our whole notion of what the relationship between art and its audience was. Until then I suppose I had kind of an elitist notion that art—true art—was essentially avant-garde and that its quality was measured largely by its distance from the average audience. But the New Wave and Andrew's reinterpretation of the American cinema changed all that.

Q: Part of what seems so exciting about this collapse is the way that certain artists and critics became avant-garde by rethinking the tradition rather than simply moving away from it.

BENTON: It was exciting this reversing your field, this turning around and heading right back into the territory that everybody else is fleeing. But it wasn't as easy to manage as it might sound. For one thing, this was all radically new at the time. I don't know if, after all these years, that the auteur theory has been part of our culture, that I can convey the sense of boldness of newness of those films and ideas.

Of course, Pauline Kael, for one, mistrusted theories about film, and while I don't completely disagree with her on that, I can't imagine talking about painting or literature or whatever without talking about the formal issues involved or without considering a work's relationship to others that have come before it. Her position was against a kind of literacy, assuming that if you gave up literacy, you would get a kind of powerful, primitive response. It was like the noble savage going to the movies. But I don't buy that, maybe because I never like the noble savage anyway. And about something as rich, and complicated, and constantly changing as movies, this anti literacy seems ludicrous to me.

Now having said that, Sarris's approach did not always work to my benefit. When he wrote his review of *Bonnie and Clyde,* which was not a great review, he said, essentially, that it was a kind of interior decorated, glitzed-up version of *Gun Crazy.* And I can't entirely disagree with that because Truffaut had us go see *Gun Crazy* before we started to write. Pauline's review of

Bonnie and Clyde was, of course, very enthusiastic, and we appreciated it, but Andrew understood immediately where it fit in.

Q: When your first film, *Bad Company,* came out, you and David Newman were interviewed in *Film Comment,* and you said, "We're both devout auteurists." You were probably the only screenwriters in America that felt that way. There was tremendous resentment about auteurism among many screenwriters, especially since this was a time when a number of young writers were not property.

BENTON: I still believe in auteurism. But it's my understanding of the auteur theory that, though it's usually the director, the auteur of a film can be anybody. The auteur can be Gregg Toland, or Garbo, or Ben Hecht, or whoever has the power. And I don't mean the political power, I mean whoever's presence informs the film. Sarris was interested primarily in directors, but that doesn't discount others. Richard Corliss wrote a wonderful book, *Talking Pictures,* about American screenwriters, which he modeled on Sarris's book. And Corliss's arguments are convincing. But Sarris's work was the initiation of a rethinking, a reassessment that, I think, has to take place as an art form ages.

Q: But you do believe that the results of auteurism have not all been good.

BENTON: As important as it was, there was a huge misreading of the auteur theory. That misreading has resulted in everyone wanting to have artistic control and to always exercise it because their assumption is that, if they're the director, they're an auteur. Well, you're not the one that decides you're an auteur. You don't get that vote. And since the key elements in the auteur theory are style and personality, directors often feel like they have to make style and personality conspicuous or else they won't be thought of as auteurs. So it has caused many filmmakers to become self-conscious about their work. For example, one of my favorite movies is Sam Peckinpah's *Ride the High Country,* which is a simple, straightforward, beautiful work. Nothing conspicuous. He's not trying to be Kurosawa; he's not trying to get into the pantheon. But once Peckinpah became aware of himself, he tried to get styled up, and the styled-up Peckinpah of *The Getaway* is nowhere near as good as the simple Peckinpah of, say, *Junior Bonner,* which is a wonderful movie.

Q: What you're bringing up here is the other side of Sarris the Bazinian.

BENTON: The antimontage side of Bazin fits perfectly with what I mentioned earlier: the pleasure and real value Andrew finds in being able to simply watch things, whether it's watching an actor move or perform, or enjoying the mystery of a great camera setup. The great thing about something like the kitchen scene in *The Magnificent Ambersons* is that Welles just lets it go. He lets you feel that space, and he lets the actors have the scene.

Q: But unfortunately, many filmmakers take Welles as the example of the great controller, and they don't see what *The Magnificent Ambersons* has in common with, say, *Open City*. In other words, they miss the other sensibility that Bazin and Sarris loved so much that relinquishes some control and avoids always imposing itself. This sensibility does not seem to have had much effect on contemporary filmmakers.

BENTON: No, it really has not. Renoir expressed it in his analogy about the two ways of building a house. When you're laying the foundation and you come across a big rock, you can either blow it up and keep to your original plan or you can build around it and incorporate it. It's about, on the one hand, keeping total control or, on the other, letting events, to some extent, work with you. Sometimes you have no choice in this. We had no choice, for instance, regarding the snow during the shooting of *Nobody's Fool*. Other times you do, and you pray to God you'll have the sense to incorporate when it's appropriate. With every film you make, you fight a battle with reality, and if you're lucky, you lose. So many directors today fight tooth and nail to beat reality, and they end up with a totally artificial film. Sometimes that's appropriate, but often times it's not.

Q: This sensibility was kept alive in the new wave films. And it always struck me how, while on the one hand they had to fulfill as filmmakers their ideas about directing and authorship, on the other hand they remained always aware that the cinema is a technology that writes even in the absence of an author.

BENTON: The new wave was always working that documentary fiction opposition. Movies that allow that documentary quality retain a kind of primitive element. They retain the kind of energy that the first movies had, when it was exciting simply to see things appear and move on screen. And in contemporary movies that do this, it's as if real life is always threatening to take over the fiction. It never does completely, but the threat is always there, and it makes for a thrilling tension.

Q: This beings me to something related. In Sarris's "Notes on the Auteur Theory in 1962," he wrote that the ultimate premise of the auteur theory has to do with the tension between a director's personality and his material. Many people read this as meaning that it's better if a director is forced to use material that's not his own or that he doesn't like, and they read this as a contrary to the *Cahiers* critics call for writer-directors.

BENTON: But Sarris is right. There is a kind of tension between a director and his material, and I don't mean an antagonistic tension. It's the productive tension between the artist and the work. And even if you've written your own script, there's a point where that script has a life of its own. It's a kind of dynamic entity. Plus, there is the material of your collaborators: the cinematographer, the actors, the location, and so on. Some filmmakers work best, their auteur status is strongest and clearest, when surrounded by certain collaborators, certain other tension factors. For example, the films Martin Scorsese made with Paul Schrader, Robert De Niro, and Michael Chapman (*Taxi Driver* and *Raging Bull*), I think, show his strengths better than any of his films. And he's made some other very good films, but there's something about that unit that is capable of extraordinary work. Scorsese and De Niro working without Schrader (*Mean Streets, The King of Comedy*) come up with a very different kind of movie. Or Schrader and Chapman working without Scorsese (*Hardcore*) come up with something very different.

And this difference isn't so much about quality as it is, perhaps more interestingly, about tone. If you could make a revision of the auteur theory, it would be interesting to explore the chemistry between a few key figures. Hawks's work with Leigh Brackett or with Jules Furthman, for example, was not exactly like his work with other people. Billy Wilder's work with I. A. Diamond is utterly different than his work with Charles Brackett. And in spite of his focus on directors, Sarris was acutely aware of these variations and he wrote about them.

But auteurism, like any complex theory, gets oversimplified as it gets disseminated. Sometimes I read people making reference to auteurism, and it's as if they got their information from one of those little graphs that appear on the front page of *USA Today*. And that's why so many people, both directors and critics, think it's about the one person and it's about total control.

Q: I know that it was after many years of reading Sarris that the two of you became friends. When did you first meet?

BENTON: It was not long after *Bonnie and Clyde*. Molly Haskell and Betty Rollin, who were roommates at the time, were having a party. There was some big film festival going on. David and Leslie Newman and Sally and I went, and that's where I first Andrew. Also, Helen Scott, who had been at the French Film Office, knew David and me and also knew Andrew and Molly. And Molly ended up taking over for her when she left. And eventually, we became friends.

Q: Normally the relationship between artist and critic is a distanced one. How has it been to have a good friend review your work?

BENTON: Well, Andrew has always been extraordinarily straightforward. When he's reviewed the movies I've directed, he's always been up-front about the fact that our friendship is a part of what he's writing about. And he's been very generous to me, but he's also been very candid about what he thought when it wasn't positive. I suspect he will always err on the generous side, and I obviously like that, but that's his nature anyway. He's never been mean-spirited, either personally or as a critic. And he has for many of the members of what you might call the second generation of American filmmakers. And he's maybe been less impressed with us than a lot of other critics have been.

And in a way that's appropriate because Andrew created us, and I'm not sure if he really knows this. First he created us as an audience, as the readers he wrote for at the *Voice*. I suspect he could not have done that had he been writing for the *Times* or *Variety* or whoever. And as part of that audience, I can say that we didn't know that we were part of a group until he started writing.

But he also created us as the second generation of American filmmakers. He began writing when the first generation of directors like Hawks and Ford and Hitchcock were at the ends of their careers and when the second generation of European directors were getting started. And in helping us to understand both, he created the second generation of American filmmakers. Of course, there would have been a second generation anyway. But it probably would not have been this kind of mixture of modern European and classical American filmmaking. It might have had more to do with the English arty movement of the period—from directors like Karel Reisz, Lindsay Anderson, Tony Richardson. And in the way that I can reduce everything to the Gloria DeHaven–June Allyson opposition, there was a similar, fundamental opposition in the early sixties between the British New Wave and the French New Wave. They really hated each other. Truffaut remarked once that the term *British cinema* was a bit of an oxymoron. And Lindsay Anderson, who I dearly love, never forgot that. He would always refer to him with a sneer as "Your friend Truffaut . . ." So maybe the second generation might have been more British influenced than French influenced if it hadn't been for Andrew.

Q: There's a certain irony to the fact that, as you pointed out earlier, in the example of *Bonnie and Clyde*, he wasn't as crazy over this second generation as other critics.

BENTON: But in a way it doesn't matter whether Andrew liked *Bonnie and Clyde* or not; it matters that he helped to create it, and he helped to create a lot of American cinema after it. I don't know how he would feel about that, and I'm not sure if it's something he would want to take the credit for, but it's true.

Advantage, Andy

Richard Schickel

*W*hen Andy Sarris played tennis—this was back in the seventies—he would usually take up a position a few feet in from the baseline, not generally regarded as an ideal place, strategically speaking, to cover the court—but one that worked uncannily well for him. Somehow he seemed to reach just about everything hit in his direction by moving just an efficient step or two forward or back, left or right. His contact with the ball was not elegant— more of a swat than a stroke if I correctly recall those long-ago doubles matches, but his shots were smart and deft, and often enough winners. Anyway, he made you scramble to return them while he projected a serene, unruffled, almost genial air, unless, of course, he and his partner (usually his wife, the lithesome Molly Haskell) fell into muttered critical dispute over who should have been covering a ball that somehow skipped between them.

There was, I thought at the time, an analogy between Sarris the tennis player and Sarris the film critic. His stance on the court was not entirely unlike his stance as our leading practitioner of auteurism: firmly committed to a carefully chosen position, which he defended with a nice blend of passion, good nature, and individuality—above all, the latter.

I continue to think there is probably a kernel of truth in observation: tennis and criticism are both games that test and reveal the character of those who play them, tennis probably more clearly than reviewing, since it offers no opportunity to cover your mistakes or perception and judgment with a nice diversionary phrase. But I don't want to trap Andy (or myself) in so limited and limiting an analogy. He deserves better than that. Anyone who has stayed the course as long as he has does, particularly if he or she has maintained surpassing grace under the pressure of unrelenting controversy for so many years.

111

It was, in fact, as a controversialist that I first heard of Andy. Before I became a movie reviewer, he had written his famous article "Notes on the Auteur Theory in 1962" in *Film Culture,* a magazine then totally unknown to me. Like a lot of people (as Andy would ruefully admit), what I knew of it was Pauline Kael's famous assault on it, which was written in 1963 but which caught up with me in 1965, when she included it in her first collection of essays, which for my sins I reviewed favorably in the *New York Times Book Review.* She was even then a devastating polemicist, with a special gift for making anyone who disagreed with her look not just wrong but foolish. The portrait of Andy that emerged from her piece was of a sort of idiot savant desperately hammering together a theoretical structure—in my mind's eye (or maybe hers) it looked something like the Our Gang clubhouse—to shelter what she implicitly identified as an arrested passion for old Hollywood crap.

She shared the same passion, of course. Everyone who writes about the movies—with the possible exception of John Simon—inevitably does. That was especially true in those days, when the movies everyone—well, anyway, the better critics and knowing audiences—cared for most and remembered best were always getting pulled over by the middlebrow culture cops and failing their sobriety tests. We were all groping for words—a new critical vocabulary, if you will—that could be used to capture and define on the page this self-evident, but until then sternly denied, reality of the movies and our relationship to them.

Kael and Sarris were unquestionably the leaders in this effort. You didn't have to choose between them at first (though even in those days Pauline was busy recruiting that little cell of not entirely secret agents that eventually came to be known as the Paulettes). But you did find yourself drifting toward one camp or the other.

At first I leaned toward her, partly because I met her before I met Andy, and there was something curiously compelling—even (I hate to say it) inspiring—about this almost demonically possessed little woman; partly because in those days—before the meanness, hysteria and power tripping took over completely—she wrote so entertainingly; partly because I was coming at movie reviewing from the same direction she was—that is to say from an essentially literary–political–moralizing direction—and did not fully apprehend the possibilities of other approaches, of which auteurism, with its stress on the manner in which directorial personalities asserted themselves on screen through visual metaphors, was by far the most interesting. (It was also because of the unusual stress it placed on critical vocabulary as it attempted to translate these metaphors into words, by far the easiest to make fun of.)

My understanding of what Andy and his co-religionists were up to dawned rather slowly, and only after I met him. This was sometime in the fall of 1966, at one of the founding meetings of the National Society of Film Critics. It was greatly aided by the fact that I immediately found him such a likable guy—especially in this slightly lunatic context.

We had come together, about a dozen of us who wrote for magazines, because at the time the only significant association of movie reviewers was the New York Film Critics Circle, which then confined its membership to writers working for the city's daily papers. They were a stodgy crowd, unresponsive to new ways of making and seeing movies—this was, after all, the ascendent age of Bergman and Fellini, Truffaut and Godard—and generally exemplars of what Andy at one of our early meetings dubbed "creeping Crowtherism," after the hopeless Bosley, who had been the *New York Times*'s lead reviewer for almost three decades. His—their—idea of a good movie was the old Hollywood's idea of a good movie: something with a sobering social message or maybe a careful literary adaptation.

On the whole, we were right about our competitors. They were not very good critics, so it was probably useful to raise an alternative organizational voice against them. On the other hand, I'm not certain that we were made of stuff all that hipper and finer. We were surely more actively aware that movies had suddenly become a hot topic in the better New York intellectual circles, where there was much talk (a lot of it rather patronizing, I thought) about this "new" art form. Personal experience—invitations to appear on public broadcasting panel shows, not to mention academic and church basement forums—had taught many of us that it was possible to earn more than a living out of this work, that some sort of a public career could now be made as a movie reviewer. Our group activities—publishing an annual anthology of our writings, issuing statements on issues of concern to the film community (mainly involving censorship questions)—very marginally added to such social esteem and intellectual authority as we were suddenly enjoying. But, frankly, the first thing we thought of doing was giving awards like the big guys did: throwing a party, rubbing up against movie stars, having some fun, for god's sake.

Alas, in those early years, we kept giving our prizes to Ingmar Bergman and his gloomy, faraway ilk, a habit that tended to dampen our festivities. But no matter. Our names got in the paper, people—especially movie people—started to reckon with us a little bit, and our modest fame grew a trifle more. This was, I think, particularly gratifying to Kael. She had been the prime mover in the foundation of the society, cheerily making common cause with reviewers she fundamentally held in contempt, because she wanted to enhance the status of her occupation (*profession,* with its impli-cation of definable standards of competence, is too grand a word for movie reviewers), and believed that in numbers there must be power. This was to some degree understandable. She had been wandering the fringes for decades, writing film notes for the theaters she managed, broadcasting on nonprofit radio, contributing to obscure magazines. Belatedly—she was in her midforties at the time—she was beginning to gain national attention, writing for a variety of national magazines before settling down at the *New Yorker,* and she was determined to enjoy it to the fullest.

Andy's history, though he was a decade younger than Pauline, was not dissimilar. Indeed, of the society's twelve founding members, he and Pauline were the only ones who were at the time fully committed, professionally and emotionally, to movies as a topic. The rest of us were just passing through. Or so we thought. Some of us were slumming novelists. Others—me among them—had journalistic agendas more "serious" than opining about movies for the rest of their lives. In other words, this was for most of us a part-time and, we guessed, short-term occupation, a way of piecing out our incomes and looking sort of "with it" as the saying used to go. What did we care about the long-run status of movie critics? In the long run, most of us imag-ined we would be doing something else.

Andy, of course, knew otherwise, knew that he, at least, was a lifer. Given his background and his commitment to film, I'm sure he enjoyed the modest celebrity now being thrust upon us as much as anyone. But he had taken a message quite the opposite of Kael's from his previous experience. He was a self-described "cultist"—I think *purist* is a better word—of the cin-ema and had no desire to transcend that status, may even have thought that to do so would be to betray his calling—and his better nature. He had ob-served, he would later write, that most of the people who had previously made names for themselves in this field were widely perceived in much the way most of the National Society's membership perceived themselves, that is as "being too good to be reviewing movies." In contrast, people coming out of the little film journals, as he had, "were not considered much good for anything else."

This was fine with him. And liberating. For as he would also reflect, "the cultist does not require the justification of a career to pursue his pas-sion, and the careerist does." He understood perfectly well that the main-stream press, which at the time was either hiring movie reviewers for the first time or trying to raise its standards in this realm, were not going to engage him except on an occasional basis, simply because he was so dauntingly, scar-ily knowledgeable about his subject. Besides, this being the sixties, when all

American institutions were generally supposed to be in a prerevolutionary condition of some sort, editors—and their trendier readers—wanted a kind of literary performance that was outside his range: an edge of out-with-the-old malice, a sense that the medium was in crisis like everything else and that virtually every movie could be seen as an event with a potential either to deepen or redeem that crisis.

Surprised and delighted to find himself making a decent living doing what, given his ardor, he would have done—and often enough had done—for no fee at all, he was serenely content with his lot. Indeed, he once swore me to secrecy on this point: editors must never know, he said, that most of us would write without recompense, so pressing was our need to express ourselves on this topic to which we were so deeply committed.

I'm not certain that I entirely agreed with him about that, though, on the other hand, here I am writing about Andy for free just because I care about the subject, so surely I knew what he was talking about. In any case, there's not the slightest doubt that my good feelings about him began at those early meetings of the society, where he presented himself as a serious man, deeply engaged in his work, but utterly without pretense or guile.

In the group's squabbles, of which there were many, he would speak his piece in a high-pitched rush of words, intelligence and, I thought, a kind of innocence—anyway a lack of calculation—attractively combined. He was like an adolescent who had just discovered ideas and his own skill with them. His capacity to excite himself with his own thoughts combined with his obliviousness to the way that excitement might be perceived in a crowd very concerned with the weight, measure, and ironic assay of their own words was wonderfully refreshing. He did not love arguments—seemed to me rather abashed when he found himself drawn into them, and entirely lacking Kael's killer instincts—but he did not shrink from them either. For he understood that his passionate intellect was bound to get him into troubles that the rest of his rather sweet nature would have preferred to avoid, and that he had no choice but to accept this contradictory and often discomfiting state of affairs.

His lively sense of his own marginality led him to a sense that the whole critical enterprise was a marginal one. He had to embrace it because, it seemed, that was his fate (he is a Greek, after all). But he did not believe that group action was likely to elevate his status or that of movie criticism in general, even imagining that this ragtag squadron was up to such a task. Certainly he did not imagine that we were up to a revolutionary reformation of the entire motion picture industry.

Kael, I think, did—and maybe one or two others among us as well. At this time—remember, we're still in the sixties—she was always insisting that the studio system was on the verge of collapse and just needed a few strategic pushes to make it tumble into a heap. She advanced at the time a notion that the leading filmmakers might organize themselves into some sort of cooperative that could find creative bliss outside the industry as it was presently constituted.

This loopy notion grew out of Kael's essentially Manichean view of the way the system worked. Though she often struck the poses of a populist, she was ever a nervous one. The movie audience was, in her view, basically guileless, therefore defenseless against exploitation by a soulless and "rotten" industry. Worse, because it was bereft of moral and aesthetic vision, that industry, as she saw it, corrupted not only the audience but all whom it employed. Or almost all. For within it there toiled a few artists of exemplary integrity, lonely rebels pursuing their singular visions against desperate odds, in the process rendering themselves virtually unemployable. When they were occasionally allowed to work, their films, their visions, were almost always subjected to cuts and revisions by the vile studios. Many of these filmmakers—not all of whom were quite what she believed them to be—she personally befriended and tried to keep on the path of righteousness. All of them she was quick to defend, and to urge us as a group to defend, when they claimed irreconcilable artistic differences with their employers.

They were only a few, these favorites. With those who stood outside her charmed circle, she was usually brutal. And not only in print. In our early hubris, we took to inviting directors to join us in off-the-record dialogues, which took place on Sunday evenings in the Algonquin Hotel dining room, which was not open for business that night but which, without cooking smells to cover it, always smelled of cat piss. The idea was to suggest that the relationship between critics and creators need not always be a hostile one, that perhaps we could make common cause against the Philistines.

In theory, this was admirable. In practice, it usually deteriorated into a catfight. Or should I say a pissing contest? And it was usually Kael, one of whose favorite epitaphs for her unfavorite moviemakers was "whore," who started it. I don't recall her actually using that word in these sessions, but sooner or later she would, under the guise of free and open discussion, launch into a vicious assault on our guest.

We were used to it, of course—we had all, at one time or another, been the victims of these near-psychopathic outbursts—but they shocked people who had come expecting a polite exchange of ideas. David Lean was so distressed by his evening with the critics that he would claim (with considerable melodramatic license) that it prevented him from making a film for fourteen years. John Frankenheimer, bless his heart, gave back as good as he got. Others fell somewhat befuddled between these two extremes, but the tone Kael kept setting subverted the purpose of these gatherings, and we soon abandoned them.

Andy, perhaps needless to say, always did his best to keep these dialogues on a courteous track. That was his nature, however blustery he might grow in advancing or defending his own positions. It was also a signal of his indifference to Kael's reformist zeal. The system's products had, after all, provided him with much pleasure over the years, and it had supported many careers that were in his view entirely admirable. Even if revolutionary overhaul were a practical possibility—which, of course, it was not—he was clearly not certain that it was such a great idea or that the National Society of Film Critics could provide the cadre to carry its banners.

In this period I began to see why Kael's animus against him, and Andy's answering passion, were both so deep. If he was right, if coherent and worthy authorial careers could be created and sustained in the motion picture industry as it had for radical reform were pointless. If, on the other hand, she was right, then his heroes must partake of the system's corruption, which would render their careers (and his enthusiasms) suspect.

Beyond that, it stood to reason that if the industry was as bad off as she insisted, they required not just a Savonarola—a slot she was happily filling—but an intellectual, a czar, a job for which she was self-nominated. Her favorite critical locution, that imperious "we" in which she attempted to sweep all readers up into her response to a film, thereby banishing argument by implying that none could possibly exist, was the tip-off. So were her confident imputations of shabby motives to filmmakers, which sometimes had mere gossip for backing, often enough not even that—just wild surmises. She also liked to pull stupid and pretentious quotations from press releases, a form in which no one is at his best, and use them against filmmakers.

Taking nothing away from her gifts—she was usually very good on performance, for example, with a talent for characterizing an actor's work in vividly evocative, often implicitly sexual, ways—she remained, I've always thought, a critic for people who didn't go very much to the movies but knew what they thought of the medium—also not very much—yet loved to overhear falsely knowing conversations about them. This crowd had no need for a defined critical position; they had neither the time nor the inclination to track or question Kael's outrageously overstated, baroquely rationalized prejudices for and against various moviemakers. Just as they ignored her when she was in her Madame DeFarge mode, they failed to observe her highly personal, hugely eccentric enthusiasms. They didn't notice, for example, her peculiar devotion to her journeyman pal Irvin

Kershner, didn't recall for long her dippy assertion that being present at the New York Film Festival debut of *Last Tango in Paris* was like being there for the premiere of Stravinsky's *Rites of Spring*. What did they care about difference between a momentary sensation and a watershed event in the history of modernism? It was enough for them to enjoy the spritz, the performance, and move on to their next diversion.

It is not entirely fair or agreeable to keep measuring Andy's performance against this one, and I apologize for it. On the other hand, one of the unexamined premises of careless writing about film these days is the notion that this woman was "the greatest film critic who ever wrote." I want to suggest that there are other possibilities. I also want to suggest that for that weird notion to be even remotely plausible, this reviewer would have had to build a body of work out of a premise somewhat more complex than the "sexiness" of the medium—though it was useful of her to publicly acknowledge that formerly dirty little secret—to build her pieces on something of more lasting interest than how a movie succeeded or failed in turning her on.

In truth, Andy was much more full-hearted about movies, a much more mature lover, if you will, in that he was far more patient with the object of his affections, infinitely more forgiving of mistakes, especially if they were committed by an artist he had admired over the years. Nor was his regard affected by gossip or speculative innuendo, real or imagined personal slights. This cool, but scarcely dispassionate, manner was a projection of his serene historicism. His work always implied that the movies would survive the latest stinker (and the latest putative masterpiece, too), and that society and culture—along with the ordinary moviegoer—would probably do the same. He was maybe an evolutionist, but only as far as individual careers, not the medium itself, were concerned. He was definitely not a revolutionist. Indeed, one of our points of contact was that we were both anti-Stalinist liberals, therefore naturally suspicious of the kind of revolutionary posturing that was so much a part of sixties cultural rhetoric.

Given that premise, we deplored other kinds of democratic centralism. There never was, and never would be, an Andrew's sisterhood comparable to the Paulettes. There's an irony here. Of all contemporary critics, Andy is most committed to what we might loosely term an ideology, a defined body of principles that inform the bulk of his judgments, but that was his thing, and he had no desire to make it your thing. There are only two reviews of books of mine that I treasure, not because they were generally favorable, but because their writer seemed to understand not just their texts but their subtexts. That writer was in both instances Andy, and in the case of the second volume he forgave a couple of rather snappish attacks on his own writing to pursue what he felt were more important matters. Such generosity, I'm here to tell you, is not all that common among our—um—colleagues.

Andy called his WBAI radio program and his column in the *Village Voice* "Films in Focus," and that said it all. He had a gift for contextualizing movies, placing them accurately in the long run of a director's or actor's career or a genre's development. I have nearly always learned something I needed to know—indeed, should have known—from Andy's reviews. I also learned from him that the least important thing a good critic has to offer is his opinion of the work at hand. Andy was not shy about expressing them. And I was not shy about disagreeing with them. But that never interfered with our friendship—or my respect for him. For early on I began to see, from his example and my own instincts, that broad judgment—thumbs up, thumbs down—was less interesting than the process of arriving at it, the range of reference you brought to it, the sense of how film culture interacted with general culture to produce the work under discussion.

I also began to see, as he ranged across the past in his writing, how tyrannical the here and now was in considering movies. By this I mean that Andy, more than any other critic, made you see that however carelessly and crassly the movie as an economic institution had been managed, however shabbily (or, equally damaging, however indulgently) it had treated some of its talent, something we could call art, and some people we might call artists, had emerged from all the previous crises the medium had endured, from all the chaos that must attend creation in an industrialized context.

He specifically argued against applying the idea of progress to the movies, insisting that the cinema rises and falls "in relation to the artists involved," that is to say, on the basis of individual achievement, not on the basis of industrial conditions or climate of opinion at any given moment. These may or may not influence a true film artist in a variety of ways, but they are incapable of distracting him from his fundamental obsessions. The obvious corollary to this argument is that there are no golden ages in the history of this (or any other) expressive form. And no ages of brass or lead, either. There are only filmmakers, struggling harder or less hard, depending on their mood and the atmosphere of the moment, to place their visions before us.

Andy was naturally aware that some people's careers had been at various times inhibited by the working conditions in Hollywood. He was equally aware of the havoc that shifts in fashion—which are not made unilaterally in Hollywood, for which critics and the general public also bear responsibility—can wreck on individual artists. But in the long run of history, the work abides and ultimately makes its value (or lack of value) clear to the discerning observer. "Formal excellence and visual wit are seldom appreciated at first glance as are the topical sensations of the hour," he wrote.

That was in *The American Cinema,* which Andy published in 1968. Bravely published, I might say, given the reception granted (not by Kael alone) to his previous essays in auteurism. Bravely published, I might also add, given the arguments he must have known it would engender. The issue was not so much seeing film history exclusively through directorial careers. By this time, I think, most of us were consciously or unconsciously doing so. It was a great convenience—a thread through the morass—and it was in the largest sense just. Directors did have their preoccupations and their stylistic signatures. These did very often prevail over studio manner or genre conventions, and you could perceive what they were over the long run of their work—and make critical judgments about it on that basis. In a sense we all became—probably had been from the start, if we were all serious about movies—auteurists. Even Pauline. Even, eventually, the jokiest TV reviewer, cramming his opinions into a minute toward the end of the local news.

No, the problem was those damned rankings of his. For three decades now, I've been having half-serious, half-satirical conversations with colleagues over whether this or that old favorite should be up (or down) graded from, say, "Lightly Likable" to "The Far Side of Paradise." Whether, in fact, some of the guys in "Less Than Meets the Eye" belonged in "Strained Seriousness" or vice versa. By me, Preston Sturges is a "Pantheon" director and Orson Welles is a "Fringe Benefit." Or not. Depends on when you ask me. Same with Josef von Sternberg, that master of "Expressive Esoterica." And Fritz Lang, whose seriousness sometimes seems pretty strained to me.

But finally all that is beside the point. Andy has himself revised his opinions, if not his book, making his peace in later articles with the likes of Billy Wilder and John Huston, whom he had underestimated. And the book continues to reside, tattered and battered, on my reference shelf, within arm's length of the word processor—for the essays on the major figures Andy considers are gems. After all these years, they continue to stir fresh thought— something the old pieces of only the best critics accomplish—as well as admiration for the aptness of the examples chosen to illuminate a director's style, appreciation for the forthrightness of his arguments—you always know where the writer is coming from—and pleasure in the mannerly confidence of their judgments. When he speaks ill of a body of work, Andy does so without malice and with an earnest effort to find its saving graces. When he speaks well of a career, he does so with seductive generosity. In either case, he leaves you room for principled argument.

If I were to categorize movie reviewing in Sarrisian terms, I guess I'd call it "expressive ephemera." Given the power of any film to command mass attention on its initial release, and the rise in recent times of venues where, however erratically, these works can be kept alive endlessly, one has to know that even the worst movie is going to persist and influence people in ways that the best, most thoughtful review of it never will. Given this hard reality, a critic's only hope of creating something of lasting usability is somehow to evade the tyranny of the purely topical, to put movies not merely into "focus" but into long-range perspective.

I speak with fresh feelings on this matter for I recently spent some years writing a biography of a contemporary actor-director. This work naturally sent me back to the reviews that had greeted his films, and it was an appalling experience. The carelessness and superficiality of the judgments, the refusal to look for, let alone find, thematic or generic resonances in the movies, the preoccupation with side issues (if I read one more stupid word about violence in the movies, I think I'm likely to resort to it myself) were deeply depressing. And that says nothing of the motiveless malignity in much of this reviewing, particularly by Kael and her acolytes. In that sere country, it was Sarris—and few others, most of them not regular reviewers—who provided the oasis. Or perhaps one should say some high ground from which one could calmly survey the landscape in which life I was trying to reconstruct had been lived.

I don't suppose any critic consciously sets out to provide such services. We are, like the actors and directors we write about, bound by the limits of our natures and our sensibilities. But we can certainly learn to aspire beyond those limits. And learn to conduct ourselves, as Andy has, with decency and discretion and a respect for the feelings of our subjects. "Movie love," to borrow a phrase, is OK; it is, I guess, within the realm of more or less normal human experience. But like all passions, it needs to be tempered when we go out in public by the knowledge that history—to which movies, like everything else we make, are eventually subject—is a dispassionate judge. It doesn't care what the maker's motive was, or what his circumstances were at the time, or even what he thought his message might be.

Auden's famous lines about history ultimately forgiving Paul Claudel his political sins because he wrote so well definitely apply. So does something Alfred Hitchcock of the Pantheon once said to me. An artist, he remarked, would be a fool to wonder whether the apples he was painting were sweet or sour: "Who cares? It's his style, his manner of painting them—that's where the emotion comes from." All of Andy's criticism, it seems to me, was aimed at that kind of judgment, the anatomizing of manner, not morals.

I began with an image of Andy at play. Let me close with another one. Some years ago, he and I were both invited to an extraordinarily grand New York party, given in honor of a new book's prominent author. Its site was one of those endless apartments in the Dakota, every room of which could have been used as a set for a glamorous movie about Big City swells. They were out in force; movie stars, television personalities, media powers. Arriving alone, I was overwhelmed by the dazzle and wandered about, slightly panic-stricken, looking for someone closer to my own station in life. Eventually I penetrated the kitchen, where a bar was set up and canapés were being served. There, thank God, was Andy. He was seated at a table. He was reading the *New York Post,* which, newspaper junkie that he is, he had prudently brought with him. Oblivious to the hubbub swirling about him, he was patiently awaiting the arrival of his wife, who is much better at these occasions than he is—or I am.

What were they to him, these preening and chattering celebrities and wannabes? He knew who he was, which was perhaps more than he had dared dream he might be when he started out to do what he wanted to do, but not less than he had dared hope to be either. This is a huge advantage for anyone, but it is especially so for a critic. It purifies his gestures of ambition, frees them of strategic considerations, and permits him simply to state his case—for whatever modest good it may do his soul, whatever quite unpredictable and certainly unprogrammatic good it may do in the world.

On a Critic and Criticism

Charles Champlin

In the grand days when I used to report the Cannes Film Festival each May, one of its great rewards was that Andrew Sarris was often there, and Molly Haskell and Rex Reed and Kathleen Carroll of the *Daily News* and Roger Ebert in his pre-media-star days. All of us, and outlanders like Alexander Walker of the *London Evening Standard,* saw a good deal of one another, magnetized by a colorful gent from New York named Billy Baxter, whose manic hospitality Roger later celebrated in his book about Cannes. We also met during one festival on Lord Lew Grade's yacht, which was not larger than an aircraft carrier, and often at his annual luncheon on the terrace of the Hotel du Cap in Cap d'Antibes. Those occasions were memorable because they were probably the only times when we were all in the open air at once. I once remarked in print that at Cannes our set never suns.

The diet of available films included not only the festival's various selections but the five hundred or so offerings in the Marche du Film, in which nuggets of excellence were to be found buried in some of the ghastliest international exploitation fare this side of the old 42nd Street.

Andrew Sarris was, to no one's surprise, indefatigable in his attendance upon the festival's bill of fare. He retained the true moviegoer's indoor pallor, untinted even by the occasional need to walk from hotel to cinema and cinema to cinema. We had met before, but I remained in awe of him. If I experienced a disappointment, it was that there was very little intercritical conversation. The standard query at every gathering was, "Seen anything you like?" And the customary guarded answers ran to few words, "The Bulgarian thing has its moments," or, "Ah, that Roemer, as blissfully obscure as always," or, "What has come over you? I mean, please."

Playing opinion cards close to the chest was de rigeuer, as it usually is among critics immediately after screenings. It is different, of course, once the reviews are in print. Then points of view can clash like swords. Hollis Alpert once told me he had to cease holding meetings of the New York Film Critics Society at his home because the damage to his furniture was severe, especially if John Simon showed up.

But this is about Andrew Sarris, and the preamble is simply to establish the awe I felt in his presence—this sturdy indoorsman, pale and hollow-eyed, with dark circles that you could fantasize had been burnt there by the reflected light from a thousand screens. The awe was indeed partly—predominantly—because of the literally thousands of films I knew he had watched, thought about, analyzed and *had opinions on*. Not an "I think," or a "could be" or a "possibly" or a "conceivably" in a carload. Even to say he has an opinion on a film is misleading. They are given as irrefutable judgments, papal bulls issued *ex cathedra,* Supreme Court decisions from which there is no appeal, no stay of execution.

Sarris is not alone in this confidence, of course. In her writing days—now, sadly, over—Pauline Kael took no prisoners either. To defy either of hem was to challenge the Dead Sea Scrolls and the U.S. Constitution rolled into one. Pauline tended to rise above the fray and not counterattack (film criticism is not brain surgery, I believe she once remarked). But one of the wicked delights of Sarris's work is that he is a great competitor, defending his ground as an auteurist and suggesting that anyone who disagrees with him is likely a person of diminished capacities. I speak of print; in person, in my experience, he is amiable and even reticent.

"Abstract aesthetics, especially on cinema, is generally the unreadable in search of the indescribable," Sarris wrote in a devastating assault on Lawrence Alloway. "Pop Go the Movies!" reprinted in *The Primal Screen.* Challenging Alloway's assault on auteur theory, Sarris cheerfully admitted that "any critical theory carried to extremes is absurd." He is, it may be, only a relative absolutist. I think of Sarris on abstract aesthetics every time I have the misfortune to bump up against the writings of semioticians.

What suffuses all of Sarris's criticism, as it does Kael's, is a manifest love of the movies, a surpassing, transcendent love of the medium that embraces the best of what was and is open to whatever comes next (and will place the new in the context of what has been, sorting out innovation from limitation with an unerring eye and pen—not that anyone uses a pen any more).

My great admiration for Andrew Sarris is toned with high envy for all the films he has been able to see and has dedicated the time to see. Growing up in a village where the foreign film were by either Frank Buck or Martin and Osa Johnson, and where the splices on worn subsequent-release prints were certain to give way at least once every night, I have been playing catch-up ever since, trying to see all the films that have defined the possibilities of the medium.

Not least, Sarris is part of every critic's and every would-be critic's education, or the education is necessarily incomplete. He is not alone. No one I think, can write good film criticism who has not read and absorb the compassionate, insightful spirit of James Agee. And for sheer pleasure, combined with exposure to a quite different critical temperament, who can *not* read Kael? I find her easier to disagree with than Sarris, yet even in disagreement I have very often found that she has looked at a film in a way that had not occurred to me. She is instructive even when one disagrees with her.

And though you step more gingerly in arguing (from a safe distance) with a Sarris dogma, it is wonderfully daring, like diving off the high board for the first time. This is most particularly of Sarris in what for me is still his most remarkable achievement, *The American Cinema,* with its no-quarter-given rankings of directors, from the "Pantheon" (only fourteen, Chaplin to Welles) to the dismal darkness of "Miscellany" (twenty-six poor souls, from Michael Anderson to Terence Young by way of Josh Logan), you are tempted (I have been) again and again to say, "Whoa!" or "Yes, but . . . I mean, Preminger higher than Alexander Mackendrick, and both of them higher than Luis Bunuel and Francois Truffaut?" (The latter two were admittedly grouped with other foreigners as "Fringe Benefits.") Ah, well, perhaps even Sarris has tinkered with his listings in the two decades since he wrote; a lot of film has gone through the sprockets in twenty years. Yet it amazing how many of his judgments hold up, as uncomfortable as we may be confronting his tough but thoughtful, well-grounded, and hugely readable verdicts.

A critic's standards are formed by all the movies he or she has seen and thought deeply about. But a critic is formed as well by all the other critics he or she has read and whose work he or she has measured against the films under review. In the end, the critic is all alone in the darkness, responding to the images with a unique sensibility and later a unique voice. But the presences of other critics, living and dead, are in the theater as well, and the flickering ghosts of remembered films.

For the generations of critics who have come to maturity reading him, and I have been one of them, Andrew Sarris has become a conscience, insisting by example that we watch more penetratingly, think more deeply, measure the historical context more knowingly, celebrate more wisely. I acknowledge the debt, with affectionate gratitude.

Part Four

Sarris and Film Studies

$\mathcal{A}$ former student of Sarris, Richard Corliss recalls how "with high expectations and a touch of the shakes," he walked into the first class of Andrew Sarris's history course in the graduate film program at New York University. "By this evening in September 1967, Sarris was well on his journey from cult item to cultural touchstone. As critic for the *Village Voice*, contributor to *Film Culture*, editor of *Cahiers du Cinema* in English, host of his own WBAI movie schmooze show, and member of the New York Film Festival selection committee, he had hacked a path of wit and originality through the thickets of Bosley Crowtherland. Film reviewing, he had proved, was not just a game of handing out laurels to pictures of the armchair humanist stripe. Men like Hitchcock and Howard Hawks directed more than traffic. Movies, even especially Hollywood movies, were art, dammit, and Sarris was their chief curator and connoisseur. . . . That class in 1967 was for me the beginning of many beautiful friendships."

Andrew Sarris and Molly Haskell got married in 1969, the same year that another film couple married: Mary Yushak of MoMA and Richard Corliss "of no fixed abode." When Mary and Richard set up house, they brought along their personal and intellectual luggage. As Corliss notes: "Each of us had files of favorite things (her opera scores, my baseball scores). One thing, it turned out, we both had saved: clippings of Sarris reviews from the *Voice* and *Film Culture*. That seems as good a basis as any for a lifelong marriage. I wonder if Molly Haskell, in stint in the mid-1960s at the French Film Office and the National Society of Film Critics, had an Andrew Sarris file."

If film professor Jeanine Basinger had to choose one person who's the most influential film critic/scholar of the past fifty years, she would without hesitation select Andrew Sarris. As she explains in her essay "Andrew Sarris: Father of Film Study," "Not Andre Bazin, whose worked is largely ignored or forgotten by young people today. Not Henri Langlois, who loved films and saved them but absentmindedly lost them again. Not Kracauer or Agee or Kuleshov or Greene or Arnheim or Pudovkin or Ferguson or Balazs or Metz or Munsterberg or Farber or Eisenstein or Wollen or any of the other greats, all influential, important, but largely unknown outside the academy. Not even Pauline Kael, Sarris's archrival and frequent nemesis, who has influenced a new generation of film critics, but whose work did not reshape education significantly."

The title of John Belton's essay, "Dear Mr. Sarris," is inspired by a fan letter Belton wrote to Sarris back in 1963, one "full of embarrassing effusions about how much I liked his columns in the *Village Voice* and how great he was." At sixteen, Belton was introduced to Sarris's weekly column through the father of a high school friend. As fate would have it, Belton shared an office at Columbia with Sarris, from 1978 to 1986, an experience that came close to "a fan's fantasy: I was playing on the same team as Mickey Mantle."

In the 1960s, the serious study of cinema was being undertaken not by film historians or academic but by college film societies, such as that at Dartmouth, and by "journalists," such as Sarris. As Belton observes, "Film culture was centered around the *Village Voice,* where Sarris and Jonas Mekas shared the task of mapping the terrain of current film practice. . . . The film community was a genuine community, and figures such as Sarris, Mekas, and William K. Everson were at its center." Like Basinger, Belton designates Sarris as the father of film studies—and leader of a lively film community.

In "Sixteen Fragments on Auteur Theory, or Sarris's Revenge," Good Machine producer and Columbia professor James Schamus describes how the introduction of the auteur theory by Sarris in the 1960s "helped to make the academic study of cinema a legitimate discipline." Before then, as Schamus points out, "there was the odd 'Ingmar Bergman and the Disappearance of God' course offered in the English department or divinity school. But now, films that had once been 'westerns' or 'John Wayne' movies became 'Fords' or 'Hawkses' expressions of individual artistic sensibilities."

Confessions of a Sarrisite

Richard Corliss

$\mathcal{W}$ith high expectations and a touch of the shakes, I walked into the first class of Andrew Sarris's history course in the graduate film program at New York University. By this evening in September 1967, Sarris was well on his journey from cult item to cultural touchstone. As critic for the *Village Voice*, contributor to *Film Culture*, editor of *Cahiers du Cinema* in English, host of his own WBAI movie schmooze show, and member of the New York Film Festival selection committee, he had hacked a path of wit and originality through the thickets of Bosley Crowtherland. Film reviewing, he had proved, was not just a game of handing out laurels to pictures of the armchair humanist stripe. Men like Hitchcock and Howard Hawks directed more than traffic. Movies, even especially Hollywood movies, were art, dammit, and Sarris was their chief curator and connoisseur.

Great critics are not necessarily great teachers; writing and talking are antithetical as performance arts. Sarris's prose was wonderfully elliptical and precise; it stressed grand generalities ("The cinema is a window and a mirror.") and epigrammatic balance ("Billy Wilder is too cynical to believe even his own cynicism."). Many of the appraisals of directors' careers in his 1963 *Film Culture* masterpiece "The American Cinema" took only a paragraph; they were often shorter than the directors' filmographies. The famous Sarris concision of style had me anticipating a two-hour class of maxims punctuated by excruciating Pinter pauses. Threat would surely hang in the air as the brighter students struggled to play Sarris's Socrates and the rest of us wriggled to avoid getting drilled by the Master's laser stare.

Which hints at the second presumption I carted into that course: my vision (never seen in the flesh) of the brilliant critic. He'd be thin and intense, a hawklike visage on a scarecrow body, wrapped in tweeds and a scarf that blew dramatically even when there was no wind. His intellectual energy would have burned away excess calories. Imagine an American Basil Rathbone or John Wood or maybe a more dapper Jonas Mekas. Of course, this was an idiot notion. It ignored the givens of a film critic's professional life: sitting on his butt watching movies and sitting on his butt writing about them. So I should not have been surprised at the figure standing behind the long table in that trapezoidal classroom.

He was a panda man, a large fellow just shy of forty with sad eyes and an air of genial melancholy. He seemed unaware of his eminence, wearing his legendary status as uneasily as his anonymous dark suits. There was a tentative note in his high, musical voice, as if the bolts of wisdom he was hurling at the grad students were the merest suggestions, submitted for our approval. We expected fire and fury; we got a puppy dog, of the basset breed, on his haunches to please.

Yet Sarris was a superb teacher, a charismatic guide to world cinema. I wish that like nearly everyone who took Vladimir Nabokov's literature course at Cornell in the 1950s the better to record their recollections of a dazzling Mr. Chips, I'd taken copious notes in Sarris's classes or at least saved what notes I did take. What I do recall is the format and the impact. Each week Sarris would show, on a rickety 16mm projector, a classic film (Ernst Lubitsch's *Angel,* for example). Before the screening, he offered remarks that sketched, with the acuity of a Daumier, the director's achievements; afterward, he'd have a colloquy with the class. Sarris never failed to persuade often of the film's greatness, always of his own powers of analysis and rapture.

Some of the students aspired not to the nattering parasitism of the professional film critic but to creative careers in acting and directing, and these rebels within the course could be dismissive of great films beyond their ken. Only then did Sarris exercise the majesty of his outrage. Once he stopped a screening of D. W. Griffith's *Broken Blossoms,* whose swooning romanticism in the dead gestural language of the silent film had provoked giggles and loud yawns from the actor auditors. "You can go outside for the next hour," Sarris warned, "or sit here in sullen silence. But Griffith deserves if not your good will, then a show of good manners."

What these future De Niros might have recognized is Sarris's transcendence as a performer. His lectures weren't rough drafts for next week's *Voice* column or for an essay in a film magazine. They were intellectual happenings, Coltrane-worthy improvs on the evening's theme, with detours and flashbacks that brought the artists to like as Kane did Kane. Beyond being a font of information and opinion, he was an inspirer. And often he was moved as we were. He'd get revved up, fueled by his eloquence, and almost literally levitate, taking his students on the super-Sarris ride.

I remember one of these flights in a later seminar on film criticism. He started talking about some 1968 film, possibly Robert Aldrich's *The Killing of Sister George,* and soon riffed on the kinship of acting and homosexuality. (The connections that he might not make today were self-love and self-loathing.) Then he subsided, spent, and looked around at us, muttering wistfully that he had pissed away his insights to an audience of twelve. At that moment we felt like a homely girl Warren Beatty had wasted an energetic evening with, sad that we hadn't satisfied his expectations, thrilled that he had exceeded ours.

Eulogies, like elegies, are typically more about the speaker than about the roastee or dearly departed. I haven't (quite) the ego or the IQ to make this little memoir an elevated personal essay of the highbrow or Lopate variety. But I should fill in a few blanks in my cinematic autobiography. It will help explain Sarris's beguiling influence on me.

As a kid (I was born in 1944), I went to movies all the time. For nine summers I worked in a theater on the Jersey shore that showed five films a week. And each Sunday, after Mass at Saint Madeline Sophie's Parish in Philadelphia, I'd scan the Legion of Decency ratings to see whether any of the films my family had taken me to were on the condemned list. One, *The Moon Is Blue,* was; we must have been either brazenly liberal or fetchingly naive (answer B).

In my early teenagery, I caught on to foreign films and saw that they were art. Here, finally, were movies worth studying, parsing, using as the subjects of term papers. Ingmar Bergman might be saying God was dead, but for me Bergman was God. I still like and admired Hollywood films (on my top five of 1959, *Some Like It Hot* and *Imitation of Life* peacefully coexisted with *The Seventh Seal*), but I didn't think of tracking down old Wilder or Douglas Sirk movies with the diligence that I lavish on early Bergman. Classic Hollywood films must have been aired in the wee hours on Philadelphia TV stations, but except for the horror movies hosted by the ghoulish Roland (known as John Zacherle when he moved to New York), I wasn't interested in midnight matinees of 1930s films. To me the late show was Jack Paar and then Johnny Carson.

I was also, from the late 1950s, a subscriber to the *Village Voice.* After seeing *Psycho* (six times in three nights at the Avalon Theatre), I thought, "I like it, but is it art?" Then I read Sarris's rave review. This man said it was art. Hmmmm. A provocative, possibly profound statement (which resonated, thirteen years later, when I wrote about the film as my all-time number one for the Philip Nobile anthology, *Favorite Movies*). Second thought: Aaaaah, anybody can saying anything in the *Voice;* that was its lure and its limitation. Reading Sarris became an agreeable habit, but more for the pleasures of the text and an early clue to European films than as a call to arms for commercial movies. For all the seductions of Sarris's prose, it didn't convince me to see Hawks's *Hatari!* or Ford's *The Man Who Shot Liberty Valance.* Westerns were just not for me. Auteur research couldn't overcome my grudge against certain genres.

Back I went to Bergman and Francois Truffaut and Akira Kurosawa and to others of lesser quality on whom I innocently inflicted snob appeal. I was the sort of kid who pronounced Jules Verne's name as if it were American and Jules Dassin's as if it were French. Dassin was making Greek tragedies and Jesus parables in modern dress, and at the time "Strained Seriousness" was right up my alley. A few months later, I was reading *Film Quarterly* and got bonked by the brick of Pauline Kael's scorn for *Phaedra;* she compared it, invidiously, to a Bette Davis weepie. From opposite coasts and politiques, Kael and Sarris were saying the same thing: that art isn't only what comes from Europe, and that kitsch wasn't a Hollywood monopoly.

Even as a graduate student in film at Columbia (my thesis subject: The Legion of Decency), I didn't plunge into American cinema. In one burst of invincible ignorance that haunts me still, I opined that Barbara Stanwyck had never been in a good movie. But I had begun camping out at the Museum of Modern Art film programs, with their sprightly blend of modern international and older U.S. films. I also had a job at Brandon Films, where employees held afterhours screenings of American and European classics from the company's vast catalog. Dawn was finally visible on my Hollywood horizon.

The light came from reading Sarris, reading him more closely than I had a few years earlier. By then Sarris's status had changed with the *Film Culture* publication of "Notes on the Auteur Theory in 1962," and the first version of "The American Cinema" a year later, and by the angry response to these essays and researches. As he wrote in the introduction to his 1970 collection *Confessions of a Cultist,* "In 1963 I rose from obscurity to notoriety by being quoted out of context (by Kael). . . . The first inkling that I had acquired a position of power came when I was attacked by other critics. Ironically, my enemies were the first to alert me to the fact that I had followers."

I was not so much a follower as a fan. From the MoMA library I excavated the *Film Culture* texts and other choice Sarrisiana. My favorite: his interview with himself in the *New York Bulletin,* with its proclamation of enlightened horniness ("If I must choose between beautiful people and ugly problems I will choose the beautiful people and leave the problems to the politicians."), its prescient promotion of Catherine Deneuve (then eighteen), and its summing up, in three words, of Sarris's conception of the cinema ("Girls, Girls, Girls"). Phrasemaker and iconographer, high priest and satyr, this was a man worth studying. By the time I walked into his class at NYU, I was ripe for acolyte status.

Conversation, stoked by his lectures, came swiftly. I was now famished for what he grandly called "the American cinema." I attended William K. Everson's and other bootleg showings of vintage Americana and frequented auteur retrospectives at revival houses. *TV Guide* was my new missal, as I caught up with the canon on TV. Revelations cascaded. *His Girl Friday:* okay, I get Hawks. *The Searchers:* a western could be a deathless masterpiece. Preston Sturges: wow!

In the year before taking Sarris's course, I had been writing professionally for *National Review, Commonweal,* and (on rock and roll) the *New York Times,* and had begun contributing to *Film Quarterly*—Bergman, of course. Gradually Sarris connected the skulker in the third row of his class with the occasional byline about movie reviews. "You're not a student" he said to me once. "You're a competitor!" Com-pe-ti-tor! Maybe he didn't use the exact words that Spencer Tracy directed at Katharine Hepburn in *Adam's Rib;* nonetheless, I took the jibe as a compliment. A mentor might become a colleague.

In 1969, Sarris left NYU and returned "in triumph" as he put it with bald glee to Columbia as a professor. For Andy, 1969 was a miracle year in two other respects: he married Molly Haskell, and he published the book version of his sacred *Film Culture* text as *The American Cinema: Directors and Directions 1929–1968.*

By its format, the book automatically exalted opinion. The directors in it were not listed alphabetically but only under categories that were either honorific ("Pantheon" for Hawks, "The Far Side of Paradise" for Gregory La Cava) or proscriptive ("Less Than Meets the Eye" for Wilder, "Strained Seriousness" ouch! for Stanley Kubrick). Hence a judgment was forced on readers before they ever began reading. *Film Quarterly* editor Chic Calenbach, in reviewing the book, aptly called this "an insane mnemonic device." And it worked. A bit more than thirty years on, I can still recall the place settings for each director at Andy's banquet.

I have always thought list making to be the obsession of a disorderly man, in part because I am a slob who loves to impose arbitrary priorities on my aesthetic whims. There is something both godlike and childlike in making movie lists: their compiler is a higher IQ version of the baseball nerd. Sarris's ranking (in both senses of the word) of Hollywood directors and their films struck me then, and still does, as stats with attitude. In the "Directorial Chronology" appended to the book, we find *Operation Petticoat, The Angry Hills,* and *A Hole in the Head* rated as better films than *Some Like It Hot.* Huh? and Whoa!

This rating hints at two hallmarks of the Sarris brand of auteurism (which is like saying "the Jesus brand of Christianity," for both are radical systems that become orthodoxy, and both have been exploited for commercial purposes). One is its genesis not just in sympathy with the French proponents of director worship but in antipathy to the comfortable stodginess of Crowther and other mainstream reviewers of the day. As much as Sarris wanted to canonize Samuel Fuller and Nicholas Ray, he needed to cauterize the work of directors laureled by frontline movie reviewers. This made Crowther the hidden auteur of the "Less Than Meets the Eye" category, a Hall of Shame that Wilder shares with, among others, John Huston, Elia Kazan, David Lean, and Joseph L. Mankiewicz. These directors can be accused of either a dead eye or academic pictorialism, but so could Sturges and Stevens, to name just two who dwelt in "The Far Side Of Paradise." The only thing the "Less" directors had in common was praise from Crowther, and that, I suspect, sealed their fate.

Until they got old. And here is the second law of Andyology: when a director becomes eligible for Social Security, he enters that "Melancholy twilight" phase of his career that Sarris finds profoundly touching. So *Ryan's Daughter* redeemed Lean, and *The Private Life of Sherlock Holmes* elevated Wilder. Politique polemics gave way to intimations of mortality and creative immortality.

Back in the 1960s, I was skeptical of Sarris's gerontophilia, his belief that advancing age can stoke genius, and a high hack can grow, not decline, into an auteur. I agreed with Fitzgerald about second acts in the lives of American artists. But now I am touched by Andrew's sentiment. It points to his respect for antiquity, for the old movies and old (as in long-gone) moviemakers he both rescued from anonymity and secured as worth cherishing in part because he cherished them. As Disraeli said and Andy loved to repeat, "In the long run, we are all dead." That is true. It is also true that, thanks to Sarris, some directors and films will never die. He is the prime reviver of our ragged, treasured art.

Over the decades, Andy has been pestered to update *The American Cinema.* I suggested that he enlarge it to include other potential auteurs, not just screenwriters but producers (David O. Selznick), actors (James Cagney), cinematographers (John Alton), craftspeople who dominated the films they made. Once, in the late 1970s, he said his plans were to reduce the categories to two: "Pantheon Directors" and everyone else. But three decades have passed without a second edition of this invaluable work of criticism, and Sarris recently told me there would never be one. I still find the insights and writing things of beauty, but I'll bet he sees the book as a creature of its time, even as the films he wrote about were creatures of another age. Besides, he has been refining and redefining his vision on the book's directors and their successors in his columns in the *Voice* and now the *New York Observer*, a living history of world cinema in weekly installments.

By 1970, the teacher and his balky admirer from the NYU classes were writing for each other; I as a fourth string reviewer at the *Voice* (specializing in the oeuvres of Russ Meyer and Radley Metzger), Andy as a valued contributor to *Film Comment* (including several pieces I hope will reemerge in his long promised study of Hollywood in the 1930s). The lead article in my first issue as *Film Comment* editor was Sarris's "Notes on the Auteur Theory in 1970," in which he restated his affirmative action policy toward directors, took a swat at me for something I'd written about *Psycho,* and waded once more into the Kael maelstrom. Clearly he had tired to "playing good old Charlie Brown to Miss K's Lucy"; clearly her old slights still rankled. "And that is about all that can be said on the subject," Sarris wrote, before spitting another few hundred words in her general direction.

Kael's attack on the auteur theory had helped make both critics stars, but it galled Andy to be linked with Kael and, I'd guess, to see her collections reviewed on the front page of the *Times Book Review.* "People were always telling me," he wrote in *Confessions of a Cultist,* "that I was lucky to be attacked in print and that the only thing that mattered was the correct spelling of my name." But the slurs hurt. It must have been painful too that Kael's 1963 screed was subtitled "Joys and Sarris," that she had punned on a mispronunciation of his name, which of course rhymes with Harris, not Doris. (Wilfrid Sheed, I believe it was, dubbed Andy's followers "Sarrisites," which at least got the pronunciation right.)

Kael was a proselytizer of the Pauline gospel. She wanted people to see the films she liked and to see them as she did; a different opinion was evidence of apostasy. I once asked some friends of hers what her reaction was when they disagreed with her. "It's never come up," they said. Sarris was not so doctrinaire; he welcomed debate on issues he was steeped in; he enjoyed challenges to his critical credo as he did a good game of tennis. (But that's Richard Schickel's area of expertise.)

For years after my classes with Andy, I was a Sarrisite, junior grade and with reservations. I shared his love for old Hollywood films but not his take

on every film or director, and felt no need to. Andrew could easily have considered me an antagonist, since, as a part-time salesman for the idea that the
screenwriter deserved honorary mention as a creator of Hollywood movie
art, I was either extending auteurism or debunking it. Andrew never took
my work as a slight; indeed, he gallantly wrote the introduction to my 1974
book, *Talking Pictures.* For Andy, the fiercest dialectic (if it didn't involve
Kael) was all conversation, which he loved. I think it was in his review of *My
Night at Maud's* where he wrote that there was nothing more cinematic than
the spectacle of a man and woman staying up all night talking.

In another life, Andy and Pauline might have been those two people—
but not in this life. Sarris often told of the time, it was about 1965, Kael having just moved from San Francisco to New York to write for *McCall's,* when
she invited her rival for a chat in her West Side apartment. "It's like *Woman
of the Year,*" he said to his friend Eugene Archer, then a critic at the *Times.*
After the rendezvous, Sarris told Archer, "She's no Katharine Hepburn," and
I can almost hear him exhaling the sigh of a fellow who, against his better
instincts, hoped that a blind date would work out. Archer famously replied,
"And you're no Spencer Tracy."

Andrew was not exactly Spencer Tracy. Over the years, he reminded me
of Gene Hackman (with his large man's grace and weight of movement) and
FDR (the rings around the eyes, the fate-defying upward tilt of the head).
Once he, I, and Richard Roud, our leader at the New York Film Festival, simultaneously declared that we imagined ourselves to be the Jean Renoir
character in *The Rules of the Game,* at least when Renoir was wearing his
bear costume.

But Andy found his Hepburn, as much Audrey as Katharine, in Molly
Haskell. Gifted, gorgeous, chic as Chanel, Molly also had that Sarrisish sand
in the oyster feeling of an outsider at the marvelous party to which her
celebrity had made her an honored guest. These qualities proved ideal for
Molly in her new role as Andrew's companion, critic, and keeper. She gently instructed him in the proper volume for dinner conversation. Her aristocratic feminism perfectly complemented his informed, starstruck romanticism for most things female. Her laugh, as knowing as Rosalind Russell's but
warmer, lent perspective to his occasional hot flashes and blue moods. She
was his nurse and good humor woman through his bizarre, catastrophic illness in 1984, even as he worked heroically to jolly her through her illness
that immediately followed his recovery. Under her loving care, Andy evolved
into Andrew.

Within a year of their marriage, they had contributed tandem rhap-
sodies to *Vogue,* each extolling the other's brilliance, sanity, mother, and fa-

ther wit. It was the sort of public declaration of love that leads a couple's friends to fear the worst; we figured they'd be Reno bound in no time. But they confounded the Cassandras by remaining exemplarily independent and interdependent. What Sarris wrote of Mankiewicz in *The American Cinema,* that "his vibrant women . . . shine with special brilliance from midnight to the three o clock in the morning of the soul," might be meant as a paean to his own vibrant woman. Andrew and Molly are the couple of the year from 1969 till now and forever.

There was another film couple married in 1969: Mary Yushak of MoMA and Richard Corliss of no fixed abode. Mary occasionally crashed Sarris's NYU course; she cooked dinner for his fiftieth birthday; she wished him a later happy birthday while standing at his hospital bed. The Corlisses have spent memorable days and nights with the Haskell-Sarrises in Cannes, Sarasota, Portofino, and some of the swankest homes in Quogue, Long Island. That class in 1967 was for me the beginning of many beautiful friendships.

When Mary and I set up house, we brought along our personal and intellectual luggage. Each of us had files of favorite things (her opera scores, my baseball scores). One thing, it turned out, we both had saved: clippings of Sarris reviews from the *Voice* and *Film Culture.* That seems as good a basis as any for a lifelong marriage. I wonder if Molly Haskell, in stint in the mid-60s at the French Film Office and the National Society of Film Critics, had an Andrew Sarris file.

Andrew Sarris: Father of Film Study

Jeanine Basinger

$\mathcal{I}$f I had to choose one person I consider to be the most influential film critic/scholar of the past fifty years, I would without hesitation select Andrew Sarris. Not Andre Bazin, whose work is largely ignored or forgotten by young people today. Not Henri Langlois, who loved films and saved them but absentmindedly lost them again. Not Kracauer or Agee or Kuleshov or Greene or Arnheim or Pudovkin or Ferguson or Balazs or Metz or Munsterberg or Farber or Einsenstein or Wollen or any of the other greats, all influential, important, but largely unknown outside the academy. Not even Pauline Kael, Sarris's archrival and frequent nemesis, who has influenced a new generation of film critics, but whose work did not reshape education significantly.

I would choose Andrew Sarris, because of three things: (1) his film criticism for the *Village Voice;* (2) his contributions to the New York Film Festival; and (3) his 1968 book, *The American Cinema, Directors and Directions 1929–1968,* which introduced the concept of auteurism to a wide audience in America. The last of the three brought about the emergence of a total reassessment of American film and ended up legitimizing film study indirectly. It was Sarris, to my mind, who took the motion picture out of the dark and brought it into the classroom, and without him, people like me could not have had the careers we've had.

Thirty years ago, film was not widely taught in American universities, and there were no actual film majors. Some schools had production courses, and more than a few had foreign language departments using movies as a crutch for students attempting "conversational" skills, but for the most part, film study was limited to what was termed "film appreciation." Maybe it was one big class . . . or just a small seminar . . . and maybe it was taught by a drama professor or a literature professor or an art professor, but "film appreciation" meant a class in which participants discussed movies on a "serious" level, which meant pretending they were almost as good as books or plays. It meant talking over their literary value or talking about them in humanistic or political terms.

One thing it almost never meant was discussing film-as-film, and the films discussed were not going to be popular Hollywood movies. Maybe *Our Daily Bread* and *The Grapes of Wrath* or *The Great Dictator* could be included, but forget about *Miracle of Morgan's Creek* and don't even mention *The Lady from Shanghai,* which had been written off as a complete failure. Mostly, such classes worked with foreign films, such as *Children of Paradise* and *Grand Illusion,* or documentaries, such as *Night Mail* and *Nanook of the North.* Then along came Andrew Sarris and the publication of *The American Cinema* and, suddenly, everyone was rethinking everything and running out to look at as many Hollywood movies as could be found for screenings.

About this time, 1969, I began teaching film at Wesleyan University in Middletown, Connecticut. I was first invited to sit in on a "film appreciation" type of class to see what "serious" appreciation was all about, and to my surprise, the class was looking at a black-and-white print of *For Whom the Bell Tolls.* No one involved in the class at any level knew the film had been made in color, or that it had won the Oscar for Best Color Cinematography. The name of Ray Rennahan—the man who had shot it—was unknown.

The serious discussion paid tribute to the fact that this was a "distinguished motion picture," because it was based on a "literary masterpiece." Then everyone pointed out how much better the book was than the movie. (Well, in fairness, the book was better than the movie, but the discussion concerned the book, and not the reasons *why.*) Right away, I knew my work was cut out for me! The campus was alive with intelligent, motivated students who wanted to see everything, and as Sarris's book appeared in the bookstore, I grabbed it up and started waving it like a flag. Soon everyone had his or her own copy, and everyone was busily crossing off titles as they were seen. A film series was formed to show rare material. Car pools were organized for trips to Boston and New Haven and New York for screenings. Plots were laid on how to get hold of obscure titles.

Then it occurred to one of our most enterprising students (Larry Mark, now a successful Hollywood producer) that we should go to the source: get Andrew Sarris on campus. I well remember the excitement this generated, as we all rushed around laying plans for the big event. Would he come? How could we contact him? After negotiations worthy of a summit conference,

the proud announcement was bruited about the campus: ANDREW SAR-
RIS, IN PERSON, NEXT WEEK, IN MIDDLETOWN, RIGHT
UNDER OUR NOSES. The faculty flew into a nervous twitter over who
would entertain him, who would get to meet him, with everyone jockeying
for position as only faculty can do. The students fought back in an "he's
ours" move, trying to give the dinner party themselves. The faculty won, and
a pompous dinner for a mob (with about three students invited) took place
at a wealthy townsman's home. Sarris arrived and held up beautifully, but the
high point was his talk, which took place in front of a packed auditorium.

Over the years, we've had many big names at Wesleyan, but we've never
had a bigger crowd than the one we had that night. Every seat was taken,
and there was standing room only at the back of the house, with students
seated on the stairs, creating a fire hazard that everyone seemed to feel was
well worth it. Sarris talked for over an hour, and then answered questions for
another hour and a half. When he finished, he was surrounded by students
pressing forward to meet him, to shake his hand, to ask more questions, and
to thank him. Mostly, they just wanted to continue the conversation in some
way, in any way at all.

Throughout all of this, Sarris was never anything but gracious and
eager, and the thing that stood out most of all about him was his generosity.
He had humor and intelligence and a deep and abiding love of the movies
and a stunning knowledge about them, but most of all, he shared all openly
and generously. And he never made fun of a movie to prove his own superiority, nor was he snotty or mean or small. He was open-minded and never
put anyone down, unless, of course, he was forced to. Then he was clever
about it and not unkind, but the person knew to back off and back off fast.

What times those were! Everyone at Wesleyan was energized by the
visit. Students were eager and willing to learn, and I soon found wonderful
colleagues who took film seriously. The excitement with which everyone
embraced learning about movies went forward for the next two decades. I
often thought about Sarris and called him for support, because it wasn't always easy to get financial aid for booking movies, and it wasn't always easy
to find respect for film study. During the period in which *The American Cinema* reigned supreme, there was a great thirst for information and opinions
on unfamiliar film titles that most people had not seen.

Since I had started going to the movies by 1940, I had seen many of
these movies, and I made every effort to bring as much obscure material to
campus as possible. Many people on campus had grave doubts about my
credibility. ("She's over there showing old Jimmy Cagney movies," someone
once said, inadvertently revealing their own lack of knowledge. To them,

Cagney was obscure. And so was *Bringing Up Baby.* In my circles, obscure meant *The Big Combo, Gun Crazy, Colorado Territory, Pickup on South Street, Tarnished Angels, Ramrod, Angel Face, Driftwood, Wives Under Suspicion, Terror in a Texas Town.*) However, I was always saved by the reputation of Andrew Sarris. When criticisms hit me directly, I pulled out Sarris's book. "But look," I could always way, "Sarris lists the director under 'The Far Side of Paradise' or 'Subjects for Further Research.'"

It should never be forgotten that, in the beginning, the general attitude in the academy was that Hollywood films were not worthy of serious consideration, and that all genre films were bad. It was hard going for all of us, and Sarris took many public beatings on our behalf. It was strange, but true, that some scholars who would encourage openness in their own fields, and who would caution students against closed minds, handed down dogmatic judgments about the movies that they were basing largely on their own adolescent viewings. They pronounced film study as worthless in general, but film study of American movies worthless in particular. What was equally scary, however, was that people with no knowledge of film history, the economics of the studio system, or the details of film production in any form began teaching film courses because they were closet movie fans. Many of these people had very limited viewing experience, and even today most film courses are based on a narrow list of "approved" titles. No credentials were required to teach film, and what a blessing that was for me, but also what a nightmare as I confronted misinformation in my own classroom. (I'll never forget one of my students telling me that he had been taught that there was no sound in movies to begin with because the addition of sound had not occurred to Edison. This "he just didn't think of it" school of information—linked to the man who invented the phonograph—defines the level of awareness that was prevalent.)

Sometimes, too, professors teaching film set up competitions: American movies versus foreign movies, encouraging students to embrace the good foreign films and discard the bad Hollywood product. This, despite the fact that, as war loomed in Europe during the 1930s, almost all of the major European talents came over to America, so that the Hollywood movie practically *is* the foreign movie for a period of time. And despite the fact that the postwar generation of European filmmakers always generously admired and respected American films, citing them as major influences on their own works. All this Sarris warned against and helped us all in our attempts to cope with it. I remember once talking to him on the phone and having him muse aloud that he found it interesting that most people who love Hollywood movies also love foreign films, but that the reverse is not always true.

We smugly agreed, with laughter, that the Hollywood fan is thus the truer movie lover!

As the 1970s moved forward, the really serious film study began, and the first Ph.D.s in film were offered. Throughout the 1980s, a marvelous generation of young film scholars emerged, passionate about their discipline, well prepared in all areas, and eclectic in their tastes. When these people began teaching in the universities and colleges of America, film study went to a new level and began to gain a more solid footing as a necessary part of the curriculum. Those of us who had entered in the 1960s basically had credentials that said: FILM NUT, HAVE SEEN EVERYTHING, JUST ASK ME. Now we were joined by scholars who had grown up with the idea that teaching movies was okay, that all kinds of movies were worthy of serious study, and that serious study meant approaching the movies from many different points of view: cultural, feminist, theoretical, historical, formalist, and so forth.

As the history of film studies in America unfolded, Andrew Sarris was an oasis of sanity and someone we all counted on for support and guidance. His book was a map to discovery, and his writings and lectures encouraged everyone toward openness, sharing, and discovery. It should not be forgotten that in the first decade, when there were no academically trained scholars to teach, there were pioneers who fought for the programs that now exist. Sarris grounded everyone-scholars and general audiences—in a love of movies, a dedication to reevaluations based on actual viewings, and a desire to define standards and criteria. Sarris was a catalyst for a movement toward serious study, one which ultimately challenged and changed attitudes toward the role of film studies in academic curricula.

To remember him only as a champion of auteurism is wrong. Sarris's brand of auteurism had less to do with calling the director the only artist in film and more to do with identifying artists, whether they be actors and actresses, producers, studios, screenwriters, cinematographers, editors, set designers, or directors. It had everything to do with taking movies seriously, with reevaluation, and with facing down suspicions and criticisms about the importance of the movies in the twentieth century.

Andrew Sarris is the father of film study as we know it today.

Dear Mr. Sarris

John Belton

$\mathcal{B}$ack in 1963 or 1964, I wrote Andrew Sarris a fan letter. I can't imagine what was in it. It was probably full of embarrassing effusions about how much I liked his columns in the *Village Voice* and how great he was.

From 1978 to 1986, I taught film studies at Columbia and shared an office with Andrew. I felt a bit strange. It was like a fan's fantasy: I was playing on the same team as Mickey Mantle.

About four or five years after my initial act of idolatry, I actually got to meet Sarris. I was teaching, as a grad student, a course on Hitchcock and wrote to Sarris to ask his permission to reprint his reviews of *Marnie* and *Torn Curtain* in a course packet I was preparing for the students. When I moved back to New York City in 1970, I had the chance to get to know Andy a little bit better. I contributed a couple dozen film essays and reviews to the *Village Voice,* where Andy was chief film critic. I had been reading the *Voice* since 1962, largely to find out what Andy had to say about current movies. What I learned about writing from reading Andy was to try to say something about the nature of the cinema in every piece, to use the film review as a point of departure for discussing the larger issues of film aesthetics, history, and theory.

I became interested in film in 1961, when I was sixteen. The father of one of my friends in high school owned a Bell & Howell 16mm projector and ran a film society on Friday nights in his home. He subscribed to the *Village Voice* and introduced me to Sarris's weekly film column.

At that point in the history of film studies, the serious study of the cinema was being undertaken not by film historians or academics but by (college) film societies, such as that at Dartmouth, and by "journalists," such as Sarris. Indeed, Sarris was the only voice regularly speaking about the cinema whose comments and insights were always stimulating, intelligent, and original. Film culture was centered around the *Village Voice,* where Sarris and Jonas Mekas shared the task of mapping the terrain of current film practice.

Back in the 1960s, the film community was a genuine community and figures such as Sarris, Mekas, and William K. Everson were at its center. They/we all went to the same screenings, whether it be to see underground films at the Charles or the FilmMakers' Cinematheque (as a colleague of Mekas and as an associate editor of *Film Culture* from 1955 to 1965, Sarris saw as much "new" American cinema as he did old American cinema). We also went to retrospectives of commercial films at MoMA, the New Yorker, or the Thalia; to foreign films at the Little Carnegie, the Bleecker Street Cinema, the Eighth Street Playhouse, the Paris, the Baronet, the Beekman, the Sutton, and the New Yorker; and to rare, old 16mm films at film societies such as the Theodore Huff Society and various university film societies. We defined the cinema broadly; it encompassed everything, ranging from Bergman, Fellini, Rossellini, Antonioni, and films of the New Wave to Hawks, Hitchcock, Ford, Fuller, Sirk, Cassavetes, Brakhage, Deren, Rice, Smith, Anger, and Breer. We all talked to one another, argued with one another.

Today, the film community is highly fragmented. Academics no longer read, much less talk to, journalists. Those interested in narrative cinema tend to ignore independent or avant-garde films. Film historians and theorists speak different languages, and neither of these languages make sense to either filmmakers or the public. Now writing for the *New York Observer,* Sarris continues to speak as he always has, but his audience is now more diverse, more contentious, less willing to become a community.

Sarris would probably never view himself as the center of a community. He always relished the role of the outsider and the iconoclast. His pioneering work, *The American Cinema: Directors and Directions 1929–1968,* was highly polemical, designed to disturb the geological profile of traditional American film criticism. It challenged the sociological approach to the cinema, exemplified by Agee and others, that valued "serious," highbrow art films that dealt with social issues and dismissed lowbrow, popular Hollywood genre pictures that appealed to mass tastes. Thus Sarris's polemical stance echoed that of Truffaut, who, in a famous 1954 article for *Cahiers du Cinéma,* had attacked the "tradition of quality" in French cinema—artsy adaptations of classic works of French literature—and celebrated instead the energy, style, and personal vision of Hollywood program pictures.

In the spring of 1963, Sarris published a sixty-eight-page draft of *The American Cinema* in a special issue of *Film Culture* (no. 23). A few months later, in December 1963, *Cahiers* followed suit, publishing a special issue on American cinema with filmographies and brief, 100- to 250-word essays on 90 producers and 121 "Metteurs en Scènes" (directors). The differences between the American and French publications were significant: the essays in *Cahiers* were organized alphabetically and written by a variety of authors; those in *Film Culture* were all written by a single author—Sarris—and arranged in hierarchical categories ("Pantheon Directors," "Second Line," "Third Line," "Esoterica," "Beyond the Fringe," "Fallen Idols," "Likable but Elusive," "Minor Disappointments," "Oddities and One Shots," etc.). The inspiration for Sarris's polemical categories may have come from a May 1962 issue of a British film magazine, *Movie,* which merely listed directors (without brief essays) in highly subjective groupings, ranging from "Great," "Brilliant," "Very Talented," and "Talented" to "Competent or Ambitious" and "The Rest."

The 1968 publication of *The American Cinema,* a revised and expanded version of Sarris's *Film Culture* piece, transformed the landscape of American film study. It was probably the most important film book ever written in that everyone read it, everyone talked about, and everyone used it. It's hard to say that about any film book published before or since (save, perhaps, Leonard Maltin's invaluable home-movie reference book *TV Movies,* which, though highly used, is not quite read in the same way).

The polemics of Sarris's project drew considerable attention to Sarris through a highly publicized attack upon him and the "auteur theory" by Pauline Kael in the spring 1963 issue of *Film Quarterly.* But the chief virtue of the project was not its controversial promulgation of the idiosyncratic and transcendent "personal vision" of commercial filmmakers, whom the critical establishment regarded as "Hollywood hacks." Rather it was the remarkable fact that, as William Paul has pointed out, Sarris took Hollywood cinema seriously and his writing conveyed the conviction of that virtually unprecedented gesture. The publication of *The American Cinema* coincided with a rediscovery of classical Hollywood cinema and energized a new generation of film viewers who took up Sarris's enthusiasm and passion for a previously unappreciated and scorned cinema.

The American Cinema proved to be one of the mostly highly used film books. Although it mapped a previously uncharted terrain, its boundaries remained flexible. It was a starting point for those who wanted to see films and think about the cinema as a cinema of directors. It did not trace a fixed history of Hollywood or set forth a grand theory of the cinema that would arm the book's users with a specific theoretical perspective. In other words, it did not do what the subsequent academicization of film studies would do in the mid-1970s—it did not lay out the field. There was something open-ended and unfinished about the book; it set film students off in different directions.

Sarris was no empire builder. He was not interested in converting a new generation of film critics into auteurists. At the *Voice*, Sarris functioned more as a magnet than as a missionary. He was followed, but he didn't lead. Young critics and scholars were drawn to him; the film section of the *Voice* featured regular contributions from Molly Haskell, Tom Allen, Stuart Byron, Richard Corliss, William Paul, Michael McKegney, Jim Hoberman, George Morris, James Stoller, and others as well as occasional pieces by Stephen Gottlieb, Elisabeth Weis, me, Stephen Handzo, Richard Koszarski, Tom Costner, Terry Curtis Fox, Marvin Deckoff, and others.

Sarris is a phenomenologist. In his columns, he writes about essences, capturing the spirit of a film through a description of his engagement, as subject, with a particular aspect of a film or object. That description often comes in the form of an insight about one feature of the film—its essence-which then elliptically stands in for the whole. As a phenomenologist, Sarris rejects systematic analysis, refusing to dissolve the object away by viewing it through the structures of a methodological grid. As a phenomenologist, he remains wary of institutions and organizations that seek to organize or rationalize the field of film study. His relationship with the film program at Columbia University reflects that wariness. He had no interest in the academicization of film studies. I don't believe he ever chaired the department. He never developed an academic agenda. He read and followed the developments of what David Bordwell and Noel Carroll have recently called "Grand Theory" (Lacan, Althusser, Barthes, Metz, et al.) but retained a journalistic skepticism toward it and other attempts to "organize" the field.

Andy's teaching tends to be phenomenological as well. In his lectures, he constructs a "horizon" of objects and issues to discuss, making unexpected and amazingly insightful connections between disparate and seemingly unrelated objects along this horizon. His classes were filled with synaptic flashes. Students could often learn more about the cinema from one brief insight in one of Andy's classes than they could from an entire course taught by someone else.

Though Andy has little interest in empire building within the academy, he remains fascinated by its politics. He may not have the organizational skills to run a department, but in the byzantine power plays, thrusts, and parries of the typical department meeting, Andy emerges as the diplomat's diplomat, presenting the most elegant and stirring arguments ever mustered in defense of his field, his colleagues, or his students. We may not have won all these battles, but Andy was our best spokesperson and, as Red Auerbach used to say, when you lose, you should lose with your best players on the court.

Years ago, Liz Weis and I played doubles with Andy and Molly on some tennis courts in Central Park. We lost. I would slam in my serve as hard and as flat out as I could—with nothing on it—but Andy (and Molly) would always get it back. Andy's serve had a lot of spin; I hit it out more often than in. You can tell a lot about someone's personality from their tennis game. Andy's was stylish (the serve), yet also scrappy and tenacious. His ground strokes were quite consistent, and his returns were really well placed. The guy seems so casual, relaxed, and lackadaisical. He even describes himself in interviews as kind of lazy. But, believe me, he's not. He's concentrated and driven.

In other words, Sarris is phenomenological to the core (even in his tennis game). His engagement with the moment is focused and intense. Beneath his cynically urbane manner and Wildean wit, Sarris is a genuine Romantic: he writes and lives passionately and for the moment. Perhaps that is why he is so drawn to Lola Montes and Lady Hamilton.

I trust that my fan letter of thirty-some years ago has long since found its place in oblivion. If I were to rewrite it today, it might look something like the above. Or it might look something like everything I've ever written about the cinema, including my next-to-last book, which shamelessly borrows the title of Andy's most famous book and which remains intellectually indebted to it. Everything that I do or have done is, in one way or another, a response to Sarris's writings. This is my fan letter to him.

Sixteen Fragments on Auteur Theory, or Sarris's Revenge

James Schamus

1. *H*ere, it is called "auteur theory." But in France it is called "politique des auteurs." Hence the confusion in the 1970s and 1980s experienced by us (post)structuralist, psychoanalytic, feminist, Marxist theorists, who were hard put to account for how all our French colleagues could by day expose the "apparatus," the "ideology," the "regime" of the cinema, while by night savoring the delights of the latest Don Siegel or Bob Swaim.

2. It is by now a well-rehearsed history how the introduction to the United States of "auteur theory" by Andrew Sarris in the 1960s helped to make the academic study of cinema a legitimate discipline. Before then, there was the odd "Ingmar Bergman and the Disappearance of God" course offered in the English department or the divinity school. But now, films that had once been "westerns" or "John Wayne" movies became "Fords" or "Hawkses," expressions of individual artistic sensibilities. Great films bore the thematic and stylistic signatures of their authors; bad films were produced without the imprints made by the weight of an individual artistic character (with the exception, of course, of *Casablanca*). Suddenly, out of the wasteland of Hollywood, a canon of great works arose, discerned using criteria easily recognizable by humanities scholars in all disciplines. But soon came theory.

3. The founding gesture of the version of film "theory" is the evacuation of the question of individual human agency from the study of the production and consumption of films. Two words—*ideology* and *apparatus*—exemplify this move. To spend time tracing the stylistic residues that may or may not mark an individual film text, as opposed to studying the cinema as an institution, seemed at best frivolous and at worst a belletristic obfuscation. What any film might "mean" is far less important than how it means, how

it positions the spectator in an imaginary relationship to the real ways in which meanings and ideologies are produced and behaviors enforced. The classical Hollywood cinema, no matter how many its various authors, was (and still is) a regime, an institution, producing not only individual films, but, more importantly, an unconsciously reproduced mentality and appetite for commodified spectacle in all the subjects who come under its sway. No individual film text can change this system because it is already a part of it, and it is the system, the entire apparatus, that is therefore the proper object of study, not individuated film–text, whose fetishized appreciation is, after all, simply one more commodified experience.

4. But even throughout the dark years of Theory, one could hear the occasional auteurist mumble: great films are the textual battlefields on which authors won.

5. Interestingly, human agency has returned to film studies not so much in the form of a revived auteurism as in a renewed respect for viewers as decision makers whose experiences selecting, viewing, and discussing films empower them to create identities and meanings. If, upon the death of the Author, it was first the critic who appeared to take the role of active agent and producer of meaning, it wasn't long until the critic gave way to "the audience" or "the fans," contemporary cargo cultists whose rituals and mysteries are seen as the locus of meaningful cultural agency.

6. Soon, however, the critic needed to go one step further, abandoning the politically and philosophically suspect position of armchair anthropologist, whose objectifying discourses and exploitation of native informants gave a somewhat condescending air to this new critical enterprise. Now it was important not simply to study specific communities of interpretation (teen fanzine readers, Star Trek groupies, pornography junkies), it was necessary to confess, indeed profess, one's own membership in such communities. Theoretical authority was achieved not by identifying with people whose pleasures appeared to be unmediated by academically sanctioned critical and theoretical discourses but by identifying oneself as such a person.

7. The next step was a natural. It was to show that such communities are far more theoretically sophisticated and empowered than one might suppose them to be—even, at times, more sophisticated than the professoriate that attempts to study them.

8. So now is it not only proper to be an enthusiast, a fan, a cinephile—it is epistemologically imperative that one be so. Without such enthusiasms, we in fact have no theoretical grounds upon which to stand when regarding the object–cinema. We much love the movies, or we will never know them.

9. Or, we must love auteurs (though we can certainly lust after stars). Thus, the revenge of Sarris, and of those in America who have labored as the critical masses, whose siege of the ivory tower of theory had always been at best an occasional (and now long-gone) English department stronghold and at worst a string of adjunct auteur classes in between reviewing gigs.

10. *Cahiers du cinéma* (an English version of which Sarris brought to the States for a time as part of the auteurist onslaught), was the creation of the great Andre Bazin, who served as godfather to the journal's young critics (among them Godard, Truffaut, Chabrol and, later, Techine, Assayas, Bonitzer—these last two writing well after Bazin's early death). But Bazin is himself not much of an auteurist. Read his *What Is Cinema?* and you find surprisingly little auteurishness in it. Auteurism is, rather, a product not of the father but of the sons: Truffaut's adulation of Hitchcock, Godard's of Lang, and so forth. It recontextualizes European, specifically French, cinephilism as a generative practice, and it remakes what might be sneered at as abject fandom into a liberatory process of self-invention and engagement.

11. Taking small-scale European artisanal modes of production and grafting them, as a critical grid, onto the reading of industrial-strength Hollywood movies allowed fledgling European auteurs to see their cinema as taking place in dialogue with Hollywood and not simply in some provincial parallel or derivative universe. European cinema could be, at one and the same time, essentially in Hollywood and anti-Hollywood.

12. Euro-auteurs like Godard and Straub–Huillet could be appreciated, and their works made the object of a kind of old-fashioned connoisseurship, precisely because their work could be read allegorically as embodying the critiques of the apparatus that were being articulated in theory. American theorists could fall in line behind these enthusiasms without noticing that, in their own way, they were re-creating the same kind of canon-making gestures they had so ruthlessly attacked in Sarris et al.

13. Just as Oscars are no longer "won" but "gone to" ("The Oscar goes to Allan Smithee"), so these days is the prize of authorship. Authorship goes to directors who make low-budget "nongenre" films (that is, films that are made in genres in the middle- and higher-browed publics refuse to recognize as such—films, therefore, that can simply be called "art" films), or it goes to directors who manage to spend obscene amounts of money no matter what kind of film they make. Like animal organs, which tend to be eaten only by the rich or the poor, film authorship is not for the middle class of directors.

14. Kant, in his third *Critique,* understood well the seductiveness as well as the danger of aesthetic judgment. The danger comes from the fact that

people are no more intolerant than when they are making aesthetic pronouncements. In order to account for this, Kant came up with the idea of a "subjective universal." He knew that aesthetic judgments are subjective, not objective, but he also knew that in order to be true they must be universal, communicable, and sharable by potentially all human subjects.

By contrast, if I have a pain in my right foot, the knowledge I have of it is certainly a subjective experience and not necessarily communicable or universal as pain—I can believe that there are other people who might be more or less stoical than I under the same circumstances. On the other hand, I have the feeling that an objective truth, such as "one plus one equals two," depends for its veracity not a whit on my subjective experience. But when we say that something is beautiful, we feel at once that our judgment is subjective as well as valid enough to argue about. Thus our barely concealed contempt for differences of opinion on matters aesthetical. There's a reason to have interfaith councils and discussions, I suppose. But what's the use of arguing, let alone discussing, with someone who just doesn't "get" late Welles?

15. The rise of the "independent film" coincided with the death of the "B" movie. Young people in America who want to be directors these days must begin as auteurs, rather than, over the years, *become* auteurs. Authorship, like day care, is for the very young and the very old, and rarely for the middle-aged, of aspiring feature directors.

16. As an American independent producer (by the way, have you ever met a producer who described himself as "dependent"), I meld two approaches to the business. From the economics side, I try my best to emulate the great exploitation producers like AIP's Sam Arkoff, or Roger Corman, or William Castle—producer–auteurs who extracted surplus economic and even aesthetic value out of serially reproducible low-budget genres. But in my case, the genre is the "auteur" film. For in the absence of affordable star actors or reliable teen-oriented effects, what do I have with which to promote the film? The director, of course.

Part Five

Sarris the Provocative Critic

*K*athleen Murphy observes in "The Man Who Loved Women" that Andrew Sarris, the "latter-day cultist, critic, and Francophile," once confessed "that his conception of cinema could be summed up in three words: 'Girls! Girls! Girls!' Behind the occasional mask of the endlessly turned-on adolescent in the dark is the character of a devout cineaste for whom the screen has always been 'a window into the soul of others.' Writing of *Lola Montes,* a film Sarris once considered "the single most important experience of my critical life, the one film that has shaped my aesthetic," he "scans Max Ophuls's cinematic poetry according to the language and bent of the old courtly love tradition." Sarris adores *Lola Montes* "because it transforms cinematic expression into a religious experience for this age of increasing faithlessness and fragmentation."

A critic "who loves women with Paterian (and Truffautian) passion, Sarris consistently locates that elusive arc where the arts of appearance and apprehension miraculously hot-wire into cinema. Vide Falconetti by Dreyer (flesh luminescing into soul); Gish by Griffith (irradiating implosions of sexuality and spirit); Dietrich by von Sternberg (pure illusion spun out of screen light, shadow, texture); Garbo by anyone (a radiance in which all the world vaporizes); Louise Brooks by Pabst (feral angel sinlessly in heat); along with Barbara Stanwyck by Capra; Ingrid Bergman by Rossellini; Machiko Kyo and Kinuyo Tanaka by Mizoguchi; Liv Ullmann by Bergman; Monica Vitti by Antonioni; Jeanne Moreau by Truffaut; Anna Karina by Godard; Catherine Deneuve by Truffaut, Bunuel, Polanski; Stephane Audran and Isabelle Huppert by Chabrol; Hanna Schygulla by Fassbinder; Gong Li by Zhang Yimou."

155

In "Sarris and the Search for Style," film professor David Bordwell recalls that after his first and only meeting with Andrew Sarris, back in 1965, he came away from the session with "both the auteur's autograph ('Sincerely yours, Andrew Sarris') and the reassurance that one could talk seriously about movies without dethroning their delights." The delights on which Bordwell dwelled "were chiefly visual"—Sarris was "virtually the only critic in America . . . who treated popular movies as a visual art." Since this side of his work "has not been fully appreciated," Bordwell's "homage, is to Sarris the stylistician, Sarris put style on the agenda because he believes that the best films show the dominance of the director's individual sensibility." This auteurist premise doesn't "explain everything in all American studio movies, but it remains the best way to understand why so many of them are so beautiful." For Bordwell, Sarris's awareness of style, which is still too rare in film studies, is his "most important insight."

In "An ABC of Reading Andrew Sarris," film professor James Naremore presents a set of "notes," written in "the spirit of concision of Sarris's most important book, *The American Cinema*." They are arranged alphabetically "in a sort of dictionary, made up of key words, titles, or names." Naremore observes that Sarris was "challenging when he shows admiration for women's soap operas in addition to male action pictures, and when he places an intellectually unfashionable producer–director like Cecil B. DeMille (the very symbol of Hollywood vulgarity and right-wing bombast) on 'The Far Side of Paradise.'"

In the entry *Ford, John; Griffith, D. W.; Hawks, Howard,* which are three directors in the Sarris Pantheon, Naremore notes that "of the three, Hawks is the most 'modern,' or the closest in spirit to the pragmatic efficiency and unsentimental values of industrialized America," and that John Ford is "Hawks's dialectical opposite." The J and K entries center on *Johnny Guitar* and *Kiss Me Deadly,* two mid-1950s films "relatively ignored by the American critical establishment, that became touchstones of auteurist taste. Both were indecorous if not downright delirious in their treatment of genre conventions and, in an indirect way, they probably inspired the French to make pictures like *Breathless.* Sarris names *Johnny Guitar* as the fifth best movie of 1954 and *Kiss Me Deadly* as the sixth best of 1955. In both cases, he stresses the anarchic–romantic temperament of the director: *Johnny Guitar* is Nicholas Ray's 'most bizarre film, and probably his most personal'; and *Kiss Me Deadly* is 'a testament to Robert Aldrich's anarchic spirit.'"

Naremore's last entry is appropriately about Zinnemann, "one of the least-admired figures in *The American Cinema.* In Sarris's hierarchy, Zinnemann represents the dull director of socially significant projects, who never stooped to entertainment, and who always tried to 'deal Realistically with a

Problem in Adult Terms.'" Naremore "would not radically challenge [Sarris's] view," but when Zinnemann died, he was reminded of how much he admires *From Here To Eternity* and *Day of the Jackal.*

Like other critics, Henry Sheehan ("The One Sarris Paragraph That Changed My Career") feels that "if it weren't for [Andrew Sarris], it's unlikely that anything that has happened in my professional life would have happened the way it did." But for Sheehan, the influence was specific: "More than [*The American Cinema*] as a whole, it was a single phrase, in a paragraph about a director Sarris didn't even like, that sent me down a path from which I've yet to really diverge." The filmmaker was John Sturges, who, because of his age, Sheehan knew as the director of *The Hallelujah Trail* and *The Great Escape,* "a quintessential boy's yarn of the 1960s." Sheehan was "willing to accept Sturges . . . as a capable entertainer. Sarris, of course, wasn't, casting him into . . . 'Strained Seriousness.'"

What struck Sheehan "wasn't Sarris's description of Sturges's films as 'tortured, humorless and self-consciously social,' but another phrase referring to Sturges's use of the 'wasteful pan,' compared as a 'stock-in-trade for superficial visual analysis to Delmer Daves's 'debasing crane,' Stanley Kubrick's 'meaningless tracks,' and Robert Wise's 'IBM perforations' in his montages." Sheehan "never would have noticed this if Sarris hadn't written about it. If Sarris wasn't going to make such a comment, no one else was. References to the actual state of movies, their architecture and construction, were so rare as to be singular. For the most part, movie criticism was in a topsy-turvy state at the time, with most of the practitioners more suited to reviewing radio than cinema. The practice of tying plot summaries together with blithe comments on acting and off-the-cuff judgments wasn't likely to lure anyone into the profession. Providing the tools for analysis, tools that led effortlessly to interpretation was positively exciting." Sheehan came to realize that Sarris was "exercising judgment, the quality that makes criticism literature instead of engineering." To Sheehan, "that word, *perspective,* sums up the contribution Andrew Sarris has made, and continues to make, to film criticism."

"It's great to admire living legends, as long as the living part comes first," notes *New York Times* television (and former film) critic Caryn James in her essay, "Andrew Sarris Observes the Future," one of few pieces about the contemporary Sarris. "It is the vital, ever-thoughtful, constantly writing Andrew Sarris I value the most today, even more than I value his role as the prime mover of American auteurism." For James, Sarris's weekly column in the *New York Observer* has been "a model of how the finest critics stay fresh. Covering everything from Titanic-sized blockbusters to tiny Iranian rarities, his reviews are prescient, unpredictable, and always forward-looking."

"To praise the Sarris of the *Observer* years is not to diminish his importance in critical history." When James "came of age as a film reviewer, in the late 1980s, his influence was so vast" that she "never had to think about it." As she notes: "The auteurist theory he carried to this country in the 1960s had by then become so much a part of the landscape that I simply assumed the director was the author of a film and never questioned the significance of a personal vision. Anti-auteurist rumblings arrived with the force of revisionist argument—the ultimate sign of auteurism's hold."

James notes, "A critic with such a profound influence might easily have spent the next decades looking back, defending his turf and longing for that first moment of glory. Happily, Andrew Sarris has never done that. When he looks back, it is to reassess, to add a new perspective, to make the past part of a critical continuum with the present." For James, Andrew is "the living proof that critics do not have to head down that road to nostalgia or self-importance. We can move ahead, along with him, always embracing the future."

The Man Who Loved Women

Kathleen Murphy

> Humanity does not pass through phases as a train passes through sta-
> tions: being alive, it has the privilege of always moving yet never
> leaving anything behind. Whatever we have been, in some sort we
> are still.
>
> C. S. Lewis, The Allegories of Love

$\mathcal{B}$ack in the politically incorrect eleventh century, a lyrical, highly sophisticated style of erotic poetry sprang up in France's Languedoc province. This
aristocratic art and the lives that imitated it made a religion of love, drawing
sensual metaphor from the language and rites of the church. A woman's
beauty was epiphany, striking the soul directly through the eye, and that
epiphany became a lifelong profession for her articulate acolyte. Fleshly consummation was permitted only in simile, creating fertile ground for the exquisite forms that flowered in verses by troubadours of courtly love.

   In just such a civilized order belongs Andrew Sarris, latter-day cultist,
critic, and Francophile, who once confessed—with a puckish wink to the
groundling—that his conception of the cinema could be summed up in
three words: "Girls! Girls! Girls!" Behind the occasional mask of the endlessly
turned-on adolescent in the dark is the character of a devout cineaste for
whom the screen has always been "a window into the soul of others." Con-
templating *Lola Montes*'s public parts in Max Ophuls's sublime strip show,
Sarris lovingly traces the transfiguration of mannequin into aesthetic Mari-
olatry. Writing of a work he once considered "the single most important experience of my critical life, the one film that has shaped my aesthetic," this

philosopher/critic scans Ophuls's cinematic poetry according to the language and bent of the old courtly love tradition:

> The emphasis of the film shifts from the object of love to the cultural mechanism of love [suggesting] that the banality of a life, any life, hers, his ours, Lola's, could be given meaning and majesty by the beauty of art [S]elling for one dollar her presence to the multitudes, [Lola redeems] all men both as a woman and as an artistic reflection of their sensibilities. . . . I suppose I love *Lola Montes* because it transforms cinematic expression into a religious experience for this age of increasing faithlessness and fragmentation. (*The Primal Screen*)

As a faithful practitioner of unfashionable *Frauendienst,* Sarris sea-changes even a lesser divinity such as Martine Carol into Fassbinder's holy whore of cinema, as surely as those long-gone Languedoc ladies were dissolved into redemptive high art. Stubbornly wearing honorable critical cloth into "proudly brainless" days, he attends movies as though any one of them might be a vehicle of sanctifying light—the screened equivalent of Danielle Darrieux's diamond earrings in Ophuls's *Madame de.* . . .

A man who loves women with Paterian (and Truffautian) passion, Sarris consistently locates that elusive arc where the arts of appearance and apprehension miraculously hot-wire into cinema. Vide Falconetti by Dreyer (flesh luminescing into soul); Gish by Griffith (irradiating implosions of sexuality and spirit); Dietrich by von Sternberg (pure illusion spun out of screen light, shadow, texture); Garbo by anyone (a radiance in which all the world vaporizes); Louise Brooks by Pabst (feral angel sinlessly in heat); along with Barbara Stanwyck by Capra; Ingrid Bergman by Rossellini; Machiko Kyo and Kinuyo Tanaka by Mizoguchi; Liv Ullmann by Bergman; Monica Vitti by Antonioni; Jeanne Moreau by Truffaut; Anna Karina by Godard; Catherine Deneuve by Truffaut, Bunuel, Polanski; Stephane Audran and Isabelle Huppert by Chabrol; Hanna Schygulla by Fassbinder; Gong Li by Zhang Yimou; et al. By virtue of such Sarrisian hagiography, we've been guided by our critical Beatrice into an "illuminated dark" to take heart from morality play—ribbons of lies and truth twenty-four times a second.

When a distaff star in Sarris's pantheon offers herself up to the martyrdom of many eyes, her exposed flesh and sensibility incandesce with saving significance and grace. In a mass transaction that is also transubstantiation, auteurist advertisers serve cinematic communicants bread and wine never staled by custom. Consumed, as is Anna Karina in Godard's *My life to Live* (*Vivre sa Vie*), such saints increase; reeling away in the time machine of the cinema, they do not die.

Blessed with the spiritual and intellectual software required to recognize images of "virtual" immortality, a romantic such as Sarris can see through the apparent "physical chastity" of Karina–Belmondo–Godard's apocalyptic *Pierrot le fou:* ". . . time and time again, I felt the chilling sublimation of love into art and then the warming translation of art back into love." Our silver-tongued movie lover confides that "I have never understood whether the existence of eroticism was established by the evidence of erection or by a logical analysis of visual and verbal expression," and demonstrates how a thinking sensualist's appreciation of celluloid bodies of work can be so spiritually tactile as to touch truth spot-on.

Claiming "there is no greater spectacle in the cinema than a man and a woman talking away their share of eternity together," Sarris cherishes the kind of passionate ratiocination that drives John Donne's erotic/religious poems and makes heaven of a couple's heated discourse during Eric Rohmer's *My Night at Maud's.* While *Claire's Knee* is skin-deep paradise, its beautiful anatomy fires the "transformation of an image into an idea, sensuality into sensibility, a bit of furtive voyeurism into an obsessive illusion, and, most important of all, a suggestion of fetishism into a surge of feeling." Out of an "elderly male filmmaker's fascination—subtle, civilized moral, aesthetically rigorous—with young women who can talk a blue streak," Sarris forges a precise definition of cinema's alchemy.

Sarris's longtime and long-range interest in movies and blondes, though not always necessarily in that order, has often found enthusiastic expression in his work, sometimes in the endearingly assumed persona of a rather cerebral gentleman, say, later James Mason somewhat flustered to find in himself a sexually charged boy, and vice versa. Consider the following breathless paean: "Miss Christie's sensual–sentimental assault in *Darling* has devastated me as nothing has since Harriet Andersson bared a bosom so ample as to contradict her Cocteau face in *Naked Night.*"

Or the declaration of love that warmed his review of *Tootsie:*

> Let it be recorded for the year 2022 that in the year 1982 a bedazzled reviewer . . . suddenly decided that Jessica Lange was more a knockout than Frances Farmer ever was, that she was everything Marilyn Monroe was supposed to be in *Some Like It Hot,* and . . . that she lit up the screen with so much beauty and intelligence that [the film was transformed] into a thoroughly modernist, thoroughly feminist parable of emotional growth and enlightenment.

But Sarris has always understood that movies—"mortality in motion"—manipulate and use up the "youthful, fantasy-making flesh" of women more ruthlessly than that of men. Thus, he surmises wisely that the witch-burning frenzy that once attended amour for Bergman and Rossellini, Mary Astor and George S. Kaufman, had less to do with sin and more to do with outrage that goddesses of the silver screen could be carnally besotted, and, worse yet, by "ugly" men. Of Astor, Sarris writes with characteristic tenderness: "There was something in the frankness of her screen image that suggested to a vicarious sensualist like me a sexuality so generous and so merciful as to qualify for a sainthood of sublimated flesh."

Frequently in his essays (with nothing like the cruel prurience of a John Simon), Sarris calculates an actress's age, its bearing on her role and her star status, its significance vis-á-vis her male co-star. Thus we learn that the sexiest movie scene of 1943 (necking on a brownstone stoop in *The More the Merrier*) was achieved by "crack-voiced comedienne" Jean Arthur, reportedly thirty-seven, with lanky, thirty-seven-year-old Joel McCrea. For Hollywood and fans, indiscreet celluloid sexiness in a lady verging on forty was bad enough, but Sarris reveals that Arthur was really forty-two at the time, a wholly inappropriate age for virtually "inducing a collective orgasm in the audience."

Similarly, he pays pointed tribute to Jamie Lee Curtis in 1994's *True Lies:* "When she describes the plight of a 35-year-old housewife and mother aimlessly watching her life pass by, the poignancy of her predicament is enriched by the Bazinian reality of a 35-year-old sexpot actress trying to get a big score before the male-dominated industry tells her that ninth inning has come and gone." Particularly, one might add, when Curtis's interrogator audience—behind a one-way mirror—is "husband" Arnold Schwarzenegger, whose exaggerated physicality kept him bankable even as he was well on his way to fifty.

In an apologia for his "anachronistic" view of relations between the sexes, Sarris once braved the tide of "relentless ideology" in a mannerless era:

> The ancient codes to which I cling govern the gallantry of romantic love, the rites and rituals of which are justifiable not so much in terms of "nature" and "normality" as of culture and history. The clinical or scientific temperament may argue that the myths and legends of romantic love are beautiful lies which conceal certain ugly truths . . . but I believe in gallantry and civility in the relationship between a man and a woman (with) an implied duality of the mind and the body and implied conflict between love and lust, an implied subordination of consummation to sublimation.

Typically, if one racks focus on Sarris's medieval philosophy of relations between the sexes, his critical aesthetic comes to the fore, an aesthetic that embraces the relations between women and movies, movies and reviewers, reviewers and readers, readers and civilization—everything that (to paraphrase Sarris) Delphine Seyrig conveys in her gaze when she looks out of Resnais's *Muriel* "past her visible companion to some ideal replica." But such relations and transformations—in art or in the flesh—require courageous souls in the stalls, and "most moviegoers would prefer to linger on the surfaces of the screen and not burst through beyond it.

"For beyond the screen lurks the very perplexing otherness from which the moviegoer is in full flight." Sarris penned that insight more than two decades ago in his foreword to *The Primal Screen*. Since then, our culture's seductive surfaces have coarsened and hardened, and moviegoers' retreat from otherness has been rendered largely irrelevant by the leveling of authentic dialectic and working metaphor on the parts of literalist filmmakers and critics alike to a wasteland of transient, repetitive, unresonant gestures, bereft of ceremony or grace.

We've come to live in fundamentalist times, when illiteracy and revisionism breed arrogant amnesiacs who don't have time for suspect aesthetic pleasures of the past. Trapped in the tyranny of Now, film reviewers spew out sophomoric puns and connect-the-dots pop-cult allusions, dish gossip or publicist piffle, all in the kind of snake-oil rant that instantly self-destructs yesterday's news. Film scholars scuttling to hammer disreputable art into upscale sociopolitical and scientific forms are as vigilant as any Inquisition against the heresies of personality and pleasure in critical writing.

The thought police have banned the stylized dance of sublimated sex, and for many right-thinking feminists, the contemplation of women onscreen and offscreen is automatic anathema along with aesthetic that would morph them into the very stuff of dreams and human aspiration. Critical discourse has degenerated into immature vulgarity, so hiply jaded by humanity's fallen state that any informed, compassionate celebration of our attempts to touch angels ranks as "corny."

In such a season, sample Andrew Sarris's review of a 1968 movie that falls short of masterpiece: Michel Deville's *Benjamin* concerns a young male virgin's "initiation into the rites of love by a society (18th century France) that lives for little else. . . . The sentimental and sensual education of a young man prepares him for a lffe through which he will pursue women till he finds the dark at the end of the tunnel." *Benjamin*'s eventual epiphany must be quoted at length:

> Benjamin's and the film's finest moment comes at a rendezvous less with
> beauty than with truth in front of a mirror at which Michele Morgan's

jilted countess surveys her own faded charms (Miss Morgan's beautifully stark cheekbones in *Symphonie Pastorale* have finally dissolved into mushy makeup; her eyes have lost their austere luster to make the Pirandellian pathos of her performance complete). Benjamin looks into that same mirror and tells the countess that she is the most beautiful woman of the region, and at that moment he finds his soul by perceiving the pain and vulnerability of another human being. *(Confessions of a Cultist)*

This is sweet chivalry, in the service of actress, cinema, memory, salvation. Covenant, too, that Andrew Sarris's critical Language, only momentarily under siege by barbarians, endures as haven, a clean, well-lighted place where cherished cinematic illuminations shine, not only as this week's entertainment but for the renaissance that must always follow our dark ages.

Sarris and the Search for Style

David Bordwell

$\mathcal{I}$n high school I had devoured the American Directors issue of *Film Culture,* so when in 1965 Andrew Sarris and another critic came to my campus for a "debate," I had to be there. It was the only time I ever met him, but I came away from the session with both the auteur's autograph ("Sincerely yours, Andrew Sarris") and the reassurance that one could talk seriously about movies without dethroning their delights.

The delights on which I preferred to dwell were chiefly visual. In Sarris I found someone—virtually the only critic in America—who treated popular movies as a visual art. Oddly enough, this side of his work has not been fully appreciated. So my homage, in all sincerity, is to Sarris the stylistician.

As Sarris's work is usually interpreted, style might seem to be subsidiary to sense. After all, doesn't the auteur theory hold that a director communicates a "vision of the world"? And wouldn't this entail that the auteur's world—the stories, the characters' attitudes and actions—take primacy? And wouldn't that mean that the critic's task is to concentrate on interpreting plot and character? Certainly that was what the "auteur-structuralists" took as Sarris's legacy. They built large-scale thematic complexes out of his suggestions about continuities of directorial vision. And I once noted Sarris's essay on *Citizen Kane* as a key source of what have become well-practiced routines of film interpretation. I think I was right up to a point, because Sarris's thematic readings powerfully influenced his successors. Nonetheless, I didn't sufficiently emphasize the ways in which other aspects of his work pointed toward an awareness of style, which is still all too rare in film studies. Sarris puts style on the agenda because he believes, after all the qualifications are

165

granted, that most of the best films show the dominance of the director's individual sensibility. This premise won't explain everything in all American studio movies, but it remains the best way to understand why so many of them are so beautiful. Here we come to what I believe to have been Sarris's most important insight.

STYLE AND FILM HISTORY

Where does cinematic beauty come from? Sarris's answer has been straightforward: it comes from expressive style. He has argued that such a notion of style could define cinema as an art, mark out its most worthy achievements, discriminate among artists, and trace historical patterns of continuity and change. He proposes, that is, a conception of cinematic style congruent with that proven successful in the fine arts, He also offers a debatable but sophisticated account of how mass-produced popular art could bear the traces of distinctive ways of using the medium. To understand beauty in the movies, Sarris insisted, we must be sensitive to style.

Stated so generally, this is a pretty old argument. The best early commentators on cinema strove to define the techniques of the new medium, particularly as it differed from theatre. By the end of the silent era, theorists and critics had generated a rich vocabulary for talking about camera placement, composition, and cutting. Many of these ideas can be found conveniently summarized in Rudolf Arnheim's *Film* (1933) and Raymond Spottiswoode's *A Grammar of the Film* (1935).

Sarris has objected to this line of thinking for its uncritical celebration of silent montage and its contempt for the mainstream movie as an enacted story aimed at mass audiences. Still, this tradition has given him one of his most punishing polemical weapons, a tacit notion of cinematic specificity. He scorns "literary" critics who refuse to pay attention to what's on the screen. "The vertical camera movement down a tower after Arkadin's death supersedes the script and quite naturally escapes the attention of our literary film critics." And when he upbraids directors who forget pictorial expressivity, Sarris can come on like any antitalkie proponent of visual values: "As one of the breed of writer-directors, [Richard] Brooks has a bad habit of saying what he means without showing what he feels." Sarris, however, would probably protest that any ideas he borrowed from the earliest theorists of style are far less important than his debt to Andre Bazin. Bazin and his contemporaries revised and corrected silent-era ideas by arguing for the centrality of staging, camera movement, and other aspects of mise-en-scène. Undertaking his examination of American cinema after 1929 (a period that almost exactly coincides with his own lifetime), Sarris was understandably drawn to a critical perspective that saw talkies not as a betrayal of cinema's essence but as a development of some of the medium's richest possibilities.

Each line of thinking conceived of cinematic style differently, but both of them converged on the belief in a universal stylistic history of the medium as such. Many silent-film critics saw cinema as a historical actor in its own right, moving inexorably toward the full revelation of its distinctive artistic essence. The critics' emphasis on style led to an idea that cinema was evolving toward a predetermined goal, often conceived as the full exploitation of the "essentially cinematic" qualities of montage. Bazin was as aesthetically catholic as he was spiritually Catholic, but he too fell in with this habit of thinking, replacing the old teleology (development toward "pure cinema") with a new one (development toward "total cinema," the most realistic of all).

In setting out to write the history of the American sound film—Sarris's stated purpose in formulating the auteur theory—he has had no patience with either version of the "evolution of film language." He has criticized the very idea as "pyramid history," with each creator patiently putting into place his contribution to the ever-ascending medium of cinema as it tapers toward ultimate realism or absolute purity. Sarris offers instead an inverted pyramid, "opening outward to accommodate the unpredictable range and diversity of individual directors." For Sarris, a genuine history of the cinema will not be the tale of a mystical rise and fall of the medium independent of the artists who use it: "Griffith, Murnau, and Eisenstein had differing visions of the world, and their technical 'contributions' can never be divorced from their personalities."

As film history exfoliates from fairly simple and unitary beginnings, we will find that the careers of the creators diverge, overlap, and interlace in unexpected ways. We have something closer to a network than to a linear progress. In effect, Sarris champions a radical version of what historians call methodological individualism. History is made by persons; even institutions, group processes, and "impersonal forces" must be explained, finally, through the concrete actions of individuals.

True, there will be some broader trends to notice, but even these will be manifested through the interplay of directorial personalities. For example, 1930s Hollywood can be emblematically represented in the image of McCarey and Capra playfully tussling over an Oscar, a very brief moment before the surge of John Ford and Orson Welles. Stylistically, the 1930s can be summed up in Lubitsch's unnoticeable editing, while the 1940s belong to "the Wellesian resurrection of Murnau's portentous camera angles. The decade of plots

gave way to a decade of themes." And "as Lubitsch was the unobtrusive cutting of the twenties and thirties, Preminger is the camera movement and long
take of the 1950s and 1960s." It is not just the masterworks—*The Awful Truth,
Mr. Smith Goes to Washington, Stagecoach, How Green Was My Valley, Citizen Kane,
The Marriage Circle, One Hour with You, Laura, Fallen Anqel*—that make history;
in the passages I've cited, Sarris doesn't even mention the relevant titles. The
filmmakers' names come to mark the historical turning points, and the names
in turn suggest entire bodies of work and distinctive personalities. This move
is even more audacious when you consider that the careers ran in counter-
point. Ford starts making films in the 1910s, but his "surge" comes in the late
1930s; Lubitsch keeps making films into the 1940s, but as a personality he is
irrevocably tied to earlier decades. That doesn't mean that Lubitsch's later films
are negligible, of course; it is just that if his 1940s works preserve his distinctive authorial sensibility—his civilized grace, his wry tolerance—they do so
within a severely changed aesthetic milieu.

   The paradoxical result of Sarris's conception of directorial individuality
is the fact that he has never produced an orthodox linear macrohistory of
American cinema. The lists and rankings tabulated in *The American Cinema,*
he has conceded, sought at once to map an unknown region and to create a
subject worth talking about. They display the open-textured, contrapuntal
nature of his conception of film history. Yet these categories and chronolo-
gies constitute only the raw materials of a broad-based film history. Neither
argument nor narrative, they do not of themselves solve the riddle of how
American cinema as a whole manifests large-scale continuity and change.

   Still, this is probably not the riddle that really preoccupies Sarris. In my
view, *The American Cinema* represents not a study in film history so much as
a historically informed framework for doing film criticism. That is, instead
of deriving a broad historical argument from critical analysis and appraisal,
Sarris has been a connoisseur, using his vast historical knowledge to shape
his scrutiny of particular movies and oeuvres. Although I doubt that one
could build a film history by aligning filmographies, I have no doubt that
thinking of Hollywood cinema as deeply historical—that is, as displaying stylistic continuity and change within individual careers—can produce excellent criticism. Sarris's writings are dazzling proof.

STYLE AND THE CRITIC

"The unconceptualized eye is at the beginning and the end of all visual appreciation." This line from 1973 sounds a bit sixties to us now, but its

Ruskinian trust in innocent perception is characteristic of a critic who always insisted that film criticism had to attend to what was happening on the screen. One of Sarris's great gifts to American film culture has been to show how visual style is central to film as an art.

This emphasis is particularly intriguing coming from a critic determined to explore the history of sound cinema. For with the coming of the talkies, most critics lamented the death of pictorial values. The expressive compositions and dynamic cutting of the silent classics seemed ill-suited to a dialogue-based cinema. One of Bazin's major insights was that the sound film required a more unobtrusive but no less supple visual style than had developed in the official classics of the 1910s and 1920s. Bazin's godsons among the *Cahiers* gang did not for the most part pursue this line of thought. If the auteur theory indeed constituted a renewal rather than a brand-new position, it was partly because Sarris could show that expressive uses of film technique had not withered after 1928.

For one thing, he could show that the director, as the creator of the visual track, shaped the overall context that would govern how the script was taken. Given the dialogue and the situation, the director can reweight them through the performances, camera angle, camera movement, and cutting. Moreover, a producer was less likely to object to a director's shots than to a writer's words, so the director is likely to be able to inflect, nuance, even work against, the script.

Similarly, Sarris realized that what silent-era aestheticians castigated as the talkiest betrayal of film's plastic essence could be considered as "an extraordinary economy of expression." For example, sound encouraged a density of audiovisual texture. Hitchcock proved himself "alive to the expressive potentialities of every encounter, His cutting is the means by which he contradicts what people say by what they do."

Sarris refines his account by noting that each director is free to discover distinctive strategies of stylistic economy, Hawks's style serves every twist in the plot, embodying his clean-lined pragmatism; he doesn't use technique as a "reflective commentary" on the action. Ford, however, adds grace notes. "He could always spare a shot or two for a mood that belonged to him and not to the plot." The key phrase is "a shot or two."

In the brilliant scene in *The Searchers* in which Ward Bond chivalrously averts his eyes from Wayne's sister-in-law as she strokes Wayne's uniform, Ford knows just how far to go: "If it had taken him any longer than three shots and a few seconds to establish this insight into the Bond character, the point would not be worth making." The action is even more concise than Sarris indicates: we see Bond look off; cut to a point-of-view shot of the woman caressing the uniform; Ford then cuts back to Bond, already looking away from her. Even Bond's act of averting his gaze is left to our understanding. The sound cinema imposes a discipline on all directors, and the best ones find idiosyncratic ways to be at once crisp and evocative.

We can see this perspective taking shape as early as the notorious "Notes on the Auteur Theory in 1962." Although sketchy and programmatic (as a manifesto should be), this essay lays out some key premises for the study of authorial style in the cinema. I want to consider them briefly, because although they are well-known, Sarris's insights remain worth mining today.

Sarris envisions authorial expression as a series of concentric circles. The first circle represents the premise that a director's "technical competence" is a fundamental criterion of value. "A great director has to be at least a good director." In *2001,* for instance, Kubrick fails "to tell a story on the screen with coherence and a consistent point of view. Kubrick's tragedy may have been that he was hailed as a great artist before he had become a competent craftsman." By contrast, the classical period of Hollywood cinema was characterized by a "relaxed craftsmanship" sadly absent from the screen of the 1960s (not to mention the decades ever since).

The criterion of craft is not such an obvious point of departure as it might seem. By taking technical competence as a baseline of inquiry, Sarris obliges the critic to understand what collective norms are operating in the director's milieu. The critic must watch a lot of movies to gain a sense of what is minimally acceptable. Although Sarris did not pursue this avenue, this quest for tacit craft knowledge can become a legitimate pursuit for the student of style. We can shed light on how movies are put together by studying a period's prevailing practices—the rules of thumb, the taken-for-granted procedures. Astruc outlined the possibility as early as 1946.

> On the soundstages of Hollywood there was passed along a sort of empirical grammar formed from the long experience of highly devoted artisans. They knew, for example, that near the end of a film it was better to increase the number of close-ups in order to raise the degree of emotion. They also knew that the *plan Américain* was the most efficient shot, permitting the greatest economy of editing. This technique may have lacked ambition, but it was faultless and sure. It would still be interesting today to analyze its smallest details.

More recently, some scholars have taken up the Astruc–Sarris challenge, investigating what constituted technical competence in different filmmaking milieus.

To stop at this circle, though, risks turning us into "forest critics," those generalizers interested only in collective convergences and not individual idiosyncrasies. Hence the need for a second concentric circle, dialectically correlated to the first. This criterion of value is "the distinguishable personality of the director." Sarris notes that the director is known chiefly through the films (and not, say, the lived life), but just as important, the personality is grasped in large part through the films' style: "Over a group of films a director must exhibit certain recurring characteristics of style which serve as his signature." And this style is, as we have seen, primarily visual: "The way a film looks and moves should have some relationship to the way a director thinks and feels."

There is much to say about this premise, but to belabor Sarris for using the term *personality,* as so many academic critics have, is probably not fruitful. The chief point is that of all the hands working on a film, directors do have the best opportunity to blend a film's ingredients, and visual style is probably the most salient route through which this takes place. And who is to deny that a director's habitual ways of orchestrating the diverse materials of the medium do not reflect something of the director's personality? It is hard to believe that Ozu was not sensitive to the evanescence of life, that Dreyer was not outraged by intolerance, that Griffith did not (in some part of his being) prize unsophisticated innocence. Directorial signatures are thus to some extent ways of knowing the people who made movies; but they are also ways of knowing the movies more intimately. And by seeking personal signatures we can confirm our sense of the expanding diversity across film history, the "inverted pyramid" that is actually a tree spreading from its roots.

One useful way to sharpen the critic's sense of stylistic differences is to find a common problem that two directors solve in different ways. Sarris astutely contrasts Chaplin's and Keaton's treatments of a rudimentary gag involving statues, and he distinguishes Milestone from Vidor through their handling of the stock situation of enemy soldiers confronting one another on the battlefield. Craft conditions create shared problems; directorial personalities solve them in ways that reveal subtle differences of purpose and attitude. Once more, style—a rich ensemble of concrete choices about camera work and lighting, performance and cutting—becomes the center of concern.

A distinguishable personal style is a necessary but not sufficient condition for being an auteur: "Visual style is never an end in itself. . . . Any visual style can be mechanically reproduced." There must also be a distinct expressive quality arising from that style. Here, at Sarris's third circle, is where we encounter the premise that aroused so much controversy. What does it mean to say that a true auteurist work manifests "interior meaning."

I find Sarris's account of "interior meaning" rather obscure. The term has been taken to be something like "the deepest significance" or "the most abstract meaning" we can assign to a film or oeuvre. But Sarris is quite insistent that interior meaning is not paraphrasable. "It is ambiguous in any literary sense because part of it is imbedded in the stuff of cinema and cannot be rendered in non-cinematic terms. Nor is it exactly a vision of the world or a director's attitude toward life."

It seems to me that interior meaning is best understood as an expressive quality that arises from the differences we can recognize among directorial personalities. And while this expressive quality may pervade an entire work, as nostalgic melancholy suffuses Ophuls's films, it is just as likely to show up in privileged moments. Sarris's example is the moment when in *Rules of the Game* Octave turns and hops in response to Lisette's call, then continues "his bearishly shambling journey" to Christine. No other director but Renoir, Sarris suggests, would have Octave break the scene's rhythm in exactly this way (and in a manner, Sarris hints, that anticipates Octave's dressing up in the bear costume for the climactic party). The nonchalant, slightly awkward grace of this interruption epitomizes Renoir's entire style of filmmaking. The gesture cannot be adequately described; it is "imbedded in the stuff of cinema." The critic can merely point to those privileged moments where interior meaning shines forth.

Elusive though such a notion is, the idea that certain stylistic events can crystallize the creator's unique sensibility captures one important way in which discerning viewers watch movies. We can praise large-scale formal effects, such as smooth plot construction or consistency of performance. But what both cinephiles and ordinary viewers tend to notice and remember are those luminous instants that change our skin temperature. We come out of a film satisfied if a few aesthetic epiphanies have flashed upon us. Interior meaning is the product of craft and personality, but it can't be reduced to them. It is often a fugitive beauty, all the more precious because it can only be seen, not described.

ENVOI

Sarris's ideas are far from played out. Granted, *Variety* now uses "auteur" as comfortably as it does "blockbuster." Yes, auteurism made director studies respectable enough for publishers to support; true, the study of American cinema is now recognized as a somewhat worthy pursuit. But much has not changed.

In the university, the study of film has largely moved toward a bland interdisciplinarity in which movies matter less than theories. In 1973, Sarris wrote: "The time has come to acknowledge film scholarship as an end in itself and not merely as a means to revitalize the lesson plans of other disciplines." He could not have foreseen that a consumer technology would turn many humanities courses into movie courses (or, rather, tape courses) and convert many class meetings into amateur sociology, wishful political thinking, and film-society chat.

In the literary culture, the caricature of Hollywood remains largely the same as that circulating in the 1930s: producers are monsters, writers are martyrs, and directors are philistine opportunists. The readers of the *New York Review of Books* have all their preconceptions about the vulgarity of studio filmmaking regularly reaffirmed by the anecdotal reminiscences of Vidal and Dunne. For the educated public, the American cinema remains of interest chiefly as a reflection of imperial grandeur and folly. To the condescensions of pop, camp, and trivia, about which Sarris warned us long ago, has been added a patronizing postmodernism and a populist cultural studies, each of which takes each summer's blockbusters as an occasion to celebrate the fragmentation of culture. As for auteurism, everybody knows the word, but when Oliver Stone and Quentin Tarantino are pressed upon us as having a vision of the world, we can only recall Sarris's melancholy speculation from 1968: "In ten years or less there may be no American cinema of great artistic significance."

For those of us who learned so much from Sarris, there remains much to do. In particular, although "style" as sensory bombast has become part of a movie's packaging and marketing (*Batman Forever* and *Natural Born Killers* order up Technique in forty-gallon drums), viewers remain almost completely unaware of *Batman* style in any rigorous sense, let alone of its nuances and subtleties. "The auteurists," Sarris remarked over thirty years ago, "are still fighting an uphill battle to make movie audiences conscious of style." *La lutte* continue, as the French used to say.

An ABC of Reading Andrew Sarris

James Naremore

$\mathscr{A}$ndrew Sarris has been a profound influence on my own writing about movies, and I cannot hope to do him justice in a short essay. To alleviate the problem, I've decided to fall back on a set of "notes," which I hope will be true to the spirit of concision of Sarris's most important book, *The American Cinema*. Just for fun, I've arranged them as alphabetical entries in a sort of dictionary, made up of key words, titles, or names. Some letters of the alphabet are more important than others, and in these cases I've allowed myself to list more than one word. In other cases, I've whimsically combined two or three letters in a single entry. The result is an "ABC" of reading Andrew Sarris.

Auteurism; American; Academic; Amateur; Art. Auteurism, a term we inevitably associate with Sarris, is not so much a theory as what the French called a "policy" of supporting certain directors and films. Perhaps it is best described as a movement, originating in the Parisian film culture of the 1950s and 1960s, which took on slightly different implications as it entered other national contexts. One of Sarris's major achievements was to reinterpret this movement for America. Like Truffaut, he launched a polemical attack against a "tradition of quality," made up chiefly of literary adaptations and social-problem dramas; his specific targets, however, were not Autant-Lara, Carne, and Delannoy, but Huston, Wyler, and Kazan. Along similar lines, he challenged middlebrow opinion by arguing that Hollywood, not Europe, had the most artistically important cinema in the world. Meanwhile, he stressed the academic importance of auteurism. Because he was a teacher rather than a would-be director, Sarris used the auteurist debates to write a full-scale history of American movies.

One of his explicit aims in *The American Cinema* was to make film historiography less of an amateur calling—an effort that required both a serious scholarly commitment and a discriminating intelligence. The project as a whole was very much like the New Criticism in American literary studies: it placed great emphasis on personal style, and it was contemptuous of the positivists, the sociologists, and their nonprofessional allies, the hobbyists or "stamp collectors." What gave Sarris's writing special force was his ability to remain an amateur (in the etymological sense of the passionate lover) while also functioning as a critic and a scholar. Even today, in an age when most academic writing is impenetrable or dry as dust, and when journalism is increasingly dumb, Sarris is a cosmopolitan, addressing his remarks to a civilized common viewer. He is able to do so because he believes in art—the most crucial term in his vocabulary, and a different thing from science, technology, sociology, or any of the professions.

Bazin, André. Bazin was a true theorist of cinema, and a major influence on the New Wave directors who wrote for *Cahiers du cinéma* in the 1950s. He was not, however, an auteurist. He praised the "genius of the system"; he disliked Hitchcock; he wrote about literary adaptations; and he put Wyler on nearly the same level as Welles. His importance to the younger generation lay not in his critical policy but in his existential humanism, which reached an almost mystical level in his writings on photography and cinematic space. Bazin's commentaries on Renoir, Rossellini, and Welles are major contributions to the poetics of film, but they are also subtle essays about the ethical implications of the camera's encounter with the world. They influenced Sarris at many points in *The American Cinema,* especially in the brilliant entries on Chaplin, Flaherty, and Murnau.

Cinephilia; Canons. Auteurism was nourished by revival theaters, film societies, museums, and the increasing presence of old movies on TV. Above all, it grew out of the cinephilia in major cities such as Paris and New York during the decades after World War II. In a recent essay in the *New York Times,* Susan Sontag has claimed that cinephilia is dead. Perhaps she hasn't seen Quentin Tarantino's last three pictures, or visited a specialty video store, or watched satellite television. In places such as these, cinephilia is still very much alive but is always in danger of being reduced to trivia or mass camp (as in movies like *Batman*). Cinephilia needs to be tempered and shaped by criticism, because indiscriminate love is no love at all.

This is a point Molly Haskell makes in *Love and Other Infectious Diseases,* where she describes the New York film culture of Sarris's younger days, emphasizing his desire not simply to know film history but to distinguish the good from the bad. Auteurism in all its forms is relentlessly evaluative, and when applied to film history it produces canons. Part of the significance of Sarris's work in *The American Cinema* lies precisely in his attempt to name (in what he himself called a tentative or provisional fashion) the important directors and films. Ironically, just at the point when his work was absorbed into the American academy, it encountered other, more radical types of criticism that were bent on destroying both cinephilia and canons. Even so, the High Theorists kept returning to the "texts" Sarris and his colleagues had established.

We are now at a point where we need less theory and more canon building. The monuments erected by such activity are not engraved; they exist discursively, in critical debate, and they do not necessarily honor Dead White Men. Without canons, Hollywood wins; we are left with no values—only facts, box-office statistics, and quasi-scientific explanations of "systems." Film study would be greatly enlivened if we had another book like *The American Cinema,* devoted exclusively to naming the best Hollywood directors and pictures of the past thirty years. This book would of course need to be written by someone as talented and educated as Sarris—someone who knows TV as well as movies, and who is willing to put her or his values on the line.

Directors; DeMille, Cecil B. French auteurism centered on directors because many of the people involved wanted to become directors in a new French art cinema. Sarris was more scholarly and academic in his ambitions; hence *The American Cinema* is chiefly about the studio system, which was dead before the book was written. Sarris argues quite plausibly that the studios gave directors more freedom than writers, especially in genre projects rather than in Big Pictures about Important Themes. Even so, the overwhelming majority of artists in Sarris's "Pantheon" were also producers or independents, working slightly apart from studio bosses or middle-management executives. There is nothing especially unusual about a book that praises such figures. Like some of the French, Sarris is most unorthodox and challenging not when he argues on behalf of Chaplin or Welles, but when he defends certain of their movies, such as *Limelight* or *The Lady from Shanghai.* He is also challenging when he shows admiration for women's soap operas in addition to male action pictures, and when he places an intellectually unfashionable producer–director like Cecil B. DeMille (the very symbol of Hollywood vulgarity and right-wing bombast) on "The Far Side of Paradise."

Epigram. Sarris's book on American cinema is a model of critical economy, showing a great flair for epigrammatic wit and insight. The entry on DeMille is a good example: "If DeMille had the right enemies, he also had the wrong friends. . . . [He may have been] the last Victorian, although the late George Orwell would probably have held out for Salvador Dali." The one-sentence contrast between Welles and Hitchcock is even better: "Wellesian cinema is as much the cinema of the exhibitionist as Hitchcockian cinema is the cinema of the voyeur."

Ford, John; Griffith, D. W.; Hawks, Howard. Three directors in the Sarris Pantheon. Of the three, Hawks is the most "modern," or the closest in spirit to the pragmatic efficiency and unsentimental values of industrialized America. Ford is equally efficient, but in other ways he is Hawks's dialectical opposite. Sarris wrote a great deal about both directors (his book on Ford is sadly out of print), and his auteurism pays huge dividends when it puts equally compelling figures side by side, pointing out the symmetrical contrasts between them. In the background of these comparisons stands the paternal Griffith, who embodies all the paired contradictions in a single figure.

Iconoclasm. Sarris has been so influential in shaping our tastes that in some ways he no longer seems iconoclastic. It might help to recall that Bosley Crowther was still the chief movie critic at the *New York Times* when most of *The American Cinema* was written, and that Crowther had dismissed many of the pictures Sarris praised. With the exception of Mamoulian, Milestone, and Wellman, all of the directors in the "Less Than Meets the Eye" or "Strained Seriousness" categories of *The American Cinema* were quite active, and most of them were regarded by American critics as the leading artists in Hollywood. American film historians thought that Ford's greatest picture was *The Informer,* and figures like Sirk, Fuller, and Mann had nothing like their present reputations. Sarris's against-the-grain judgments on these individuals made him slightly controversial, but his true rebelliousness lay in his straightforward assertion of art as personal expression.

The idea that the best films arise out of the director's worldview is probably even more daring today and is regularly attacked by academic leftists and Hollywood insiders. Its opponents are in one sense justified, because the discourse on personal expression (as on anything else) can have pernicious effects; it can easily degenerate into a cult of celebrity, a romantic daydream, or a bourgeois ideology. Individual artists are nevertheless as much a material fact as the studio system or the budgets. To take them seriously, to make intelligent comments on their attitudes and stylistic choices, is one of the most unorthodox, socially powerful, and critically resistant things we can do.

Johnny Guitar; Kiss Me Deadly. Two films of the mid-1950s, relatively ignored by the American critical establishment, that became touchstones of auteurist taste. Both were indecorous if not downright delirious in their treatment of genre conventions, and, in an indirect way, they probably inspired the French to make pictures like *Breathless.* In *The American Cinema,*

Sarris names *Johnny Guitar* as the fifth best movie of 1954 (after films by Hitchcock, Ford, Renoir, Rossellini, and Bunuel) and *Kiss Me Deadly* as the sixth best of 1955 (after films by Rossellini, Hitchcock, Sirk, Welles, and Ford). In both cases, he stresses the anarchic–romantic temperament of the director: *Johnny Guitar* is Nicholas Ray's "most bizarre film, and probably his most personal"; and *Kiss Me Deadly* is "a testament to [Robert] Aldrich's anarchic spirit." I myself saw both films in my early adolescence, and they made no special impression on me at the time. I do not know how personal they were, but I cannot watch them today without being aware of how much I originally missed and without feeling gratitude toward Sarris and the other auteurists.

Lists. As I've just indicated, *The American Cinema* is a book of evaluative lists. Sarris lists his favorite directors alphabetically in hierarchical categories; he lists each director's films chronologically, italicizing the best ones, and, at the end of the book, he lists the best films of each year from 1915 onward (after their directors' names), italicizing the true masterpieces. His technique is once again borrowed from the French New Wave, who repeatedly used ten-best lists as a shock tactic. (Godard announced not only the ten best pictures of the year, but also such things as the "Ten Best American Sound Films" and the "Six Best French Films Since the Liberation.") Sarris expanded this strategy into a large-scale history, producing both a complex reference work and a guide to his personal tastes. We need not ask if he was "correct"; his lists are deliberate provocations, stimulating debate and making us want to look more closely at certain pictures. Every critic ought to follow his example. We have too many "Ten Worst Movies of All Time" and too many compilations of last week's box-office hits.

Modernity; Montage; Memory. Sarris is a modern intellectual because he is a strong advocate of cinema. He also has a few things in common with the twentieth-century avant-garde: a fondness for lists and manifestos; a declared affiliation with a "theory" or "ism"; and a love of mass-cultural artifacts, which he uses as a weapon against middlebrow opinion. In many important ways, however, he is critical of both industrial modernity and artistic modernism. *The American Cinema* repeatedly argues that there is no such thing as progress in the arts, and it obviously supports the romantic belief that individual artists can transcend Hollywood, protecting certain values against the encroachments of capitalism and industrial rationality. At several key junctures, Sarris attacks the pretensions of the cinematic avant-garde; and, very much like Bazin, he is skeptical of montage, the cardinal tenet of modernist aesthetics in all the arts. Despite the montage-like quality of his own book, he favors continuity and long takes. He is also fond of what might be called the cinema of memory and of directors who recall the nineteenth century. This is what makes his commentaries on such figures as Griffith, Chaplin, Ford, and Welles particularly effective.

Nostalgia; Nature. The cinema of memory is also the cinema of nostalgia, often producing a complex longing for nature or for an organically unified world. There is an obvious irony here, because the movies are products of modern industrial society. Sarris is aware of the irony and is quite good at showing how it operates in certain directors; in Robert Flaherty, for example, whose cinema, as Sarris observes, offers us "one of the last testaments of the 'cult of nature,' and, as such, is infinitely precious."

Ophuls, Max. One of the directors in the Sarris Pantheon, about whom Sarris has long planned to write a book. The entry on Ophuls in *The American Cinema* is superb, evoking the exact feel of the films and answering every possible objection to the director's work. Notice that Ophuls is in many ways quite different from Ford, whom Sarris equally admires. A European sophisticate and a director of "women's" pictures, Ophuls specialized in tragic love stories, and his style depended upon elegant camera movements, keyed to the rhythms of fashionable walks up winding stairways or across ballrooms and town squares. But Ophuls, too, was a director who expressed nostalgia for time gone by. For Sarris, the meaning of Ophulsian camera movement is that "time has no stop." Unlike montage, which tends to operate "in a limbo of abstract images," the moving camera "records inexorably the passage of time," and it shows the characters' "imprisonment in time." This theme is basic to the cinema of memory and to romanticism in general. (See, for example, the poems of Wordsworth or Yeats.) It gives a kind of poignancy to Ophuls, but also to Sarris's own writing.

Pleasure; Performance; Paradox. Like all the auteurists, Sarris conveys great pleasure in the things he discusses. He and the other auteurists are also aware that one of the basic pleasures of movies comes from watching the stars. Hence, despite his commitment to directors, Sarris makes a good many interesting observations about acting. As we might expect, he is relatively unenthusiastic about the modern performances in Antonioni or the Method-inspired directors; instead, he prefers the classic Hollywood style and is especially good at commenting on the relation between old-fashioned male directors and their female stars. He also devotes an entire section of *The American Cinema* to the comic performers, who are usually far more important than their directors. Above all, he admires the "torrents and torrents of classical acting" in Griffith. "Lillian Gish is an infinitely greater actress than Monica Vitti," he writes, because Griffith's cinema demands "a rediscovery of behavioral reality" and a sense of "psychological harmony with nature."

Sarris's pleasure could therefore be described as paradoxical, involving glimpses of behavioral reality through mechanical reproduction.

The American Cinema is equally paradoxical in the way it uses a theory of individual expression to explain an industrial art, and in the way it inverts the usual critical values, dissolving the boundaries between highbrow and lowbrow. Even its basic conception of the movie director is founded on a paradox: "The director," Sarris says, "is both the least necessary and most important component of film-making. . . . He would not be worth bothering with if he were not capable now and then of a sublimity of expression almost miraculously extracted from his money-oriented environment."

The Quiet American; Red Line 7000. Sarris was never a slavish imitator of French fashion. One of Godard's favorite directors in the 1950s and 1960s was Joseph L. Mankiewicz, whom Sarris placed in the "Less Than Meets the Eye" category of the 1968 edition of *The American Cinema.* In 1958, an annus mirabilus of auteurism, Godard ranked Mankiewicz's *The Quiet American* as the best film of the year, putting it a whopping six places above Welles's *Touch of Evil;* a decade later, Sarris listed *Touch of Evil* as the second best film of 1958 (after *Vertigo*) and wrote that Mankiewicz was "unable to cope" with the Graham Greene novel on which his picture was based. In 1966, French critic Jean Narboni, writing in *Cahiers,* claimed that Howard Hawks's *Red Line 7000* was "a masterly presentation of various ways of twisting convention—an epitome of and treatise on deconstruction." Sarris greatly admired Hawks, but he wrote that *Red Line 7000* was a disappointment and little more than a "self parody."

Style. In Sarris, the term *style* seldom refers to an abstract system of formal rules, as in "the Hollywood style." He usually employs the word in its expressive sense, reminding us of the traditional notion that "style is the man." A famous linguist once explained this usage by analogy with a tennis match (one of Sarris's favorite sports): style is the way an individual player copes with the rules of the game, managing to get the ball over the net.

Ulmer, Edgar G. If Edgard G. Ulmer had not existed, the auteurists would need to invent him. Happily, he did exist, and he is the surest single proof that an artistic temperament can transcend pulp formulas and impossible working conditions. One of the many reasons why Sarris deserves praise is that he helped call attention to Ulmer's work. "That a personal style could emerge from the lowest depths of Poverty Row," Sarris wrote, "is a tribute to a director without alibis."

Von Sternberg, Josef. Another member of Sarris's Pantheon, and another director about whom Sarris has written a book. No filmmaker in Hollywood was more out of key with the tough-guy ethos of the 1930s and 1940s (see John Dos Passos's thinly veiled parody of Sternberg in *The Big Money*), and no filmmaker was more "against nature." Surprisingly, despite the last of these qualities, Sarris responds powerfully to Sternberg's films. He is interested in their "autobiographical" quality rather than in their overt perversity, but he appropriately describes them with a series of paradoxes: surface becomes essence, trivia becomes profundity, absurdity becomes lyricism, stillness becomes violence, and all the characters behave like existentialists or Hemingway types, showing "poise under pressure" and "style under stress."

Wilde, Oscar. In introducing Wilde's name, I should perhaps make clear that I am not suggesting a latent homosexuality in Sarris or the auteurists (as Pauline Kael once did). I am aware that Andrew and Oscar are separated by a hundred years and are quite different on many levels: Sarris is a heterosexual American movie critic of Greek descent, whereas Wilde was an Anglo-Irish literary dandy with Hellenic aspirations. But consider what the two have in common: both are iconoclastic, both are fond of epigrams and paradoxes, and both validate the pleasures of performance. Two of Sarris's favorite directors—Ophuls and Sternberg—are among the cinema's greatest aesthetes and might have been admired by Wilde. The key difference, it seems to me, lies in Sarris's implicit belief in nature or a world not made by art (even if it is a world of the director's emotions). Notice also that he is resolutely opposed to Camp interpretation. Another key theme of *The American Cinema* is that old Hollywood movies should be appreciated with a "straight face" and not with the "giddy rationalizations of pop, camp, and trivia."

Xanadu. David Thomson, another auteurist, has said that he once thought of calling his biographical encyclopedia of films *The Xanadu Inventory.* That splendid title would apply just as well to Sarris's *The American Cinema.* Like an ideal investigator of Kane's estate, Sarris provides us with an immensely useful map to the bewildering and bizarre maze of American movies, separating the junk from the treasures and making sure that nobody tosses a Rosebud into the furnace. He also writes impressively about Orson Welles, and he is right to see *Citizen Kane* as the work of an auteur rather than of a studio.

Youth. The French auteurists were sometimes known as "young Turks," and their unfettered romanticism makes them seem youthful even today. Unlike such critics as Wilde, however, they never made a cult of youth. Even in their salad days, part of their sweetness and charm lay in their respect for old directors and for films that were quiet, meditative, and unspectacular. Sarris in particular has never been taken in by razzle-dazzle. He is keenly sensitive to such pictures as Ford's *The Sun Shines Bright* or Benton's *Nobody's Fool,* which have an elegiac tone and a leisurely pace that is anathema in Hollywood.

Zinnemann, Fred. One of the least admired figures in *The American Cinema*. In Sarris's hierarchy, Zinnemann represents the dull director of socially significant projects, who never stooped to entertainment, and who always tried to "deal Realistically with a Problem in Adult Terms." I would not radically challenge this view, but when Zinnemann died recently, I was reminded of how much I admire *From Here To Eternity* and *Day of the Jackal*. Zinnemann may be a pigmy compared to Orson Welles, but he is a giant compared to Renny Harlan or Paul Verhoeven. One of the beauties of a book like *The American Cinema* is that it makes us want to reexamine the major and minor directors, together with the actors, writers, and photographers. It gives a human face to Hollywood and invites us to compare notes with the author. Sarris himself has modified many of his opinions over the years, and there is no reason why we should not debate his judgments. In the last analysis, he even knows that many of the great movies had little to do with their directors. His value is that he encourages a discriminating cinephilia, challenging historians to see everything and learn about everyone.

The One Sarris Paragraph
That Changed My Career

Henry Sheehan

I have probably met Andrew Sarris face to face less than a half-dozen times in my entire life, yet there are few people who claim so much influence on it. True, that influence was remote, even invisible, at times, but if it weren't for him, it's unlikely that anything that has happened in my professional life would have happened the way it did.

Of course, that happened, as it did for so many people, through the pages of *The American Cinema,* that well-thumbed handbook for cinema hounds. But even more than the book as a whole, it was a single phrase, in a paragraph about a director Sarris didn't even like, that sent me down a path from which I've yet to really diverge.

The director in question was John Sturges, who, because of my age, was known to me as the director of *The Hallelujah Trail* and, especially, *The Great Escape,* a quintessential boy's yarn of the 1960s. In my dawning realization that movies could speak in different ways, Sturges was also the director of *Bad Day at Black Rock,* a movie that, in contemporary showings on television, had reacquired some status as a bold social statement.

Of course, even to a youth, that latter film seemed shrill, but I was perfectly willing to accept Sturges, in his less pretentious moments, as a capable entertainer. Sarris, of course, wasn't, casting him into *The American Cinema's* most hellish hole, "Strained Seriousness." But what struck me wasn't Sarris's description of Sturges's films as "tortured, humorless and self-consciously social," but another phrase referring to Sturges's use of the "wasteful pan," compared as a "stock-in-trade for superficial visual analysis" to Delmer Daves's "debasing crane," Stanley Kubrick's "meaningless tracks," and Robert Wise's "IBM perforations" in his montages.

185

There were two problems with understanding the description. First was the peculiarity of the word *wasteful*. Even a careless viewing of Kubrick's *Paths of Glory* was enough to figure out that all those elaborate tracking shots didn't amount to much more than directorial egotism. And while I couldn't remember any particularly "debasing" crane shots from *Broken Arrow* or perforations in Wise's *Sound of Music*, I could pretty much figure out what he meant.

But how could a pan be "wasteful?" Wasteful of what exactly? The only pans I thought I could remember for sure in *The Great Escape* was one following Steve McQueen on his motorcycle as he attempted to jump a fence as he tried escaping from the killjoy Germans on his trail. There certainly didn't seem anything wasteful about that.

Further investigation was needed, but that's where the second problem came in. Growing up in Boston, when I did, was nothing short of a blessing for film lovers, with a revival theater seeming to anchor (in a budding cineaste's mind, at least) every square in Boston and Cambridge. But apparently the programmers at all of them were influenced by *The American Cinema,* so that while there was plenty of Preston Sturges to see, there was virtually no John Sturges screened.

This wasn't a temporary phenomenon. At college, at the University of Chicago, I joined Doc Films, where we were too busy programming directors from "The Far Side of Paradise" and "Expressive Esoterica" to bother much with the "Strained Seriousness" crowd. In fact, even though occasional attempts were made at programming something—anything—that wasn't endorsed by the book, only a few one-shots by the likes of Robert Rossen or Richard Fleischer ever made it onto the schedule.

This wasn't simply prejudice. This was the early and mid-1970s, and there was still an enormous amount of material that lay dormant in Hollywood vaults. It seemed—and certainly was—far more important to screen works by, say, Douglas Sirk or Samuel Fuller, who themselves never failed to cause bemusement, consternation, or even hostility among the student population at large, than to look into whether *The People Against O'Hara* had wasteful pans.

What shed light on Sarris's enigmatic remark was a counterexample that came to light thanks to the Bogart cult and the rise of UHF TV. The Bogart cult was a minor phenomenon of the 1960s that, while predictably centered around *Casablanca* and *The Maltese Falcon,* led to the unearthing of most of the Bogart oeuvre. And while the cult was centered around the Brattle Theater in Harvard Square, it was soon appropriated by one of the new local stations way up high on the dial with a license to broadcast but nothing much to show.

The movie that began to emerge from the steady programming was Raoul Walsh's *High Sierra* and, in particular, the final sequences. In them, Bogart's character, Roy Earle, is on the run from the police, tearing across a California desert scape and into the Sierra foothills. He's tearing up the road in a roadster while a covey of motorcycle cops and two police cruisers chase him from not far behind.

Walsh shoots the opening chase almost entirely with pans. Not only that, he would repeat them. First, a shot opening with Bogart's car approaching in a haze of smoke, then tearing past the camera, then disappearing off down the highway. Then cut to the same opening set-up, this time with the cops, sirens wailing, approaching, passing, and disappearing.

Actually, the shots were never exactly the same; they would end somehow a little differently, either the Earle shot or, less frequently, the cop shots getting clipped before the camera could complete its arc. The result would be pans that started with an oblique angle as it looked to the right, then suddenly quite an acute one as it turned to the left.

Walsh interrupts this sequence with a brief flurry of close-up inserts of Earle in his car and, more often, traveling shots from a camera truck speeding ahead. The result was a sudden suggestion of freedom, or at least escape, as Earle plunged ahead.

But these come to a cruel end with the resumption of the pans, including an absolutely spectacular 700-degree shot, the camera pivoting a complete 360 degrees on Earle's car as it comes up a switchback and then spinning again as it catches the phalanx of speeding cops making the same circuit.

There would be more pans still, including a daunting one, when Earle is forced to leave his car and head up the mountain on foot. The camera pans just ahead and up, showing the towering dead end he's headed for. It's a bitter foreshadowing, particularly given the precision that Walsh would invoke in depicting Earle's end.

These pans, of course, were not at all wasteful. On the contrary, they were screamingly expressive, describing a course of action that was simultaneously frantic and hopeless. Try as he might, Earle—or his pursuers, for that matter—could not escape the logic of Walsh's camera, forever in motion, forever motionless, closing each and every circle.

I never would have noticed this or understood it if Sarris hadn't written about "wasteful pans." It's worth mentioning here that if Sarris wasn't going to make such a comment, no one else was. References to the actual state of movies, their architecture and construction you might say, was so rare as to be singular. For the most part, movie criticism was in a topsy-turvy state at the time, with most of the practitioners more suited to reviewing radio than cinema. The practice of tying plot summaries together with blithe comments on acting and off-the-cuff judgments wasn't likely to lure anyone into the profession. Providing the tools for analysis, tools that led effortlessly to interpretation, was positively exciting.

But if that was the first bit of instruction he gave me, it wasn't the most jarring. That came through the pages of the *Village Voice* in a review of the movie *The Hospital*. I was aghast; Sarris actually praised the collaboration between writer Patty Chayefsky and director Arthur Hiller. Some mistake, surely? Could the country's prime champion of visual flair and genre filmmaking actually be praising a movie directed by the awkward, pedestrian Hiller from a script by the hectoring Chayefsky?

With a growing sense of betrayal, I rushed through the review. I never saved it, but even now I can remember words like *middle-aged, noble, humanist,* emerging from newsprint. Tossing it aside, I figured, well, even Homer nods—or, more to the point perhaps, even a von Sternberg made a *Blonde Venus*—and determined to forget it.

Luckily, I never did. For one thing, it bugged me too much. But then, gradually, I came to realize that Sarris was exercising judgment, the quality that makes criticism literature instead of engineering.

What better to bring, after all, to the art of perspective than yet another perspective. To me, that word, *perspective,* sums up the contribution Andrew Sarris has made, and continues to make, to film criticism. He showed us a mountain to climb and how to climb it. Then he suggests that, if like him we manage some day to get to the top, we look off into whatsoever or how so many directions we'd like.

Andrew Sarris Observes the Future

Caryn James

*I*t's great to admire living legends, as long as the living part comes first. And so it is the vital, ever-thoughtful, constantly writing Andrew Sarris I value the most today, even more than I value his role as the prime mover of American auteurism. Since May 1989, his weekly column in the *NewYork Observer* has been a model of how the finest critics stay fresh. Covering everything from Titanic-sized blockbusters to tiny Iranian rarities, his reviews are prescient, unpredictable, and always forward-looking.

To praise the Sarris of the *Observer* years is not to diminish his importance in critical history. In fact, when I came of age as a film reviewer, in the late 1980s, his influence was so vast I never had to think about it. The auteurist theory he carried to this country in the 1960s had by then become so much a part of the landscape that I simply assumed the director was the author of a film and never questioned the significance of a personal vision. Anti-auteurist rumblings arrived with the force of revisionist argument—the ultimate sign of auteurism's hold.

A critic with such a profound influence might easily have spent the next decades looking back, defending his turf and longing for that first moment of glory. Happily, Andrew Sarris has never done that. When he looks back, it is to reassess, to add a new perspective, to make the past part of a critical continuum with the present.

His *Observer* columns offer a wonderfully flexible forum for that approach. Though people outside New York City may not be aware of its existence, the *Observer* is a weekly noted for its peach-colored newsprint, its upscale tone, and an impact way out of proportion to its fairly small circulation (around fifty thousand). Its emphasis on the worlds of media, Wall

Street, and high-priced real estate provides a congenial audience: its readers know what an auteur is.

Andrew Sarris's earliest columns in the *Observer* acknowledged that. They came under a title that was pure Sarris in its wryness, modesty, and savvy: "The Accidental Auteurist." You can dismiss the allusion to *The Accidental Tourist* and still appreciate this title. It is of a piece with Sarris's introductory essay in his 1970 collection, *Confessions of a Cultist,* which starts, "My career as a cultist began unobtrusively, if not inadvertently, in a dingy railroad flat on New York's Lower East Side back in the unlamented Eisenhower era." However inadvertent its beginning and cultish its cast, throughout his career he has sustained that engaging tone (at once confident and slyly self-mocking) and that absolute sense of the moment (the apparently throwaway phrase "the unlamented Eisenhower era" actually reveals the immediacy and political context he creates so deftly).

It was not Sarris's choice to toss out "The Accidental Auteurist" in favor of different titles for the column in subsequent years. Less wise editorial heads, perhaps not trusting their audience as much as they should, decided to call it "Manhattan Moviegoer" for several months in 1995. After that, to conform with other columns' titles in the paper, it became "At the Movies with Andrew Sarris." (I have been at the movies with Andrew Sarris, and it is a delightful experience, but as a title for a column it is hopelessly generic and passive; it fails to capture the spirit and energy of his writing, that of an active mind responding to film.) But whatever the column is called, each review is marked by an engagement with the film that provokes ideas in the reader, rather than badgering for agreement.

Andrew Sarris's reviews are especially cogent when he refuses to jump on some critical bandwagon. He never resists for the sake of being a contrarian. Instead, he provides an astute sense of where and why some much-hyped and overpraised films fail. Consider his response to Kirby Dick's 1997 documentary *Sick: The Life and Death of Bob Flanagan, Supermasochist,* the hard-to-watch film most notorious for its scene of the subject hammering a nail into his penis. While appreciating the film as an act of daring and an existential statement, Sarris made an important distinction most other critics failed to make: that shock tactics, however high-minded, do not necessarily make art. Though he found the film "something of a revelation," he added, "I would not rest easy if I inflicted *Sick* on any of my readers outside the S&M culture with the alibi of art. Art it is not, but a bizarre display of raw existence it certainly is." Here is a reasoned, open-minded response that takes the film on its own terms, gives it full credit for its visceral power, yet ultimately puts it precisely in its minor place.

Such rare lucidity is also applied to Hollywood. Early on, Sarris took Jim Carrey seriously enough to discern the talent beneath his sometimes chaotic comic energy, to note his debt to African-American humor, and to point out that by the time of *Dumb and Dumber* Carrey had "developed a curiously sophisticated broadness of farcical attack that could appeal simultaneously to the highest level of taste for its formal virtuosity, and to the lowest level for its scabrous content." In that way, megahit movies are born. "This high–low game," Sarris points out, "has always been misperceived by overly genteel middlebrows." And, astute as he is, Sarris knows better than to pretend to be a seer. A year later he wrote, "*The Cable Guy* may turn out to be a transitional film from one of our greatest comic talents. Then again, it may be the beginning of the end of Mr. Carrey's superstardom."

It is easy to be a fan when you agree with a reviewer's taste, of course, as I did when Andrew Sarris praised Atom Egoyan's *Exotica*. Perhaps it says more about the trenchant nature of his reviews that I read him just as enthusiastically when I disagree. His excitement at Kevin Smith's *Chasing Amy* caused me to do what the many other positive reviews hadn't: reconsider my low assessment, if not change my mind. In championing young directors like Egoyan and Smith, he helps film criticism stay focused on the future.

And when he looks back—at his own work as well as at old movies— it is with a total lack of sentimentality. That rejection of nostalgia is one of his rarest, most welcome, most characteristic qualities. There are, after all, plenty of critics eager to be nostalgic for him, pining wistfully for what they perceive as the good old days, when France ruled the film world and critics squabbled with one another in print. Having lived through those times, Andrew Sarris has better things to do than live through them again.

His pure engagement with the present is beautifully displayed in a 1997 *Observer* column that neatly segues from the rerelease of Jean-Luc Godard's *Contempt* to John Woo's *Face/Off*. Looking back thirty-three years, he recalls putting *Contempt* on the top of his ten-best list in the *Village Voice*, while Judith Crist put it on top of her ten-worst list in the *New York Herald-Tribune*. "The battles back then were more sharply defined than they are today," he writes, but his point is elsewhere. "I still admire *Contempt*, but I can't really find that much more to say about it. There are too many new critical issues to consider." From there he goes on to point out how Hollywood action films have replaced highbrow foreign films as the grist for serious criticism.

Sarris appreciates Hollywood action movies as much as the next critic, and here he is simply defining a crucial change in the critical ground, not railing against it. "As a former champion of the once neglected American action cinema, I am in no position to complain," he says, then leaps into a shrewd, against-the-grain view of the much-praised *Face/Off*, in which John Travolta and Nicolas Cage trade faces. It is not just another innocent action movie, he argues, because it "plays with the idea of identity in a solemn enough manner to impress high school kids. . . . John Woo's bogus seriousness does not make the indiscriminate slaughter of human beings harmless fun. Quite the contrary. *Face/Off* is made even more disgusting by its clumsy applications of psychological analysis." In one neat phrase he elucidates the element of the film that made me leave the theater feeling there was something deeply wrong with the world: "John Woo's bogus seriousness"! The film's pretension is as far from the Sarris outlook as it could possibly be.

In my worst nightmare, it is thirty years from now and I am sitting around some home for retired film critics with my contemporaries, everyone grousing about the good old days of the 1990s.

"Those kids call themselves critics?" someone says. "They have it easy. In our day we went to Sundance and walked through three blizzards in one week just to get to the movies."

"Remember back in '96 when we invented the year of the independent film? Critics had power back then."

"Remember when I discovered *Reservoir Dogs?*"

"You did not."

"Did too."

The best antidote I can imagine for such a poisonous vision of the future is the ongoing example of Andrew Sarris's career. He is the living proof that critics do not have to head down that road to nostalgia or self-importance. We can move ahead, along with him, always embracing the future.

Part Six

Sarris the Career Maker

A whole cohort of individuals became film critics because of Andrew Sarris and his movie writings.

In "An Auteurist Adolescence," film critic Dave Kehr observes: "When the slim white volume appeared on the shelf of the suburban Chicago library near my home, I had no reason to think it would change my life." *The American Cinema* joined a dozen volumes in the small film section. Among them were, most memorably, William K. Everson's *The Western,* Griffith and Mayer's *The Movies,* and Daniel Blum's *Pictorial History of the Silent Screen,* all of which Kehr had checked out and pored over countless times in the first burst of adolescent film buffery. But, says Kehr, *The American Cinema* was different: "It had no pictures, for one thing, and was largely concerned with a class of film artists I was just becoming aware of. As a kid, I'd loved the silent comedians, and particularly Laurel and Hardy; as a teenager I had just discovered *Citizen Kane,* with its full stock of wonderful tricks and ominous moods. Orson Welles was my new hero, and I was gratified to find him included in what the author called his 'Pantheon Directors.' But who were these other people?" Sarris's book motivated Kehr to find out who the "other" directors were.

For Kehr, Sarris's reviews in the *New York Observer* have taken a "far less polemical tone than [Sarris] did in the *Village Voice,* where confrontation was and is the house style. Sarris himself may have mellowed over the years, drifting away from the abrasive genre films he once defended.... Certainly, Sarris was always a not-quite-closeted romantic (the secret heroine of *The American Cinema* is Margaret Sullavan), but his columns in the *Observer* have allowed him to project a newfound courtliness and concern toward the

medium that has been the long-time object of his intellectual passion." Kehr
concludes: "As the cinema enters its second century, Andrew Sarris remains
its most devoted and respectful acolyte, tending the flame in the temple he
helped so much to construct."

Like Kehr, film critic Godfrey Cheshire ("My Own Private Shinbone") discovered Sarris in his formative years, as he recalls: "Though it
was a few years before Sarris taught me the word, I became an auteurist at
age eleven. The film responsible was John Ford's *The Man Who Shot Liberty
Valance,* which I saw at the movie theater nearest my home, the Colony."
Cheshire noticed the title "Directed by John Ford" and somehow decided
that this man was "responsible for what I loved about the film. And what,
exactly, was that?" Things get more tricky and self-reflexive when
Cheshire tries to separate "several versions of myself, including the child
who beheld *Liberty Valance* at the Colony, the twenty-something who
avidly read Sarris . . . on the work of John Ford, and the forty-eight-year-
old film critic writing these words."

Liberty Valance represented "the affecting mix of valor, idealism, and instinctive fear in Jimmy Stewart's greenhorn lawyer, who is called 'Pilgrim' by
John Wayne's Tom Doniphon, himself a striking figure of tragic, unrewarded
heroism. In these compelling characters, and in the film's action, comedy, suspense, and western setting, there was indeed much for a kid in 1962 to like."
Cheshire realized that it was "not the individual virtues but the overarching
vision connecting them" that explained his enjoyment. This vision constituted "a genuine, artistic myth of America and its history, a myth that comprehends certain essential things about where we have come from as a people and about what we have become: particularly, it concerns how . . .
converting wilderness into civilization entailed men like Stewart's Ranse
Stoddard—a walking middle-class civics lesson: teacher, lawyer, public hero,
senator—gaining precedence over the frontier's untamed and rugged individualists."

Gerald Peary, in "I Was a Preteenage Auteurist," can't forget "that fateful day in 1965, when, strolling about Broadway in the West 80s, I wandered
into Dan Talbot's New Yorker Bookstore" and encountered a magazine
"with Busby Berkeley chorines on the cover, . . . a remaindered issue of an
enticing-looking periodical, *Film Culture,* from spring 1962. I opened it and,
innocently, commenced reading . . . the special issue in which critic Andrew
Sarris . . . tackled the American cinema. . . . He applied something he called
the 'auteur' theory to several hundred directors, dropping them into immutably Dantean categories." Peary experienced "lightning bolts! Joycean
epiphanies! Proustian flashes! My eyes bulged, my legs shook, standing there

at the New Yorker Bookstore. New to Sarris's rhetorical mannerism, his wordplay stylistics, I'd never read film writing that described the cinema so precisely, so unusually, so authoritatively: 'Sternberg's films are poetic without being symbolic. . . . Sternberg's exoticism is . . . less a pretense than a pretext for objectifying personal fantasies.'"

"Except for Hitchcock," many of the filmmakers whose names Peary "knew best—Stanley Kubrick, John Huston, Stanley Kramer, Elia Kazan— were disparaged. That was perplexing enough. Yet who in the world were these directors Sarris was pushing in their place, unheard of, such as Budd Boetticher, Anthony Mann, and Douglas Sirk? And what about this Edgar G. Ulmer, 'whose films,' Sarris said, 'are of interest only to unthinking audiences or specialists in mise-en- scène.' Mise-en-scène! That was for me, whatever it was. I purchased the *Film Culture* issue and, in the coming weeks, read it through again and again, practically memorizing Sarris's shorthand, delightfully judgmental polemics. . . . I started recasting my aesthetic, seeking out Sarris-approved 'auteur' films on TV's late show. (Where oh where is Douglas Sirk's *Kaza, Son of Cochise*? I'd joke with my movie friends.)"

When Todd McCarthy ("Sarris and Paris") went to Europe as a student in 1970, he took with him several books. But, as he notes, "by the end of the year, only two of them were so thumbed, pored over, underlined, note-ridden, and worn that they barely survived with their bindings intact: Montaigne's *Essays and Selected Writings* and Andrew Sarris's *The American Cinema*. Montaigne was deeply impressive for his sagacious but modest self-regard, his temperance when read in overheated times, his antiphilosophical philosophy." Sarris made a stronger, more significant impression, since it had a direct and profound influence on McCarthy's aesthetic life and future career: "Like a handful of other works, fiction or nonfiction, if encountered at the right age—*The Fountainhead, The Great Gatsby, Das Kapital, Tropic of Cancer, The Interpretation of Dreams*—*The American Cinema* was the sort of polemical book that could and did leave an indelible mark. It represented such a great leap that its positions inspired repeated reading and long-lasting debates. As with other seminal books, it also made one feel the need to expand upon it, in the sense that its revelations opened up vast new territories for exploration."

When Todd McCarthy first picked up a copy of *The American Cinema* as a freshman at the Stanford University bookstore in the fall of 1968, he was "completely unsuspecting of its explosive nature." He says, "I was vaguely aware of the author's name from . . . the *Village Voice* . . . but had undoubtedly first come across his name in Pauline Kael's infamous 'Circles and Squares' attack on him, an essay in which I thought the intended victim seemed to be making a lot of sense." And McCarthy concludes: "Andy may have no idea how influential he has been, but very simply, in my case, he taught me how to write about films by example and led me to a career. It wouldn't have happened the way it did without him."

An Auteurist Adolescence

Dave Kehr

*W*hen the slim white volume appeared on the shelf of the suburban Chicago library near my home, I had no reason to think it would change my life.

Titled *The American Cinema,* it joined a dozen or so other volumes in the small film section. Among them were, most memorably, William K. Everson's *The Western,* Griffith and Mayer's *The Movies,* and Daniel Blum's *Pictorial History of the Silent Screen,* all of which I had checked out and pored over countless times in the first burst of my adolescent film buffery.

But this book was different. It had no pictures, for one thing, and was largely concerned with a class of film artists I was just becoming aware of. As a kid, I'd loved the silent comedians, and particularly Laurel and Hardy; as a teenager I had just discovered *Citizen Kane,* with its full stock of wonderful tricks and ominous moods. Orson Welles was my new hero, and I was gratified to find him included in what the author called his "Pantheon Directors." But who were these other people?

I knew Chaplin and Keaton, of course, and Hitchcock was the funny fat man on TV who made movies (*Psycho, The Birds, Marnie*) I wasn't allowed to see. I knew Griffith's name from the other books, though as nearly as I could tell, his movies could only be seen at a far-off place in New York City called the Museum of Modern Art. The others—Flaherty, Ford, Hawks, Lang, Lubitsch, Murnau, Ophuls, Renoir, Sternberg—were entirely new to me, but the implicit promise that they were the equals of Welles was enough. I read and reread their filmographies and the compact, epigrammatic essays the author, Andrew Sarris, had attached to them. For me, they were like a list of exotic destinations in a travel office window, places I hoped to visit some day but that for now were remote and inaccessible.

The city fathers of the bedroom suburb of Palatine, Illinois, had myste-
riously failed to provide facilities for a local cinematheque. There was, however, WGN, the locally owned (by the *Chicago Tribune*) television station,
which had a Sunday night late-movie slot set aside for black-and-white
films, as well as the far more erratic programming on the network affiliates.
Armed with the newspaper television listings, a well-thumbed copy of *The
American Cinema,* and a functioning alarm clock, the dedicated teenage
cinephile could see an amazingly wide range of movies, though in the dead
of night on a nine-inch screen. This was probably not the best way to encounter, say, Sternberg's *The Devil Is a Woman* for the first time (which arrived courtesy of a classic movie series hosted on the *Sun-Times* station,
WFLD, by Chicago's leading drama critic, Richard Christiansen), but I took
as much pleasure seeing it then, pressed up against the tiny black-and-white
screen in my bedroom, as I did seeing it many years later in a beautiful 35mm
print restored by UCLA.

By the time I made it to the University of Chicago in 1970, I had already seen an absurdly large number of movies. My choice of school had
been dictated first by a vague plan to earn a respectable degree in English literature that might allow me someday to find refuge from the real world
teaching in a woodsy college somewhere, and secondly by the fact that the
University of Chicago was home to the Documentary Film Group.

Doc Films, as it was affectionately and universally known, was the old-
est student-run film society in the United States, having been founded in
1932 by (as the name suggests) a coalition of left-leaning activists dedicated
to the then-fashionable notion of documentary films as agents of social
change. In the early 1960s, however, it had become the first American film
group to go whole hog for auteurism, thanks to a many fabled trip to Paris
taken by a group member who had returned with suitcases stuffed full of
Cahiers du Cinéma and *Positif.* At Doc Films, I met for the first time other
semisentient beings who not only knew who John Ford and Howard Hawks
were, but who could recite entire filmographies from memory, describe individual shots from obscure films in rapturous, precise detail, and call up
pages of complex dialogue at will.

Andrew Sarris was, of course, a god to us. Every Doc Filmser carried a
paperback copy of *The American Cinema,* usually wrapped with rubber bands
to compensate for the Dutton edition's notoriously flimsy binding, with the
titles one had seen underlined in each biographical entry. This dedication to
a sacred text made us resemble, a bit too closely for comfort, some of the
other cultists then proliferating on the proudly radical campus—namely, the
junior Maoists with their Little Red Books.

But apart from envying the sleek plastic covers that the Chinese had wisely provided for the words of their chairman, we had little to do with the political groups. Firm believers in Sarris's dedication to the trees rather than the forest, we were determined to rescue film culture from the sociologists and editorialists who then dominated the scant serious literature on the cinema. Movies at their best were the reflection of the sensibility of a single artist, a director who could combine the many elements that made up the cinematic product, both human (actors, technicians, screenwriters) and cultural (genre conventions and studio identities), into a unique vision.

A modest enough proposal, but in the early 1970s it was still enough to unleash passions and resentments on an almost epic scale—or at least enough to power a TV miniseries. The controversial aspect was not that directors could conceivably be "authors" of films—that much had been accepted by the academic establishment since the Bergman–Fellini boom of the 60s—but that claims of significance were being made for Hollywood films, one zone that had been carefully and consistently ruled out of "serious" consideration at least since the silent era. Hollywood has long since been established as the world capital of crassness, vulgarity, and rampant commercialism, and we had the word of F. Scott Fitzgerald and Nathanael West to prove it.

To suggest that films like *Vertigo* and *The Searchers* were something other than obvious potboilers, as Sarris and the Sarrisites had begun to do, was to challenge a whole system of ingrained beliefs. Among these heretofore unquestioned assumptions were that European art was automatically superior to American art, that the East Coast literary establishment had obvious moral rights over the West Coast movie crowd, that the mere fact that a cultural product was popular was proof of its inferiority to more refined, esoteric, and sparsely attended arts.

When the discussion could be lured away from the well-lit terrain of A-list directors like Hitchcock and Ford and into the dark back alleys of B-moviemakers like Ulmer and Dwan, it was generally enough for the anti-auteurist to cite titles like *Babes in Bagdad* and *The Woman They Almost Lynched* to carry the day. But auteurism, as Sarris suggested in his introduction to *The American Cinema,* has always operated more on curiosity than contempt, on respect for individual films rather than blanket dismissals of genres and schools. If *Babes in Bagdad* turns out to be, on closer inspection, a somewhat less momentous creation than *Ulysses* or *The Rites of Spring,* it is still an engagingly strange little film, poignantly illustrative of the depths to which its doomed director had fallen in his heroically single-minded attempt to keep making movies against all odds.

Looking back, it seems as if the auteurists lost a fair number of the battles—particularly when the opponent was the wily, impassioned Pauline Kael—but still resoundingly won the war. Hitchcock and Ford, if not Ulmer and Dwan, are safely installed in the syllabi of every Introduction to Film class, and even on the graduate level, where the postmodern theorists hold their sway, the films under discussion largely remain the auteurist classics despite all the theoretical assurances that the idea of authorship is only a long dead, romantic cliché. Pauline Kael may never have come around to Joseph H. Lewis and Phil Karlson, but she has been no less loyal to her own list of auteurs, including Brian de Palma, Irvin Kershner, Philip Kaufman, and Ron Shelton.

If anything, Sarris's Pantheon seems to have frozen into the marmoreal permanence of its Roman namesake, constructed in 27 B.C. and still going strong. (Though in the case of Sarris's belated induction of Billy Wilder, I'm forced to remain more Catholic than the Pope: here is a gifted writer whose flat, theatrical mise-en-scène reflects nothing like the profound film sense the category would seem to require.) Nor has critical consensus produced any radical readjustments among Sarris's other main categories. Though film scholarship has suggested a few more names for some of the outer orbits—perhaps there would be room now for Monta Bell and Alfred E. Green, and William Dieterie might be allowed to move a bit closer to the light on the basis of his pre–Paul Muni work—time has only confirmed the eerie precision of Sarris's judgments.

Robert Siodmak, no matter how many of his German, French, and early American B pictures come to light, seems irrevocably fixed as "Expressive Esoterica," and few defenders have come forward to reclaim the lost souls of "Strained Seriousness," the innermost circle of Sarris's critical inferno. Stanley Kubrick now seems to have justified himself through sheer persistence, and Richard Lester has earned respect if not immortality with his late run of self-destructively personal projects. But Sarris seems almost clairvoyant in his grim career predictions for such 1960s superstars as John Frankenheimer (toppling from *The Manchurian Candidate* to *The Island of Dr. Moreau*), Norman Jewison (*Bogus*), Sidney Lumet (*A Stranger Among Us*) and John Schlesinger (*An Eye for an Eye*).

Sarris, alas, was not all seeing. Published in 1968, which now seems so clearly a watershed year, *The American Cinema* displays few advance warnings of the coming revolution. Arthur Penn, whose *Bonnie and Clyde* would that same year sound the death knell for the studio system, appears only as a vague figure on the horizon, dismissed in a few sentences for his early, not always happy, attempts to meld Hollywood genres and East Coast ambitions.

Francis Ford Coppola, whose 1972 *The Godfather* would open the floodgates to a new generation of poststudio, film school–educated directors, receives only a brief mention for his ominously titled apprentice film, *You're a Big Boy Now.* Martin Scorsese, Robert Altman, Jerry Schatzberg, Steven Spielberg, and the rest of the young Turks who would create a "New American Cinema" for the 1970s make no appearance at all.

Perhaps Sarris subconsciously knew that the system he celebrated in *The American Cinema* had come to the end of its time; perhaps only at the moment of its passing could it be appreciated for the artistic wonders it had offered, rather than dismissed for the commercial compromises it had also produced in abundance. In any case, the system would never regain the richness and stability that Sarris described.

The 1970s first produced a period of creative anarchy, when the newly empowered young filmmakers succeeded in imposing an exaggerated, European notion of authorship on the Hollywood system. Then after anarchy came the inevitable reaction, as *Jaws* and *Star Wars* pointed the way to a brutal new commercialism. Relieved, the reorganized studios replaced the wayward auteur with an almost fanatical adherence to the rules and regulations of genre filmmaking. Ancient B-movie formulas (horror, science fiction, action-adventure), reproduced as simply and naively as possible, took over from the adult dramas of the 1970s, installing the fourteen-year-old filmgoer as king.

What went wrong? Were the gangster films and westerns of the 1930s that much more inherently complex than the slasher films and action-hero romps of today? Probably not, yet those genres managed to nourish the genius of Howard Hawks and John Ford, where contemporary formulas produce, at best, gifted stylists (James Cameron, John McTiernan, Renny Harlin) whose work self-destructs the minute it becomes manifestly personal (*The Abyss, The Last Action Hero, The Long Kiss Goodnight*). Creating an *American Cinema* hierarchy for the 1990s would be a thoroughly dispiriting enterprise, yielding an almost unpopulated "Pantheon" and a "Lightly Likable" that would swamp the rest of the book.

It's almost as if, like an Audubon working in the wilds, Sarris had succeeded in identifying a large number of native American auteurs, only to make it easier for the studio heads to hunt them down and drive the genus to extinction. The bottom-line, M.B.A.-driven Hollywood of today does its best to separate directors from the process of development; instead, projects are created around screenplays, which agents use to attract stars and producers dangle to attract investments. In this system, the most important thing is that there should be no surprises—that the film turns out to be as much like the script as possible. And yet what is filmmaking but a director's inspired response to finding himself or herself confronted with these actors and this screenplay at this moment? Directors who invest too much of themselves upset the process and are simply not hired. Far preferable are those malleable filmmakers who come from more flexible backgrounds—from television, from commercials, or from Great Britain. Best of all are those who come from all three: Tony Scott, Adrian Lyne, and Alan Parker.

There are two ways of getting around this rule. The first is to be a famous actor who decides to direct, and thus be able to back your personal projects with your own star power. Clint Eastwood is certainly the most successful example in this category (and one of the few star directors who would be skillful enough as a filmmaker to succeed on his own), though other prominent actor–auteurs include Kenneth Branagh, Barbara Streisand, Jodie Foster, Al Pacino, Diane Keaton, and Mel Gibson. The vastly talented Albert Brooks belongs to a separate tradition, that of the great filmmaker–comedians going back to Chaplin and Keaton. The common denominator in these films is, not surprisingly, a fascination with the self (how often that mirror metaphor appears!), a subject that can yield fascinating results (as in the harsh self-criticisms of Eastwood and Brooks) but too often collapses in narcissism. At a time when practically every character actor with a reasonable resume, from Danny DeVito to Kevin Spacey, is being asked to take up the megaphone, there is the risk that film directing will become exclusively a question of working with performers, leaving the once crucial questions of framing, lighting, and composition entirely to the cinematographers.

The second way is to come up through independent filmmaking, raising your own money through the force of your personality. This is a field that tends to produce hypertrophied auteurs, films so stamped with "authorship"—Quentin Tarantino, Spike Lee, Joel Coen, David Lynch—that the signature practically obscures the subject. A handful of indie-style "star" directors, such as Tim Burton, has been allowed to cross over to the mainstream, where they are allowed to author such big budget follies as *Mars Attacks!* on the condition of producing the occasional *Batman*. But these days, the biggest independent distributors, such as Fine Line and Miramax, seem to prefer no-name directors to the potentially difficult indie stars. Perhaps the only true independents are those hearty regionalists who, like Victor Nunez, Richard Linklater and John MacNaughton, exist so far outside of the LA–NY axis that they have had to develop their own lines of finance and their own systems of support.

When I think of what it means to be an auteurist critic in the 1990s—and I continue to think of myself that way—I think less of an urge to uncover new personalities (Is Stephen Herek an auteur? Is Dennis Dugan? Does it matter?) than a continuing commitment to film as a unique and special medium. To me, that attitude will always be Sarris's most important contribution to film culture—his willingness to see movies, not as illustrated novels or canned theater, but as objects of art sufficient unto themselves, with their own logic and aesthetics. If that commitment meant valuing *The Man Who Shot Liberty Valance* and *Merrill's Marauders* over *Lawrence of Arabia* in 1962, as Sarris did, it also means elevating the purified, classical mise-en-scène of *Mother* over the computer-enhanced baroque of *The English Patient* in 1996. There are those movies that call on the visual, aural, and rhythmic properties of the medium and those that simply provide pretty pictures, and it is a distinction increasingly in need of defense and reinforcement.

In his work for the *New York Observer*, Sarris has taken a far less polemical tone than he did in the *Village Voice*, where confrontation was and is the house style. Sarris himself may have mellowed a bit over the years, drifting away from the abrasive genre films he might once have defended and toward those more genteel pastures where dwell such sweet trifles as *The Whole Wide World* and *Marvin's Room*. Certainly, Sarris was always a not-quite-closeted romantic (the secret heroine of *The American Cinema* is Margaret Sullavan), but his columns in the *Observer* have allowed him to project a newfound courtliness and concern toward the medium that has been the long-time object of his intellectual passion. As the cinema enters its second century, Andrew Sarris remains its most devoted and respectful acolyte, tending the flame in the temple he helped so much to construct.

My Own Private Shinbone

Godfrey Cheshire

*F*our boys are at play in that shimmering but soft-edged field called memory, refracting an actual field in Raleigh, North Carolina, when I was eleven years old. The field, the actual one, is near my house. I am one of the boys (a sentence that cries out for qualifications that cut to the uncertain heart of what I am about to relate here). Two of the boys carry toy pistols; the other two toss a toy rifle between them. The game, which they—we—repeat over and over, exchanging roles each time, mimes a nighttime gunfight on the main street of a fictional western town called Shinbone. It goes like this: one boy with pistol comes reeling down the street and confronts his opposite number, the blustering bad guy, gets shot in the arm by him, and drops his gun, at which point he looks very much like a goner. Yet across the invisible street the third boy tosses the rifle to the fourth, who carefully shoots the bad guy at the same instant that the wounded boy fires the pistol he has just picked up. The bad guy dies spectacularly, in a prodigiously elaborated sprawl and collapse; this was every boy's favorite part to play and was well worth the wait.

Though it was a few years before Andrew Sarris taught me the word, I became an auteurist at age eleven. The film responsible was John Ford's *The Man Who Shot Liberty Valance,* which I saw at the movie theater nearest my home, the Colony (it is now the Rialto, an art house). I have told the story above, about how my friends and I would reenact the film's climactic shoot-out, so often that I have become a little suspicious of it. Did it really happen this way, or has my mind embellished the memory—as legend famously becomes fact in Ford's film—to fit the heading "how I became an auteurist"? Actually, I think it did happen like this. What strikes me now, in trying to examine the recollection more closely than I have before, is that it does involve a significant duplicity; yet this belongs not to the tricks of memory but to the incident itself, which has, and always had, two components, two separate faces—call them the communal and the private. Why are they so connected?

The communal happened in the movie theater, but was transmuted, affirmed and fixed in memory in that twilit, actual field. More bookish than outgoing as a kid, I have few vivid memories of playing like this with friends, and there must have a special thrill for me in the sense, glimpsed retrospectively, that I effectively functioned as director, actor, and critic in the reenactment (surely I was the one who suggested the game and explained to my pals why the scene was so great). The memory's private aspect also began in the movie theater, in my own enjoyment of the film, and it continued afterward in a recognition that—unlike that game in the field—has a very obvious bearing on why and how I "became an auteurist." That is, I noticed the title "Directed by John Ford" and somehow decided that this man must be responsible for what I loved about the film.

And what, exactly, was that? Here, things get a little tricky when I try to separate several versions of myself, including the child who beheld *Liberty Valance* at the Colony, the twenty-something who avidly read Sarris and other critics on the work of John Ford, and the forty-eight-year-old film critic writing these words. Surely, just as I was drawn to the movie by Gene Pitney's theme song on the radio, I responded to things about it that were not particularly profound: the thrilling menace of Lee Marvin's violent, sarcastic villain (Tarantino has spoken of how the startling combination of terror and comedy in *Abbott and Costello Meet Frankenstein* led him to *Pulp Fiction*).

Liberty Valance was my equivalent; the affecting mix of valor, idealism, and instinctive fear in Jimmy Stewart's greenhorn lawyer, who is called "Pilgrim" by John Wayne's Tom Doniphon, himself a striking figure of tragic, unrewarded heroism. In these compelling characters, and in the film's action, comedy, suspense, and western setting, there was indeed much for a kid in 1962 to like.

Yet I think that even at the time I realized that it was the combination of these things, not the individual virtues but the overarching vision connecting them, that explained my enjoyment. More than that, I sensed—however obliquely—this vision as constituting something that might be called a genuine, artistic myth of America and its history, a myth that comprehends certain essential things about where we have come from as a people and about what we have become: particularly, it concerns how the process of converting wilderness into civilization entailed men like Stewart's Ranse Stoddard—a walking middle-class civics lesson: worker, teacher, lawyer, public hero, senator—gaining precedence over the frontier's un-tamed and too-rugged individualists, whether rapacious criminals like Valance or stoic vigilantes like Doniphon, who both represent the wildness that is conquered by law.

Did I understand, too, the aspect of psychological fable here, the sense in which Stoddard stands for the adult, socialized being that emerges from the childishly aggressive and antisocial impulses embodied by Valance and Stoddard? Did I grasp the depths of the sexual contest over Vera Miles's Hal-lie, which pits Stoddard's bumbling but successful suitor against Wayne's self-sacrificing loner, with Valance looming constantly as the threat of violation, of rape? Let us just say that at age eleven there was surely lots about the film that I may have felt but didn't necessarily understand. Yet *Liberty Valance* is a film in which feelings are at least as important to understanding as cerebra-tion is: this is part of what makes it art and myth rather than a schematic his-tory lesson.

It opens with the aged Stoddard and Hallie arriving in Shinbone and going to visit the remains of Tom Doniphon, which lie in a simple coffin surmounted by a single rose. Did Hallie once love Tom? Does she still? From here the story's motion is a constant plunging back through waves of time and memory and regret, into the past—a past that is revealed as itself du-plicitous, mixed of nobility and deceit. That past's historic heart is reached in a flashback within a flashback which shows—this is the scene that my friends and I reenacted—that the slaying of Valance, which would be credited to Stoddard and make him a hero and later a successful politician, was in fact accomplished by Doniphon (the fourth character in this scene, who tossed Doniphon the rifle, was his servant, played by Woody Strode). So the legend, which was taken as fact and became, one might say, the myth, was a lie. Does that make it untrue?

Liberty Valance begins where all philosophy begins: with the sense that things are not as they seem, that there is a hidden reality lying behind and informing the apparent. (The secret here, since this American myth has a strong Christian component, involves death, self-sacrifice, guilt, transference and at least a hint of redemption.) Yet the film is not cynical about myths; rather, it has a complex, poetic grasp of their ambivalences and costs. The portraits of Lincoln and Washington, in the frontier schoolroom where the young Stoddard teaches children the meaning of democracy, remind us that myths are nutritive, sustaining, tales that represent a people's highest aspira-tions and most crucial values. What makes the film itself an "artistic" myth is that it adds to this communal aspect a personal dimension, in two senses: it shows us the private ravages and realities behind the (necessarily distorted) public image, and it conveys Ford's own feeling about the story. To say the film is rich with personal feeling would almost be an understatement. Ford's elegiac lyricism is as potent as that of Proust or Henry James, even if the film's form has the austere elegance of a frontier church.

The communal aspects of *Liberty Valance* imply the audience as crowd, while the personal imply the viewer as solitary sensibility: the apparent paradox, or duplicity, here is that of cinema itself, and of anyone who becomes captivated by it. At age eleven, I was thrilled by the chance to be part of the gang by acting out that gunfight. But my fellows had gone to the movie because of Gene Pitney's song and came away with memories of heroism and villainy and gunplay; only I took away "Directed by John Ford." Two years later, when *Cheyenne Autumn* opened in Raleigh, it had no John Wayne and no theme song on the radio. Moreover, it played a downtown theater that formerly had separate entrances for whites and blacks but now was being integrated, which for a while caused many whites to avoid it. I couldn't persuade any of my friends to go, so I went alone.

Four years later, when I was seventeen, my first movie review was printed in the student newspaper of my school. It was of *2001: A Space Odyssey,* another very American tale about how frontiers transform their conquerors. Like Ford's film, Kubrick's suggests a hidden order behind the outward progress of history; in demanding interpretation, it creates a place for the critic, giving him the role of mediating between artist and viewer and between a movie's communal and private aspects. Yet in looking back now at the brief time separating these two movies of the 1960s, I am struck that they seem to belong to two wholly different eras and to be divided by a crucial watershed. *Liberty Valance* issued from a Hollywood veteran who would never have called himself an artist; *2001* was the product of a maverick New Yorker who clearly coveted that mantle. While auteurism appreciated the former film, it helped create the latter.

However, in France auteurism spawned a generation of filmmakers; in America, a generation of critics. Why? Perhaps because differing cultural notions of authority and authenticity decreed different approaches to the metaphor of movie authorship, the French inclining toward *writing* (that is, making movies oneself), Americans toward *reading* (understanding them). Inevitably, Truffaut's *politique* underwent a sea change when Andrew Sarris whisked it across the Atlantic and turned into a theory, suitable at once for college syllabi, museum curatorial catalogs, and the publicity machinery of Hollywood. Directors became stars? Producers and screenwriters fumed? Lesser critics lacking theories railed and threw mud? All very true. But this is news of the late 1960s and the 1970s. Notice what has happened more recently. Thanks in large part to the auteur theory, critics gained a prominence in the culture that continues today, yet the stock of directors has fallen. Directors have a prized job because they make lots of money and rub shoulders with stars. They are often considered minor celebrities; less frequently are they viewed and esteemed as *artists*.

Artistry, in pure Sarris's auteurism, implies one thing above all: a "private communion" linking moviemaker and viewer, like that between poet and reader. For Sarris, cinema's finest essences are distilled in these "privileged moments," which find an unbeatable emblem in a wordless passage in Ford's *The Searchers* that Sarris describes this way in *The American Cinema:* "[A character played by Ward] Bond is drinking some coffee in a standing-up position before going out to hunt some Comanches. He glances toward one of the bedrooms, and notices the woman of the house tenderly caressing the Army uniform of her husband's brother. Ford cuts back to a full-faced shot of Bond drinking his coffee, his eyes tactfully averted from the intimate scene he has witnessed. Nothing on earth would ever force this man to reveal what he had seen. There is a deep, subtle chivalry at work here, and in most of Ford's films."

In that woman's tender caress is all the drama any movie could ever contain, conveyed with poetry's radical concision. And in Bond's stoic gaze is Ford's attitude toward that drama, an attitude compounded of both strong personal feeling and a complex of traditional ideals (chivalry). Auteurism presumes that we are at least as much interested in that attitude, that gaze, as we are in any drama it might comprehend; the point of this art, its very definition, lies in one-to-one contact between the individual sensibilities of director and viewer.

What is to be said of a such a definition in 1998? First, that it's now clearly identifiable not as the definition destined to supersede all others, but as a special case that belongs to a certain period of cinema, primarily the 1960s and 1970s. Movies were born as mass spectacles; apocryphal or not, the tale of spectators fleeing the Lumieres' arriving train is a comedy of mass terror, with nary a hint of privileged gazes or private reading. And movies have become so again. *Titanic* exemplifies an era where films mimic thrill rides, audiences derive meaning from public experience rather than inward communion, and no one cares a whit about the director's feelings or imputes to him any form of higher sensibility, much less chivalric wisdom. James Cameron? He's famous because he made the film. The film isn't famous because it expresses him or connects us to him.

Since southerners understand at a primal level the romance of lost causes, I think I may value auteurism now more than on first reading *The American*

Cinema, when it seemed both necessary and inevitably triumphant. Today it is discreetly bracketed as a privileged moment belonging to cinema itself. Was it bound to fail, if failure means being misread? Perhaps, since its emphasis on private reverie and projected identification easily can lead to the closed loop of self-obsession. It is this form of arrested development, or heresy, I submit, that leads some to the mistake of preferring *The Searchers* to *Liberty Valance, Citizen Kane* to *The Magnificent Ambersons, Vertigo* to *Rear Window.*

Myself, I continue trying to link private fascinations back to the public weal, to the ongoing democratic drama that has as its greatest cinematic poet John Ford. In that and in other critical tasks, I have found no more eloquent, generous, helpful, or inspiring guide than Andrew Sarris, whom I tend to identify with Ford when I read a passage like the following on the film that literally changed my life, a passage that sweeps me back along the lanes of memory to a field where four American boys mime the actions of giants: "The heroic postures of Wayne, Stewart and Marvin form a triangle in time. The conflicting angles, the contrasting plays of light and shadow, the unified rituals of gestures and movements and, above all, Ford's gift of sustained contemplation produce intellectual repercussions backwards and forwards in film time until, on a second viewing, the entire film, the entire world of John Ford, in fact, is concentrated into the first anguished expression of Vera Miles as she steps off the train at the beginning of the film, and everything that Ford has ever thought or felt is compressed into one shot of a cactus rose on a coffin photographed, needless to say, from the only possible angle."

I Was a Preteenage Auteurist

Gerald Peary

*H*ow can I forget that fateful day in 1965 when, strolling about Broadway in the West 80s, I wandered into Dan Talbot's New Yorker Bookstore, a second-floor adjunct to his legendary New Yorker Theater? There was a circular wire carousel in the middle of the store containing back copies of film magazines. I swung the carousel around, and there before me, with Busby Berkeley chorines on the cover, sat a remaindered issue of an enticing-looking periodical: *Film Culture* from spring 1962.

I opened it and, innocently, commenced reading . . . the special issue in which critic Andrew Sarris, whom I'd just started following in the *Village Voice,* tackled the American cinema. All of it! He sliced it, diced it, spun it on its ear, and weirdly classified it. He applied something he called the "auteur" theory to several hundred directors, dropping them into immutably Dantean categories. The "Pantheon" cineastes floated on high, along with "The Far Side of Paradise," while "Expressive Esoterica" knocked hopefully at the empyrean gates. "Lightly Likable," "Oddities, One-Shots and New-comers," and "Subjects for Further Research" bobbed in limbo, whereas poor "Strained Seriousness" and "Less Than Meets the Eye" dropped into the muck below.

For me, the gentle reader: lightning bolts! Joycean epiphanies! Proust-ian flashes! My eyes bulged, my legs shook, standing there at the New Yorker Bookstore. New to Sarris's rhetorical mannerism, his wordplay stylistics, I'd never read film writing that described the cinema so precisely, so unusually, so authoritatively: "Sternberg's films are poetic without being symbolic. We need not search for slumbering allegories of Man and God and Life, but rather for a continuous stream of emotional biography. Sternberg's exoticism

211

is, then, less a pretense than a pretext for objectifying personal fantasies. His equivalent literary genre is not the novel or the short story or the theatrical spectacle, but the closet drama unplayable but for the meaningful grace of gesture and movement."

Wow!

Except for Hitchcock, many of the filmmakers whose names I knew best—Stanley Kubrick, John Huston, Stanley Kramer, Elia Kazan—were disparaged. That was perplexing enough. Yet who in the world were these directors Sarris was pushing in their place, unheard of, such as Budd Boetticher, Anthony Mann, and Douglas Sirk? And what about this Edgar G. Ulmer, "whose films," Sarris said, "are of interest only to unthinking audiences or specialists in mis-en-scene."

Mis-en-scène! That was for me, whatever it was.

I purchased the *Film Culture* issue and, in the coming weeks, read it through again and again, practically memorizing Sarris's shorthand and delightfully judgmental polemics. I was definitely persuaded. I started recasting my aesthetic, seeking out Sarris-approved "auteur" films on TV's late show. (Where oh where is Douglas Sirk's *Kaza, Son of Cochise?*, I'd joke with my movie friends.)

As for new movies in the mid-1960s, I now swore weekly allegiance to Sarris's film section in the *Village Voice*. There the contemporary cinema was discussed by critics who spoke out—and this was very radical then—from an intensely personal point of view. Gay rights and women's rights and film history and underground cinema all were in the wonderful mix. I solemnly believe that there has never been a more splendid, talented group of critics working for a newspaper. A Golden Age: Sarris, Molly Haskell, Stuart Byron, William Paul, and, additionally, Jonas Mekas. Awesome!

But was it a coincidence that I was so swept away by all of this? Or, more likely, character being fate, wasn't it inevitable that I would be smitten?

THE ROAD TO ANDREW SARRIS . . .

Without knowing it, I was a preteenage cultist, whose taste as a movie-crazed child was truly madly deeply prematurely "auteur." Many years before Sarris had brought the "Politiques" from Paris, I was, amazingly, already drumming to their ★★★★★ (Masterpiece!) beat.

The precocity of a future film critic: the movies I loved best as a tiny child were made, almost inevitably, by what would be Sarris-designated "auteurs."

The film that brought vivid nightmares to a four-year-old in 1948 was Joseph Losey's *The Boy with the Green Hair*. A fabulous birthday party I attended of second-graders in 1952 culminated in a movie trip to see children lost in the Alaskan wilderness in Joseph H. Lewis's *Desperate Search*. In Phillippi, West Virginia, a tiny mountain town where I lived, some Hollywood movies arrived many years late. That's why this eight-year-old saw, first-run in late 1952, Fritz Lang's 1940 *The Return of Frank James.*

And so it continued, as my family moved me to Columbia, South Carolina. I fell hard for Nicholas Ray's *Johnny Guitar,* Don Siegel's *Invasion of the Body Snatchers,* George Stevens's *Shane,* Cecil B. DeMille's *The Greatest Show on Earth,* Hitchcock's *Rear Window.* If you'd asked me in 1956, when I turned twelve, what were my three favorite films of all time, you'd find a formidable challenge to Francois Truffaut. I adored Nicholas Ray's *Rebel Without a Cause,* Howard Hawks's *Land of the Pharaohs,* and, most of all, John Ford's *The Searchers.*

Enraptured, I watched *The Searchers* four days in a row at the theater at its original release. Thirty screenings since, it's still my favorite.

But I had no idea who directed all these great movies, or what a director was, except for the ever-visible TV host of *Alfred Hitchcock Presents.* When I did learn about directors, it was a different bunch, foreign language masters—Fellini, Kurosawa, Antonioni, Wajda—from avidly reading my first magazine film criticism in the early 1960s: Hollis Alpert and Arthur Knight in *The Saturday Review* and Dwight MacDonald in *Esquire.*

I was reborn as a foreign film dandy. Ingmar Bergman was my most cherished filmmaker and, for several years, *The Searchers* was forsaken for new all-time greatest films, *Wild Strawberries* and *Jules and Jim.* As an undergraduate, I wrote my first film paper, which was on the "alienation in the modern world" of *La Dolce Vita.*

My film taste was becoming rarefied and elitist. The only movies that could "mean something" had subtitles. I desperately needed to be shook up! Thank you, Andrew Sarris! We're back to *Film Culture,* spring 1962. We're back to Sirk and Ulmer, and me, regaining my cine-soul, taking American movies as thematically seriously as European ones. Bergman might be obsessed with the death of God, but Nicholas Ray, said Sarris, demonstrates that "every relationship establishes its own moral code, and there is no such thing as absolute morality." Sarris showed me that, without abandoning my continental tastes, it was very cool to love and admire *The Searchers* above all. Talk about Pantheon "auteur" mise-en-scène: *The Searchers* was directed by John Ford!

Pursuing a Ph.D., I traveled to the film-nutty town of Madison, Wisconsin, where, in the mid- to late 1960s, Sarris's aesthetics had already hit the Midwest. Among the students were future critics Michael Wilmington and Joseph McBride, who collaborated on the Sarris-indebted study *John Ford.* The film section of the school paper, the *Daily Cardinal,* was totally auteurist. (I was arts editor in 1970.) Most important, we students began our own amateur film magazine, *The Velvet Light Trap,* which combined Sarris-style auteurism with something new: "studio studies" (RKO, Warner Brothers) and leftist-revisionist film history.

At the "Berkeley of the Midwest," we Madisonians of draft age were battling American involvement in Vietnam. Some of the most passionately auteurist film freaks were also the most politically occupied. Me too. I do recall that, for several heated years, I felt out of sorts with Sarris's more centrist liberalism. I identified myself then as a leftist–auteurist, and I veered toward personal directors whose work had a socially activist bent: Pontecorvo, Godard, Arthur Penn, Hal Ashby.

However, I also remember that one of the most Marxist–Godardian–Ultraleftist of the film aficionados, Tony Chase (now a law professor), brought Sarris back into the fold. Well, more than that: one day he decided that Sarris's old *Film Culture* categories (by then recast in book form for 1968's seminal *The American Cinema*) went far beyond a way of placing films. Instead, they offered a veritable cosmology, a way to classify *anything:* friends, American presidents, gods, you name it.

Chase proved his abstract point by arriving at Madison's student union one morning with an elaborate Sarrisian chart, ranking about fifty candy bars! Hershey Bars and Mr. Goodbar were "Pantheon"; Reese's Buttercups were "The Far Side of Paradise." Several popular candy bars that Chase disdained, he classified as "Less Than Meets the Eye." I remember that "Chuckles" headed the category "Here Come the Clowns"!

FROM MADISON TO THE WORLD . . .

I flash ahead fifteen years, to 1986, when I was a Fulbright scholar in Belgrade, Yugoslavia. I don't think that Andrew Sarris had ever visited there but, amazingly, everyone in film circles knew his aesthetics, and many lived by his book *The American Cinema.* This was under Communism, but the local cinematheque chose its films from an "auteurist" point of view: Sundays were always crowded John Ford nights! As for the film school, it was the only place in Eastern Europe with a course in Howard Hawks.

As someone steeped in Sarris, I became a valued source for information about the cult U.S. directors whom the Yugoslavians had read about but had no idea how to pronounce. There was that amusing day in Belgrade when I was surrounded by Sarrisian film freaks who wanted to know: "How do you say 'Borzage'? How do you say 'Boetticher'?" Afterward, I was at the triumphant class in westerns at the university where, for the first time, the teacher informed his students confidently about the wonderful "auteur" filmmaker of *Commanche Station*.

(Curiously, the Sarris–Pauline Kael critical battles were also a topic of interest in Belgrade, though everyone I met was closer in thinking to Sarris. I recall a conversation with a Yugoslav who was annoyed to discover that a certain critic in *Rolling Stone* wrote virtually the same reviews as Kael. How could that be? I introduced him to the term *Paulettes*.)

The Australians also wanted to know about Sarris and Kael, but firsthand. Another flash forward, to summer 1995. A literal Tribute to Andrew Sarris, a main event at the Sydney Film Festival, as Sarris, now working for the *New York Observer*, was flown from Manhattan to talk, to reminisce. Fortuitously, I was teaching Boston University film students in a special summer-in-Sydney program, so I was asked to host the exciting event.

What an honor, to converse one-on-one with my mentor, Sarris, on a huge stage before an immense audience of rapt Australians. I began with the story that began this essay, the discovery of Sarris's *Film Culture* writings that changed my life. And then, to enthusiastic crowd applause, I introduced The Great Man himself. It wasn't long before, by request, he launched into the famous tale of his first meeting ever with Pauline Kael, in which he daydreamed beforehand a kind of Adam's Rib banter and attraction. "Alas, I was no Spencer Tracy," Sarris joked, "and Pauline was certainly no Katharine Hepburn."

Sarris had a deservedly wonderful time in Australia, that I do believe. "Auteurism" seemed alive and thriving Down Under, and the audience listened especially intently when Sarris, the American, was asked to rank Australian filmmakers. He's still the man!

The Sydney days ended at a wind-down dinner in which, I recall vividly, the subject came up to nominate the sexiest screen performance ever for a female star. I was shamelessly modern and campy and joined a young Chilean at the table in voting for Ann Margaret snarling away in *Kitten with a Whip!* Sarris could only shake his head at such a meretricious pick, such overstated eros. He and the French film critic Michel Ciment, editor of *Positif,* made a far classier, gentlemanly choice: Kay Francis's dazzling victim of jewel thieves in the 1932 *Trouble in Paradise,* by, naturally, a Pantheon director, Ernst Lubitsch.

Yes, Sarris loves Ernst Lubitsch, and what he notes about Lubitsch in *The American Cinema* says what I think of Andrew Sarris: "We shall never see his like again." Salutations on your seventy-second birthday!

Sarris and Paris

Todd McCarthy

*W*hen I went to Europe as a student in 1970, I took with me any number of books. But by the end of the year, only two of them were so thumbed, pored over, underlined, note-ridden, and worn that they barely survived with their bindings intact: Montaigne's *Essays and Selected Writings* and Andrew Sarris's *The American Cinema*. Montaigne was deeply impressive for his sagacious but modest self-regard, his temperance when read in overheated times, his antiphilosophical philosophy; among the numerous great French moralists and theologically oriented thinkers, he was also the most accessible, the most genial guide to the manner and means of refined thought and expression.

All the same, there is no question that Sarris made a far stronger and more significant impression, since it had a direct and profound influence on my aesthetic life and my future career. Like a handful of other works, fiction or nonfiction, if encountered at the right age—*The Fountainhead, The Great Gatsby, Das Kapital, Tropic of Cancer, The Interpretation of Dreams, The American Cinema*—it was the sort of polemical book that, in the late 1960s, could and did leave an indelible mark. It represented such a great leap that its positions inspired repeated reading and debate that lasted for years thereafter. As with other seminal books, it also made one feel the need to expand upon it, in the sense that its revelations opened up vast new territories for exploration.

When I first picked up a copy of the newly published *The American Cinema* as a freshman at the Stanford University bookstore in the fall of 1968, I was completely unsuspecting of its explosive nature. I was vaguely aware of the author's name from having paged through the *Village Voice* on visits to New York but had undoubtedly first come across his name in Pauline Kael's infamous "Circles and Squares" attack on him, an essay in which I thought the intended victim seemed to be making a lot of sense.

By the time I was eighteen, I had already seen a lot of movies, but like most other buffs, I subsequently learned, my background in the "classics" was necessarily sketchy, proscribed by the sorts of films shown on television during the 1960s, in church basements (where I had first seen *Citizen Kane,* perhaps aptly enough), at the High Art film nights at Northwestern University in my home town of Evanston, Illinois, and enhanced mainly by Bruce Trinz's monumentally imaginative, different-double-bill-daily programming at the unique Clark Theater in Chicago's Loop. The Clark was a combination flophouse for bums and drunks (its hours were 8 A.M. to 6 A.M.), rest stop for weary women shoppers (it featured a "Gals' Gallery" mezzanine from which the occasional scream could be heard when a predatory man succeeded in sneaking in), and privileged sanctuary for the film fanatic; where else, in the preauteurist, pre–film studies mid-1960s, could one see *The Searchers* and *Rio Bravo* on John Wayne's birthday, *M* paired with *Contempt* (with Fritz Lang in attendance one night), *Dracula* and *Frankenstein* one day, and *Breathless* and *Shoot the Piano Player* the next?

Upon examining *The American Cinema* for the first time, however, my initial reaction was outrage, outrage produced principally by the insult I deeply felt (and still would maintain) Sarris directed at one filmmaker: Billy Wilder. The fact that a serious critic could actually rank someone as crass and vulgar as Cecil B. DeMille over an artist as sophisticated and deft as Wilder seemed so preposterous to me that I almost resisted buying the book. Fortunately, the author's vast erudition was evident at a glance, and I was highly intrigued not only by Sarris's advancement of directors I'd barely heard of, and certainly never had experienced firsthand—Ophuls, Lubitsch, Borzage, Fuller, La Cava, Sirk, Vidor, Preston Sturges (not John?)—but by his championing of directors I had, in my own amateur and haphazard way, been noticing since I was twelve years old without much clue as to their critical reputabilty or lack of same—Preminger, Hitchcock, and Anthony Mann above all, as well as Losey, Minnelli, Blake Edwards, Nicholas Ray, George Stevens, and Stanley Donen.

At the same time, at Stanford, near San Francisco, I could scarcely have been farther from the critical fray then beginning to convulse the national critical establishment in New York, and then the teaching of film. The Chicago I grew up in was a four-paper town, but all the film critics were, to put it bluntly, old ladies, local contemporaries of Hedda Hopper and Louella Parsons, from whom I gleaned nothing but a passing familiarity with hackneyed critical jargon and a certain prissy, prudish snobbery.

When a young man just out of college named Roger Ebert was suddenly hired by the *Sun-Times* in 1966, it was like a blast of fresh wind off the lake: here was a guy excited by what was happening in film right now, stimulated by all kinds of movies, and who used his position to rightly complain about the dreadful provincialism of film distribution in Chicago, dictated, as it was, almost entirely by the whims of the *New York Times*'s Bosley Crowther. So exciting was Ebert's arrival on the scene to those of us who loved films that I began writing letters to him at the paper that, to my astonishment as a high school student, he began printing; my first published words, if I recall correctly, were in a letter bemoaning how Orson Welles's *Chimes at Midnight* (or *Falstaff,* as it had been retitled by its American distributor) seemed destined never to reach Chicago due to its dismal reception by Crowther in New York. About a year later, Ebert and I were both there on opening night, when Welles's masterpiece finally opened at the Town Theater, a seedy venue that more commonly played home to nudie features such as *Sinderella and the Golden Bra* and a stripper named Babette Bordot.

Although I had never written a word for my high school newspaper, for some reason the first thing I did upon arriving at Stanford was to head to the offices of the *Stanford Daily* and ask if the paper could use a film critic. Unable to produce any writing samples, I was asked to do an audition review. Just opening locally was a film I had seen and loved in Chicago just a month before, during the tumultuous 1968 Democratic National Convention, *Belle de Jour.* I went back to see it again, wrote it up, was asked for a rewrite, submitted that, and thus was a career unwittingly born. (I'm not quite sure how I was able to write that review without having seen any previous Bunuel films, although I was better prepared for my next review, of Truffaut's *The Bride Wore Black.*)

The critical atmosphere at the time was immediately before the revolution. The film criticism class I took was rooted in two perennial warhorses, Arthur Knight's historical survey, *The Liveliest Art,* and Siegfried Kracauer's *From Caligari to Hitler,* neither of which I was ever able to get completely through, although Robert Warshow was held up as the most advanced thinker on the cinema. But Northern California was also Pauline country, so to offset this academic stodginess, our professor, Henry Breitrose, who chain-smoked Pall Malls through his every lecture, brought in as his teaching assistant a bright young East Coast fellow by the name of David Denby. A Paulette before the term was invented, Denby brought The Word back to the West Coast from Kael, who had only recently found her berth at the *New Yorker,* and I say this as a covert attempt to counterbalance the auteurist heresies I was beginning to spread several times a week in my reviews and columns. In 1968–69, no American arts critic enjoyed anywhere near the cache that Pauline Kael did, and Breitrose and Denby jointly used her clout to beat up on my Sarris-inspired alternative views, for which, as far as I knew, I was the only proponent west of the Hudson. Every Friday, I ran a "Film of the Week" column in which I weighed in on the dozen or so films due to be shown on campus in the coming week, and every Friday morning in class, one or the other of them would playfully run down my list, commenting, "Well, McCarthy might be right about this, but he's out of his mind about that," as I sat stoically in my seat.

Despite the best efforts, however, the pesky gnat of auteurism would not go away, so one day Breitrose and Denby, with considerable ceremony, decided to stage a Great Debate on the subject. Our professor announced that he would begin the proceedings by stating the case against auteurism, while the unbiased Denby would handle the rebuttal. The entire debate went very much as follows. Breitrose: "*Casablanca* is a great film, but Michael Curtiz is not considered a great director. So much for the auteur theory." "Well, you're right." End of discussion.

By the spring of 1970, I must have read every page of *The American Cinema* at least ten times. Thanks to Sarris's pointing the way, I had, by now, twice devoured the complete works of Buster Keaton, begun to sample the greatness of Jean Renoir, Ernst Lubitsch, and Max Ophuls, and understood how Josef von Sternberg, whose work spoke to me so deeply, might legitimately be viewed as a great visual poet rather than just a master of artifice. He had, as he modestly stated his wish in his introduction, established priorities of viewing, with his hierarchical categories providing a legitimate window through which to approach an appreciation of the history of the Hollywood sound film (which was only forty years old when Sarris's book was first published and had since expanded by another three decades).

Despite the evident sense of what Sarris wrote and my willingness to be guided by it above all other sources, I was far from being a doctrinaire disciple. I still vehemently disagreed with him about Wilder and DeMille and have always felt that he was unfairly harsh on most of the directors whom he dumped, along with Wilder, into the "Less Than Meets the Eye" category: Huston, Kazan, Lean, Mankiewicz, and Wyler in particular. I embraced auteurism, but with major reservations consistent with the attitudes of a lifelong nonjoiner, and I learned just how far from full-fledged membership I was when I visited my friends at Doc Films at the University of Chicago.

These gents, and the rare lady, were hard-core, representing auteurism at full sail. Fiercely polemical and ferociously opinionated, they were already deeply into the most obscure works of Gerd Oswald, Harvard Hart, Peter Tewksbury, Joseph McGrath, and other directors Sarris had mentioned just in passing. On the other hand, their fanaticism had its intense upside: during one week I visited Chicago, in April 1970 just prior to my departure for France, Doc Films had as its guests Fritz Lang, Nicholas Ray, and Joseph Losey. Because I was the only one there with a car, I got to chauffeur these men around, and I joined as well in the numerous screening and discussions of their work, which began providing firsthand knowledge about the reality, and not just theory, of directing movies.

In these formative years of cinemania, the decisive films for me were very nearly all French, with a heavy emphasis on the great works of the New Wave. Up to 1970, my hot list of greatest films of all time would have had to include *Shoot the Piano Player, Children of Paradise, The Crime of M. Lange, Contempt, Ma Nuit Chez Maud, Napoleon, The Young Girls of Rochefort, French Can Can, Pierrot Le Fou, The 400 Blows,* and several others. So it didn't hurt that auteurism was so deeply steeped in Francophilia, a bias I unapologetically shared with Sarris. Had the *politique des auteurs* been developed, let's say, by critics in Sweden or the Netherlands, it is doubtful its influence would have been so profound and far-ranging. There had always been a romance surrounding French intellectualism, and the achievements of the New Wave directors had not only enhanced that, but had shown all of us often solitary film buffs, for the first time, that there was a way to put theory into extraordinary practice, that there was, in a way, hope for us all. Still, all of this would have remained one step removed, and culturally too remote, had not Andrew Sarris brought it all home and, sometimes literally, translated the French into American.

And it was precisely by carrying *The American Cinema* with me to Paris that I was able to rediscover the American cinema, the films I had loved up to my adolescence but had snobbishly turned away from. Of course, I knew all about the Cinematheque Francaise, and my first visit there—to the old one in the Latin Quarter—had all the trappings of a religious experience, of a visit to Chartres, the Sistine Chapel, or Boradudor. The occasion was the first opportunity I'd ever had to see *The Devil Is a Woman* by Sternberg, one of my gods at that time (later in the year I made a pilgrimage to his birthplace in a very unfashionable district of Vienna). This last Sternberg–Dietrich creation, like so many of the films I caught up with in Europe, was all but impossible to see in the United States then.

The excitement of the crowd cramming up to the doors before they were opened was very like the opening scene in *The Red Shoes,* in which dozens of youthful balletomanes charge the balcony to secure the best possible seats. As for them, experiencing this work by one of the great masters was, for me, the most important thing in the world at that moment. As the impossibly beautiful film unspooled in a glorious 35mm print, I became overwhelmed in a way that only the greatest works of art can manage, and Sarris's declaration that it was a masterpiece was looking like an understatement. I was utterly unprepared for the nakedness of the director's confessional, the depth of its masochism, the brutality of its self-mocking.

No film I had ever seen, I decided, was as personal as this one and, after having been momentarily detracted by the buzz of gossip as we filed out that Francois Truffaut had been in the audience, I wandered aimlessly around unknown streets of Paris for hours, more transported than I had ever been by the creation of another individual, and astonished that so remarkable a film had been dismissed, then neglected, by all but a handful of discerning critics. Surely here was the absolute proof of the auteur theory's position that deeply personal work was done in the Hollywood studio system, that profound meanings could lurk beneath the surface of entertainment's artifice. How could anyone have missed the extent to which the director had made up Lionel Atwill to resemble himself, the transcendent way he had mercilessly transformed the ruins of his relationship with Dietrich into corrosively triumphant art?

Convinced more than ever that Sarris and the French were right and that the others were either wrong or as yet unenlightened, I plotted my subsequent weeks in Paris—prior to my departure for Britain and school—on the basis of the listings in each Wednesday's edition of the entertainment guide *Pariscope*. With my highly educated and refined French uncle and aunt, with whom I was staying, aghast that I wasn't spending my days at the Louvre or at the Bibliotheque Nationale immersing myself in Napoleonic history, I crammed in two or three films a day, racing from one cinematheque or revival house to another, guided above all by the priorities established by Sarris in *The American Cinema* but with extra input from the French publications I started to read.

At La Pagode, the fabulous Orientalist minipalace, I discovered the comic Hawks in *Bringing up Baby,* although I was just as quickly turned off by *I Was a Male War Bride* shortly thereafter. Sarris proved right again when I was entranced by Lubitsch's *Design for Living* at an out-of-the-way-theater where, for good measure, I was convulsed to embarrassment by the Marx Brothers in *The Coconuts,* then utterly unavailable in the United States; it became clear during the projection that very few members of the audience understood English, since I was practically the only one laughing at most of

Groucho's jibes, just a third of which were translated—or translatable—in the French subtitles.

I was awakened to John Ford by the Sarris and *Cahiers* favorite *Young Mr. Lincoln,* seduced by the measured intensity of Kazan's *Wild River,* exhilarated by the Walsh of *Gentleman Jim,* drawn into the intrigues of directorial authorship by the Windust/Walsh *The Enforcer,* and disappointed by two pictures entirely out of circulation at home, Sturges's *The French They Are a Funny Race* and Hughes's *The Outlaw.* Wisely, I checked my auteurism at the door of the Cinematheque for a screening of a childhood favorite and scored major points with a young American woman I'd recently met who had been raised overseas and had never even heard of, much less seen, *The Wizard of Oz.*

But most avidly of all, I attended the Studio Action-Republique, a long-gone neighborhood theater that, during that spring, was running an epic series devoted to the American western. I had noted that quite a few westerns, and directors who specialized in them, rated very highly with Sarris. But since I had turned entirely off the genre at adolescence and had so much other ground to cover, I had placed other priorities first. But now, faced with the enormous opportunity of two or three different double bills per week, the time for discovery and reassessment had arrived: I simply had to dive in and find out who this fellow Budd Boetticher was, why the French were so cuckoo about *Johnny Guitar,* whether my childhood instincts about Anthony Mann were correct, see some Fuller films I had sort of avoided, and go deeper into Ford country.

The series was, in short, a revelation. I'm sure the experience of seeing *The Searchers, Man of the West, Buchanan Rides Alone,* and *Run of the Arrow* and so many others benefited in some small way from having occurred systematically in a French context, and with French subtitles to boot, rather than haphazardly in an American grind house; that the sense of physical and intellectual distance enabled me to appreciate values in the western that one can easily ignore at home, and which foreigners are sometimes in a better position to notice (I will also always remember the highly civilized practice of the Studio Action-Republique of posting a notice as to the quality of prints to be shown). My experience of this series in Paris, so far from the home I had been so anxious to escape, made me see the richness of, and poetry in, the western—just as Paris as seen through Sarris made me rediscover the American cinema.

The first time I met Andrew Sarris was when he delivered the inaugural address at the Pacific Film Archive in Berkeley in the early 1970s. Over the years, we have encountered each other occasionally, at film festivals and

critics meetings, but only once have we been able to sit down for a prolonged tete-a-tete. In June of 1997, Andy graciously agreed to participate in
a discussion I led at the Museum of Modern Art in connection with the
publication of my biography of Howard Hawks, and the day before, he invited me over to his apartment for a drink. Molly was away, and we spoke
for a couple of hours.

It's never easy to tell people, especially just acquaintances, how much
they and their work have meant to you, and it is more difficult still to make
someone understand that he has profoundly influenced you; when I attempted to do so that Sunday afternoon, with the sun beginning to descend
in the direction of the Guggenheim Museum outside of his westerly window, Andy briefly thanked me but quickly brushed my humble acknowl-
edgments aside, clearly discouraging further efforts in that direction. So it
will have to be here that I tell him that, had it not been for him, I would
never have experienced the cinema in the way that I did, would not have
had a model of scholarship as well as prose excellence in my chosen field,
and would not have embarked upon my book *Kings Of The Bs* directly out
of college, a tome that, as I stated in the introduction, was conceived entirely
as an extension of *The American Cinema* and was directly inspired by his
phrase "Eventually we must speak of everything if there is enough time and
space and printer's ink." There is every chance that, had Andrew Sarris never
existed, I never would have pursued my career as a film critic or would not
have in the same way.

Andy may have no idea how influential he has been, but very simply, in
my case, he taught me how to write about films by example and led me to
a career. It wouldn't have happened the way it did without him.

Part Seven

Sarris the Creator of
American Movie Culture

*M*ichael Wilmington notes that Andrew Sarris is one of the great "taste-shapers and list makers of our time: an extraordinarily valuable movie critic who, in his ornery, stubborn, wisecracking way, has probably done more than any of his colleagues to alert us to the wonder and magic of movies—and to encourage us to keep digging, seeking, and scratching for more. We are—and I wish more of us would admit it—powerfully in his debt." Sarris was "the critic who helped us to see movies as art, to understand how they could reflect a point of view, act as a window into the soul of the artist and the world outside. Without Sarris, many of us would still love movies—but we might be shyer of speaking about them, lazier about watching them."

Discussing Sarris's opponents, such as "Pauline Kael (in her famous and hilarious demolition job 'Circles and Squares'), . . . Dwight MacDonald, [and] John Simon," Wilmington notes that "of all the assaults on Sarris, only Kael's broadside remains worth reading—because she can still make us laugh." According to Wilmington, Kael's admirers paid her "the most perverse of compliments. Instead of wanting to seduce her back, they wanted to *become* her, to copy her rhythms, her tone, her voice, her tastes. Did they think she wanted nothing around her but human mirrors? (She would go along, I suspect—if not too enthusiastically—as long as they copied her tastes.) And none of them could really catch her literary persona. Imitating Pauline without matching her wit—which none of them could—was like trying to imitate Fred Astaire without knowing how to dance." Wilmington says that Sarris "inspired a different kind of mimicry. You never wanted to copy his writing style. It was too clearly his own and his alone. But once you were exposed to his perspective, you wanted, very simply, to find all the movies he had praised or canonized and sample them yourself."

In my essay "Sarris, Kael, and American Movie Culture," I contrast the contributions of Andrew Sarris and Pauline Kael to the making of a uniquely American movie culture. Despite long-time animosities, Sarris and Kael have shared several similarities, including cinematic taste. Lively and irreverent, Sarris and Kael established themselves as the preeminent exponents of a new literary genre, movie criticism. At various times, Kael and Sarris have been called the Katharine Hepburn and Spencer Tracy of criticism—for their (in)famously heated debates but also for making the profession sexy. Both Sarris and Kael showed vast knowledge of movie history, caustic wit, flair for the polemic, and a sophisticated style. They belong to a small group of intellectuals who have shaped American culture, entering the lives of cinephiles as representatives of a new way of life, one dominated by movies.

But though both are products of their times, they are important critics in different ways and for different reasons. Sarris's career was influenced by the European cinema, particularly the French New Wave. His acute awareness of developments in the international cinema led to the assimilation of new critical sensibilities into his perception of American movies. In contrast, Kael was always the more "American" critic, both in her pop culture orientation and in her emphasis on new American directors. If Kael was romantically energetic in discovering hot American talent, Sarris was a classicist in praising the work of gifted directors, both foreign and American.

Sarris and Kael flourished during the New American Cinema, a loosely structured movement that lasted for a decade (1967 to 1976) and saw the production of stylishly entertaining movies that could be enjoyed emotionally and intellectually. Under their influence, American movies began to be perceived as personal art works rather than assembly line products. Films were no longer evaluated in terms of their stories, but as art works whose visual style and mise-en-scène were more important than their contents. Writing with fresh viewpoint, witty candor, and heightened perspective, Sarris and Kael introduced new criteria of evaluation. However different their approaches were, they contrasted sharply with the middlebrow orientation of Bosley Crowther and other "realist" reviewers.

In "Circles, Squares, and Pink Triangles: Confessions of a Gay Cultist," scholar and writer Ed Sikov concurs with the other contributors that "the battles over auteurism waged between Kael and Andrew Sarris have long been over. Sarris won. The world takes auteurism so for granted today that nobody even sees it as a theory anymore; the legend has become fact, as it often does." For Sikov, "the Sarris–Kael debates . . . take on a more personal resonance." As he notes: "I confess I'm an ex-Kaelian. I really thought she was great when I was a teenager. But the more I saw onscreen, the more I loved; the more I read of Kael, the less I liked. As a film lover, it was Andrew Sarris who was my inspiration. Sarris opened my eyes to Hollywood, to the ethos of Howard Hawks, the spirituality of John Ford, the resonant brilliance of Hitchcock. And as a gay man, after a period of disappointment and necessary rage with my two critical mentors, I now know where I stand with both of them. I'm with Andrew all the way."

According to Sikov, "Calling Kael's *Rich and Famous* [review] 'homophobic' really fails to describe the sarcasm, desperation, and overt fag baiting. . . . While she is by no means the only major film critic to fall into this kind of sewer—the ever egregious John Simon once described a Broadway play as 'faggot nonsense'—Kael's literary stature, not to mention her clout among acolyte journalists, gave her remarks added weight and smell. . . . As gay critic Vito Russo put it in his landmark survey *The Celluloid Closet,* 'Almost every time Kael reviewed a film with a homosexual theme, she told about a gay friend; after a while it came to be something of a George and Gracie routine.' "

Sundance Festival's Geoffrey Gilmore, in "Auteur Theory and Independent Cinema," notes that decades after its introduction, "Sarris's scheme for reconsidering the American cinema still stirs controversy, misunderstanding, and debate. The 'auteur' theory, as it's popularly known, is too often simplistically understood as a system for prioritizing and privileging the contributions of directors to film. [But] it misses the real significance and point of Sarris's work. Written as a polemic to invite debate as to the nature of cinema and what constituted aesthetic quality, it has sparked contentious discussion that did indeed rehabilitate the reputations of certain Hollywood filmmakers and broaden the definitions and standards as to what constituted great film and/or film art. By focusing on the central coherence of directorial authorship, in opposition to the dominance of a producer working inside a Hollywood system that imposed its constricting determinants of commerce and bureaucracy, Sarris hoped to resuscitate the classic American film from the dustbin to which snobbish and high-minded critics had consigned it."

If the genesis of auteurism was a "response to the dismissive critique of a film universe defined as 'Hollywood,' then perhaps the film universe that is independent film' is generically its antithesis, that is, a system that is ostensibly creatively positive, supportive, and sympathetic. In typifying independent filmmaking as personal, artistic, even idiosyncratic and quirky, one seems to be almost defining an ideal 'system' for auteurs, one that enables the director to be fully in control, to reflect a personal aesthetic rather than just the effect of a 'personality.' "

Gilmore raises the provocative issue of whether the independent milieu is actually a supportive system: "The independent universe is clearly not a utopia, and in reality the biggest independent distributors take no more a laissez-faire attitude regarding their productions . . . than do the studios. . . . [But] the possibilities for making films that defy easy categorization, that are not limited to the boundaries of genre, and that depend on storytelling that is compelling because of the quality of its writing, its personal nature, and its visual style, is now largely the province of the independent sphere."

The Great Taste-Shaper

Michael Wilmington

$\mathcal{A}$ndrew Sarris is one of the great guides, taste-shapers, and list makers of our time: an extraordinarily valuable movie critic who, in his ornery, stubborn, wisecracking way, has probably done more than any of his colleagues to alert us to the wonder and magic of movies—and to encourage us to keep digging, seeking, and scratching for more. We are—and I wish more of us would admit it—powerfully in his debt.

Wonder and *magic* are words overburdened with sentimental misuse, but they're appropriate to Sarris, one of the most deviously sentimental and cynically warm of writers. Other Yank critics may have beguiled us with their sexy wit (Pauline Kael), stunned us with their poetics (James Agee), stimulated us with their crankiness (Manny Farber), delighted us with their erudition (Jonathan Rosenbaum), or overwhelmed us with their omnipresence (Roger Ebert). But Sarris, more than any of his comrades, really and substantially changed the way we look at films. He helped alter, too, the way moviemakers make them. Those changes, I would argue, were almost always for the better.

He was no small achievement either—the most eloquent spokesperson for that sometimes despised occupation or obsession: movie mania. As the longtime critic of the *Village Voice* and now of the *New York Observer,* he was, for thousands who followed him, the first key guide into the labyrinth of film history, the writer who helped make the most sense of it.

Most importantly of all, he was the critic who helped us to see movies as art: to understand how they could reflect a point of view, act as a window into the soul of the artist and the world outside. Without Sarris, many of us would still love movies—but we might be shyer of speaking about them, lazier about watching them.

229

If, for example, I tried to count up everything that I personally owe Sarris—and especially to his indispensable 1968 guidebook *The American Cinema* (a book that I read at exactly the right time, in my early twenties)—I would find myself so embarrassingly in his debt, I might be tempted into some quasi-filial revolt. One doesn't like to admit that one is carrying over ideas, tastes, and whole frames of reference learned long ago from another writer.

Would John Ford, Howard Hawks, Alfred Hitchcock, and Orson Welles now be so universally acknowledged and accepted as artists of the first rank if Sarris had not canonized them and others in his private pantheon—in *Film Culture* and then in *The American Cinema?* Would we bother to categorize film history in terms of directors? (Or even know most of their names?) Would we have spent so much time and effort seeking out the movies of Sarris, other pantheon directors (Griffith, Lubitsch, Keaton, Chaplin et al.)?

Would both academic film history and film preservation enjoy their vogue? Would we be as receptive to the individual styles of the post-1960s generation of moviemakers—both in America and abroad?

Or would we still remain quaintly lodged in the conventional wisdom of the once-dominant movie intelligentsia: corseted in that narrow conviction that the vast majority of American movies are dismissible, that movies are a debased art form of interest mainly to children, neurotics, and time-wasters (and humorists like S. J. Perelman), that only a handful of foreign directors (and almost none from Hollywood) are worth a thinking person's time? (Many of those notions now hold curious sway in the Groves of Modern Academe-spiffed up in latter-day jargon: dominant cinemall and semiotics, postmodernism and the gaze, Lacan's psychoanalysis and Althusser's philosophy. But how many people who love or make movies really give a damn?)

How important was Sarris? In the 1960s, he was absolutely crucial, though, ultimately, I suspect, that if Sarris had not been the bearer of news from the France of the 1950s, someone else would have done it later. We would have been somehow apprised of the tastes and ideas of the *Cahiers du Cinema* group that included Andre Bazin, Francois Truffaut, Jean-Luc Godard, Eric Rohmer, Claude Chabrol, and Jacques Rivette—and the whole band of Parisian outsiders and cinephiles that Greek director Theo Angelopoulos calls "The rats of the Cinematheque": the movie-crazy students of Cinematheque head Henri Langlois.

And whoever that other bearer would have been, he or she probably would have been trashed and trashed, as Sarris was in the early 1960s—not just by a younger Pauline Kael (in her famous and hilarious demolition job

"Circles and Squares") but by Dwight MacDonald, John Simon, and all the rest. Would he have stood up as well? (Of all the contemporary assaults on Sarris, only Kael's broadside remains worth reading—because she can still make us laugh.)

Nevertheless, the idea would have taken hold, as it did eventually all over the world—helping spark the cinematic new waves not just of France and America but of western and eastern Europe, Latin America, and Asia. Sarris helped start a universal dialogue. I can talk to critics from France, film actors from England, or film directors from Yugoslavia and find instantly that we have something in common—something that opens up discussions and whole worlds for us. It's the list of movies and moviemakers we all got from Andrew Sarris.

A more personal note. When Joe McBride and I, in our early twenties, wrote the book *John Ford,* which set us both off on our afterward separate critical careers—it was quite obviously *Sarris's* John Ford whom we were writing about, Sarris's general view of Ford we were explicating, and probably Sarris, and not Robin Wood, to whom that book should have been dedicated.

We had spent several years researching and writing *John Ford* in the tempestuous, riot-torn campus of the University of Wisconsin at Madison—where tear gas, broken windows, and chants of "Hell no, we won't go!" eventually became a constant background. It was a strange time to he writing about Ford—not least because we were both as opposed to the war as were most of our friends and fellow students (and as Ford himself, at the time, was publicly in favor of it). While we watched and analyzed *They Were Expendable, Sergeant Rutledge,* we also regularly observed massive civil disobedience, street fights, burnings, and sometimes almost nightly rioting.

We were both teargassed on several occasions. Joe covered most of the campus riots as a reporter for the *Wisconsin State Journal.* I watched them from the gray Volkswagen of our friend Steve Wonn, darting around town in the heat of battle.

It was a hellish time, wildly exciting and madly destructive by turns. In one hectic twenty-four-hour period—amazing to recall today—I saw *Belle de Jour* for the first time at the Playboy Theater in Chicago, lost my virginity in Evanston, Illinois, to a girl I met beneath the Playboy marquee, and witnessed both the Grant and Lincoln Park riots at the 1968 Chicago Democratic Convention.

Toward the close of that volcanic twenty-four hours, Steve Wonn, I, and his girlfriend Barbara Becker saw all of the famous Lincoln Park riot from the roof of the TV camera van at the intersection of Balbo and Michigan, parked right in front of the Conrad Hilton Hotel. We were bystanders who just climbed up on the van for a better view. The riot exploded in the street five minutes later, and the TV riot scenes, in fact, were shot right over our heads.

I can still remember that five-minute-long eruption of terror, brutality, and flight: the protestors being kicked and beaten only a yard or so away from us, the screams in the street, the crash of the Conrad Hilton windows, the cries of the TV cameramen begging us to get off the van (understandably terrified we would draw the police toward them)—and the help we suddenly got from one solitary cop, who hadn't joined in the beatings but who silently pointed his club toward Lincoln Park when we asked how to get away. (Joe right at that time was watching a Preston Sturges movie on TV elsewhere in Chicago, but he has always insisted that he can see a brief shot of me on the street in Haskell Wexler's *Medium Cool*.)

What we saw from the van roof was just what Ford always claimed as the goal of his own historical movies: "what really happened." But, in the midst of all that hair-raising violence (echoed almost every night by the bloodshed on TV's nightly news), John Ford often seemed, to most of the Madison people around us, as much a relic of the past as D. W. Griffith and *The Birth of a Nation.*

The stereos screamed with The Doors, Bob Dylan's "Blonde on Blonde," and The Rolling Stones' "Beggars' Banquet." And the cinematic heroes and icons tended to be Bergman, Fellini, Antonioni, *Bonnie and Clyde, The Graduate,* Jean-Luc Godard, *Z, M*A*S*H, The Battle of Algiers,* and *Easy Rider.* Ford movies—especially the cavalry pictures like *Fort Apache* or *She Wore a Yellow Ribbon*—would be jeered at during public showings. Student audiences who knew of the massacres at My Lai and Kent State almost always saw a continuum between John Wayne's movie cavalry and the U.S. war machine.

Even worse, we had to research our book—and discover the glories of Ford—under hurried or less-than-ideal conditions: at showings of the Wisconsin Film Society, private screenings at Film Incorporated's Skokie, Illinois, offices, or, most shamefully of all, on TV, chewed up by commercials.

Almost everything pushed us culturally away from Ford. Without Sarris—or his passionate advocacy of the then largely unacknowledged classic *The Searchers*—we might not have bothered, might not have traveled all the way to Chicago, to catch a Clark Theater retrospective showing of *The Searchers:* the first time for either of us. We wouldn't have sought out all his other movies or studied them obsessively.

It was, as they say, an epic experience—and one we owed largely to Sarris. He was, at the time, the quintessential Fordian. And while he was influencing us, he was also, almost certainly, inspiring the young generation of

New York and Los Angeles moviemakers (Scorsese, Lucas, Spielberg, Schrader, and others), who would afterward proclaim *The Searchers* as a primary influence.

So, why didn't we acknowledge our great debt? Robin Wood—then a primary *Movie Magazine* writer and author of numerous perceptive and gracefully written auteurist director monographs of Hitchcock, Hawks, Penn, Bergman, and others—was my idea. Joe pushed for John Wayne. Unhappily, I prevailed. So we shoved Duke to the side and gave Sarris a high acknowledgment—and another for Britain's major Ford champion ex–*Sequence* and *Sight and Sound* critic and film director Lindsay Anderson.

I am not proud of this today. Had we somehow split the dedication between John Ford's main American and British champions, we would have been truer to our influences. And we might have spared ourselves decades of sniping from Lindsay Anderson, who probably wouldn't have liked our book any better but might have refrained from trashing us—and Sarris and *The Searchers*—at so many opportunities.

Do I still feel the same way about John Ford? Yes and no. If Joe and I were to revise or update the book, I would vote to cover many more middle-period films, especially *Judge Priest, The Prisoner of Shark Island, Young Mr. Lincoln, The Long Voyage Home, How Green Was My Valley,* and *The Grapes of Wrath. Grapes,* which Sarris low-rates, is now my choice for one of Ford's four or five best.

But to talk about these differences of opinion is to underscore how minor they really are. Before Sarris, Ford's art was regarded as a single high mesa or two rising plaintively above a desert of Hollywood bondage (where he was a prisoner). How wrong were all those detractors who felt he never made a good movie after *The Quiet Man* (or even, perhaps, after *The Grapes of Wrath*). And how right was Sarris, who defended him all the way up to *Seven Women.*

If Sarris hadn't held up a beacon—for Ford and many other filmmakers—would Joe and I have so stubbornly followed him? Probably not.

As the great champion of individual expression and artistry in mass filmmaking, Sarris has always been a guide to the infinite *variety* of movie pleasure. Rather than fixating on some smaller, more specific (political, iconographic, or literary) subset, he's one of those personalities—and critics—who encourage you to devour it all: someone who won't settle for half measures, who tries to embrace everything, understand everything.

Someone who makes lists.

Perhaps that's what most infuriated his early detractors: that the Sarris of the early years of *The Village Voice* and the old *Film Culture* seemed

capable of reducing all of Hollywood history to a series of lists and rankings—with whimsical category titles like "The Far Side of Paradise," "Expressive Esoterica," and "Less Than Meets the Eye." In his early years at
Film Culture and the *Village Voice,* he was a master list maker, ranking all the
movies he'd seen in any given year in order of personal preference: thousands of movies all pinned in their particular place, hundreds of directors
all labeled and ranked. That certainty is part of what maddened his early
detractors—some of whom tended to see auteurism as a critical equivalent
to Rosicrucianism, Satanism, or a belief that the world is flat.

But that's the special appeal of *The American Cinema.* It presents you
with categories, hierarchies, guideposts. Armed with that little book, you can
go out and start watching movies, discovering old directors—and new
ones—yourself.

Now, to the average film critic of the 1960s, and a few of the very best
(I'm thinking of both Kael and MacDonald), Sarris's all-inclusiveness was absurd—as much, I suspect, because of the fact that his list indicated he'd seen
all those movies. And since Sarris praised so highly films that many of his
most intelligent colleagues had decided in advance, weren't worth the trouble—movies with titles like *Kiss Me Deadly, Johnny Guitar, Angel Face, Bringing Up Baby, The Naked Spur, The Phoenix City Story, The Rise and Fall of Legs
Diamond, Hell is for Heroes,* and *Leave Her to Heaven*—they had a double motive in deriding him. How much easier it is to be an expert in cinema if cinema consists only of, say, twelve or fifteen films a year.

Indeed, *National Review* critic John Simon once bashed Sarris and his
ilk (Kael included) as cinematic lowbrows, precisely because he believed they
saw too many movies. (I'm torn myself between thinking the professionally
grouchy Simon sees too few movies—and that he doesn't see few enough.)

Sarris triumphed over his early critics, even winning a few of them over.
(I suspect there's no bad blood today between him and Kael.) But there's one
thing that I've never understood: Why did he seemingly abandon his project
in midstream? Why didn't he offer up regular revisions and additions to *The
American Cinema*—if not yearly, then, at least, every five or ten years?

By not doing so, by never trying to categorize the directors and movies
that came out after 1967, he relinquished his own powerful influence. Kael
and others rushed into the breach, creating pantheons of their own.

Was it because the American cinema of the Vietnam era was too con-
fusing for him, too fragmented or wrenchingly divided? Was he less eager to
lay himself on the line with later movies? Or did he simply relax after winning his earlier bloody critical battles? Whatever the reason, the contribution
of *The American Cinema*—even if you disagree with sections of it—remains

huge and growing, even as Sarris found himself, in some cases, shunted aside or underappreciated.

It's sometimes easy, unfortunately, to underappreciate him. When I first read Andrew Sarris, I was a college freshman at the University of Wisconsin. I wasn't bowled over at first sight—as I was, for example, on my encounter the same year with a piece by Pauline Kael (on *Hud*) in *Film Quarterly*. Back then, I thought Kael (not to mention MacDonald, my teen favorite) the superior writer because her sexiness and humor and self-revealing frankness were turn-ons. My experience, I think, was similar to that of many others. You didn't read Kael so much as find yourself seduced and swept away by her. Many critics have never gotten over that first mad crush.

Oddly, Kael's admirers paid her the most perverse of compliments. Instead of wanting to seduce her back, they wanted to *become* her, to copy her rhythms, her tone, her voice, her tastes. Did they think she wanted nothing around her but human mirrors? (She would go along, I suspect—if not too enthusiastically—as long as they copied her tastes.) And none of them could really catch her literary persona. Imitating Pauline without matching her wit—which none of them could—was like trying to imitate Fred Astaire without knowing how to dance.

Sarris inspired a different kind of mimicry. You never wanted, especially, to copy his writing style. It was too clearly his own and his alone. But once you were exposed to his perspective on the American films of the silent and early sound era, you wanted, very simply, to find all the movies he had praised or canonized and sample them yourself.

Once you did that, you inevitably found him one of the most reliable of all guides to that golden period: perceptive, eloquent, indefatigable, and generous. He fulfilled a critic's highest function: drawing you to the best works in his field and helping you experience them more deeply and intensely. Having done that, he supplied a framework with which you could go on seeking out the best for yourself.

It was unnecessary to agree with him on everything to learn from him. I took strong exception, and do now, to his views on some of my own personal favorites (especially Billy Wilder, Elia Kazan, David Lean, and John Huston, all relegated then to his most dubious and debatable category: "Less Than Meets the Eye"). But, disagree with him as much as you wanted to, you could still apply Sarris's ideas about directorial expression and overall career evaluations even to artists he himself didn't like or actually underrated— like Stanley Kubrick, John Cassavetes, or Sam Peckinpah.

The tastes Sarris helped foster and spread were not all original with him. Probably, he inherited many of them from the rats of the Cinematheque. But it was Sarris who distilled them, packaged them, made them approachable—brought them to the United States. Every critic who has raked over all these filmmakers and their acknowledged classics ever since then knows very well—whatever he or she says—that it was Sarris who ushered most of them into our theater of opinion.

Another personal note: Sarris himself is the subject of one of the most amazingly and painfully personal volumes ever written about a movie critic: wife Molly Haskell's *Love and other Infectious Diseases,* a sometimes hair-raising account of his serious illness and slow recovery in the 1980s. (Uncommented on by Haskell: his disgraceful final treatment by the then-editors of the *Village Voice,* who didn't even grant him a decent farewell column.) Illnesses—like the one suffered recently and unhappily by his old antagonist and now colleague Pauline Kael—are the mettle-testing tragedies of the middle-class celebrity. But when I met him and his wife, they didn't act like a couple returned from the damned. They were, instead, kind and considerate, not self-absorbed.

I've met Sarris only rarely—usually at the yearly meetings of the National Society of Film Critics at the Algonquin Hotel banquet room, where he—and, before her retirement, Kael—were regular, weighty, and not necessarily antagonistic presences. But encountering Sarris changes your slant on him. When you read him, among the things that you note are his puns, his passion, and his percussive alliteration. When you meet him, what you may notice most strongly are his sweetly avuncular smile and the great gloomy eyes that rise above it.

I'm always struck by that duality: geniality touched by melancholy. Between the upper and lower halves of Sarris's face, sometimes there's such a split that it's as if the masks of tragedy and comedy were combined in a single expression.

In a way, they are. And in his writing, too.

Because of that, Sarris at his peak remains the best of guides. He encourages you to seek out the tragedy *and* comedy of the movies—and everything else they have to offer as well. That's one of his best qualities: the way he stimulates us not just to think about movies, but to see them, and seek them out.

Without him, most of us would probably perceive American movie history—and the rest of the world's as well—in a much different way. We might not just have missed or underrated *The Searchers, Vertigo,* and *To Have and Have Not,* but also *Trouble in Paradise, They Live by Night, Broken Blossoms,* and *Sunrise.*

All of Orson Welles after *The Magnificent Ambersons* (or maybe even *Citizen Kane*) might be a fading archival memory. And names like Budd Boetticher, Jacques Tourneut, Douglas Sirk, and Edgar Ulmer—only an strange rumor. (Who cares, in the end, if Sarris low-rated a Lean, a Huston, a Wilder, or a Kazan? They weren't exactly nonentities. Nor were they, in the long run, vulnerable.)

Without Sarris, we might still see Hollywood's first five decades as many of Sarris's critical predecessors did (and as those anti-Sarris, pro-psychoanalytic academics often do today): as a popular media factory mass producing bastard works for undiscriminating audiences, coughing up art rarely and unreliably.

Our lives would be poorer.

Andrew Sarris himself would probably scoff at the claim, but it seems obvious to me that, of all American movie critics in our century, his influence has proven the most lasting, deep, and beneficial to his fellow critics and to moviemaking itself.

Does that praise seem extravagant? It shouldn't. Anyone should recognize clearly that without Sarris—derided in his early career, perhaps overly institutionalized later on—our entire concept of movie appreciation would be quite different. And that goes not just for movie critics but the smartest audiences and many of the best American moviemakers as well.

Without his lists, and with no Cinematheque of our own to educate or inspire us, we would have been on our own.

We owe him everything. And if that seems too much, we owe him, at the very least, the Pantheon, Expressive Esoterica, and The Far Side of Paradise.

Sarris, Kael, and
American Movie Culture

Emanuel Levy

It's time to recognize publicly what we have known for a long, long time: Andrew Sarris is the most influential film critic in American film history. When people talk about movie criticism in the 1960s and 1970s, they single out two seminal figures: Sarris and Pauline Kael. However, no critic, not even Kael, has changed the very way we perceive and talk about movies as much as Sarris. Sarris's profound impact on the film world is by now established. At the same time, one can't understand the emergence of American movie culture without including Kael's role. Singly and jointly, Sarris and Kael have contributed to the formation of a uniquely American movie culture. How did it happen? Neither Sarris nor Kael have published their memoirs, but since both have engaged in a more subjective mode of reviewing, their essays contain quite a few personal observations.

Lively and irreverent, Sarris and Kael established themselves as the preeminent exponents of a new literary genre, movie criticism. At various times, Kael and Sarris have been called the Katharine Hepburn and Spencer Tracy of criticism—for their heated debates, but also for making the profession sexy. Despite longtime animosities, Sarris and Kael share many attributes in common. Both showed vast knowledge of movie history, caustic wit, flair for the polemic, and a sophisticated style. Their passionate commitment to film was never questioned, even when they dismissed movies that were praised by other critics. Sarris and Kael belong to a small group of intellectuals who have shaped American culture, entering the lives of cinephiles as representatives of a new way of life, one dominated by movies.

Born in 1919, Kael is older than Sarris (born in 1928), but she began writing at about the same time, in the early 1950s. Sarris became the associate editor of *Film Culture* in 1955, a position he held for a decade. After managing two art houses in Berkeley and broadcasting radio shows, Kael achieved national prominence when her first collection of reviews, *I Lost It at the Movies,* became a bestseller in 1965. Sarris's seminal book, *The American Cinema: Directors and Directions,* was published in 1968, the same year that Kael's *Kiss Kiss Bang Bang* came out. Both Sarris and Kael were at the height of their fame and power in the 1960s and 1970s.

Both Sarris and Kael are still bemused by the serendipitous drift of their lengthy careers. Though both are products of their times, they were important critics in different ways and for different reasons. Sarris's career was influenced by the European cinema, particularly the French New Wave (Jean-Luc Godard, Francois Truffaut, Eric Rohmer, Alain Resnais). His acute awareness of developments in the international cinema led to the assimilation of new critical sensibilities into his perception of American movies. In contrast, Kael was always the more "American" critic, both in her pop culture orientation and in her emphasis on new American directors. If Kael was romantically energetic in discovering hot American talent, Sarris was a classicist in praising the work of gifted directors, both foreign and American.

THE MAKING OF AN AMERICAN AUTEURIST

A product of the depression, Sarris was born to a poor Greek-American family in Queens. Moviegoing was an integral part of his childhood, as he recalled: "Whenever dinner was done, we all ventured out to one movie house or another, and nothing that was showing on the marquee could deter us from entering. Since we almost always came in at the middle of one or the other film that was part of the double feature, there would come that inevitable moment when one of us would nudge the other with the familiar get-up and-go gesture signifying, 'This is where we came in.'"

Sarris never questioned the wisdom that "once you knew how the plot came out, there was no reason to sit through a movie to the end a second time. And it made even less sense to go back on another occasion to see the movie again. Aside from the wasteful extravagance of such an action, there was a feeling that movies were to be consumed like food. Once a movie was seen, it was somehow 'used up,' and 'old' movies were as discredited for viewing as cars in a junkyard were for driving."

By his own admission, Sarris owed his career to Jonas Mekas, editor of *Film Culture:* "Mekas brought me to the pages of *Film Culture* in 1955, and allowed me to pinchhit for him in his movie column in a new Greenwich

Village publication called *The Village Voice,* while he was shooting his film, *Guns of the Trees.* " Sarris's first *Village Voice* review appeared on the stands on August 11, 1960—the film was Hitchcock's *Psycho.* His "high-flown auteurist" critique received so much hate mail that *Village Voice* editor Dan Wold, publisher Ed Fancher, and arts editor Jerry Tallmer were favorably impressed by his ability to stir up controversy.

In his foreword to *Confessions of a Cultist,* Sarris observed: "I was the beneficiary as well as the victim of the intellectual vacuum that occurred in movie reviewing with the death of James Agee in 1955," the year in which the first issue of *Film Culture* came out. Sarris had been studying film in an evening course at Columbia, "between meandering through graduate English and malingering in Teachers College." He got his start as a reviewer and editor without pay at the age of twenty-seven.

The *Film Culture* group represented a different breed of critics. "The cultural rationale for our worthier predecessor—Agee, Ferguson, Levin, Murphy, Sherwood—was that they were too good to be reviewing movies. We, on the contrary, were not considered much good for anything else." What they lacked in prestige, however, they made up for in their passionate love for film. Wrote Sarris: "Whereas the late James Agee discovered cinema through his love for movies, too many of his self-proclaimed successors chose to abuse movies in the name of *Kultur.* " In the 1950s, critics appeared to be of two kinds: "journalistic reviewers who would be equally happy in the real estate departments of their publications, and highbrow humanists who admired *From Caligari to Hitler,* because they, like Kracauer, were more interested in Hitler than Caligari."

Years later, Sarris recalled that, "as a provincial outerborough ethnic, a bridge-and-tunnel person before my time, I was ill-prepared for the Manhattan spotlight, even though I had done my year in Paris at the crest of the nouvelle vague, had worked briefly for Mary Meerson and Henri Langlois at the Cinematheque Francais, and had attended the 1961 Cannes Film Festival, where I rediscovered Luis Bunuel through *Viridiana.* "

As the American pioneer of auteurism, Sarris devoted his career to disseminating its ideas. Auteurism is still associated with his name, having written what's considered to be "the Bible of Auteurism." Sarris's inspiration derived from Truffaut's seminal essay in the January 1954 issue of *Cahiers du Cinéma,* "Une certaine tendance du cinema français," in which "La politique des auteurs" was born as a rebuke to the French Tradition of Quality. Auteur criticism pointed to the potential tension between the director's vision and the means at his disposal for realizing it: studio pressures, genre conventions, star demands, story requirements. Auteurists felt that because of Hollywood's industrial–commercial nature, genuine film artists often came through the back door.

The publication of "Notes on the Auteur Theory" in 1962 prompted a (in)famous attack by Kael. Years later, Sarris, quoting Mario Puzo's remark after the success of *The Godfather,* said: "If I'd known so many people would read it, I'd have written it better." Actually, very few people read "Notes"— fewer, in fact, than those who read Kael's rebuttal. Nonetheless, the essay propelled Sarris from obscurity to notoriety, and for a while, as he observed, "I was a pariah among members of the cultural establishment."

In a matter of a few years, Sarris was vindicated by the widespread revaluation of unfashionable directors, such as Hitchcock and Hawks. He stage-managed an honorary degree for Hitchcock from Columbia University and defied the conventional decline-and-fall wisdom on Josef von Sternberg and John Ford with books exalting these old masters. Sarris's work took place during the new cinematic age of Fellini, Bergman, and Antonioni, whom he also admired, though never as unreservedly as his peers. As Sarris put it: "While Woody Allen was genuflecting before Bergman, Paul Mazursky before Fellini, and Mike Nichols before Antonioni, I was writing the first serious American monograph on Howard Hawks, influenced by Jacques Rivette's analysis in *Cahiers du Cinéma.*"

From its inception, auteurism was meant to be more pragmatic than Platonic. As Sarris noted: "All we young revisionist critics knew was that there were a great many good movies from the past in danger of being dumped in the dustbin of film history by an assortment of realist and Marxist historians. When we found a cluster of good movies linked by the same director, a hypothetical auteur was postulated, and the search began for an individual theme and style." Sarris insisted that auteur theory was the first rather than last stop of film analysis, but, as he later noted, "Fortunately, no one believed me, and I came to be regarded, in the late Dwight MacDonald's memorable phrase, 'a Godzilla monster clambering from the depths.'"

What brought Sarris into the critical mainstream was "The American Cinema" issue of *Film Culture,* in the spring of 1963, with its directorial chronology from 1915 to 1962 and a cover of the gloomy-looking Goldwyn Girls on a circular platform in an ancient Roman slave market from Frank Tuttle's *Roman Scandals.* Sarris had nothing to do with this outrageous Busby Berkeley metaphor for Hollywood directors enslaved by the studio system, but he was universally praised for his wonderful sense of humor.

One of Sarris's breakthroughs in terms of critical credibility came with his rave review of Richard Lester's *A Hard Day's Night* in the *Village Voice,* in 1964: "My high-brow embrace of the Beatles at this comparatively early date brought me a new kiddie-car constituency, and a great many raised eyebrows among the literati." Years later, when Sarris was hospitalized, the nurses were impressed to realize that he has become a clue in Trivial Pursuit: Who is the critic who described *A Hard Day's Night* as "the *Citizen Kane* of juke-box movies"?

KAEL'S RISE TO PROMINENCE

Kael published her first review, an appraisal of Chaplin's *Limelight,* which she called "Slimelight," in 1953. Her subsequent work appeared in *Sight and Sound, Partisan Review, Film Culture, Moviegoer,* and *Film Quarterly.* From 1955 to the 1960s, Kael managed the Berkeley Cinema Guild theaters, the country's first art houses, where she revived films by W. C. Fields, Mae West, and Busby Berkeley. In ten years, Kael earned less than two thousand dollars from film criticism, supplementing her income by working as a seamstress, cook, and textbook ghostwriter.

Kael's fortune changed overnight in 1965, when Atlantic Monthly–Little Brown published *I Lost It at the Movies,* which became the first bestselling volume of film criticism. Brash and acerbic, the book placed Kael in the forefront of American critics. In this volume, she praised such foreign films as *Grand Illusion, Shoeshine,* and *Forbidden Games,* but also American films like *Hud.* In what became one of her more personal essays, "Hud: Deep in the Divided Heart of Hollywood," Kael linked the film's values to her own experience, placing Hud's ranch up against her childhood on the farm and describing her father as both charitable and a whoremonger. Kael unmasked the ways that her friends misunderstood the film's ethics, alluding to her father's infidelities to suggest that Hud could be an adulterer and a good man too. Her agenda was to refute the charge of the *New York Times*'s Bosley Crowther that Hud was evil because he committed adultery. Kael's review of *Hud* broke grounds and exerted tremendous influence on a younger generation of critics.

In 1965, Kael was fired from *McCall's* for panning *The Sound of Music,* of which she wrote: "Wasn't there perhaps one little Von Trapp who didn't want to sing his head off, or who screamed that he wouldn't act out little glockenspiel routines for Papa's party guests, or who got nervous and threw up if he had to get out on a stage?" "I had realized that I would sock the ladies right between the ears," she later told *Newsweek,* "but what the hell is the point of writing, if you're writing banality."

In one of her fundamental essays, "Trash, Art and the Movies," Kael claimed that people enjoy movies because they lack the good intentions and moral uplift extolled by schoolteachers and other upholders of establishment culture. "Movie art," she insisted, "is not the opposite of what we have always enjoyed in movies, it is not to be found in a return to that official high culture, it is what we have always found good in movies. It's the subversive gesture carried further, the moments of excitement sustained longer and extended into new meanings."

THE NEW AMERICAN MOVIE CULTURE

Sarris and Kael flourished during—and benefited from—the New American Cinema, a loosely structured movement that lasted for a decade (1967 to 1976) and saw the production of stylishly entertaining movies that could be enjoyed emotionally and intellectually. The directors of that era—Arthur Penn, Mike Nichols, Robert Altman, Francis Ford Coppola, Martin Scorsese, Steven Spielberg—regarded themselves as artists; in the studio system, most directors were perceived as craftsman. These filmmakers adopted the formal devices of the New Wave—fractured narrative, freeze-frame, slow motion—never before seen on the American screen. Their innovations and self-awareness represented a radical break from Hollywood's classic paradigms.

Film criticism underwent changes, too. Under Sarris's and Kael's influence, American movies began to be perceived as personal artworks rather than assembly line products. In 1966, as charter members of the National Society of Film Critics, Sarris, Kael, and several others created an association to counter the middlebrow sensibility of the New York Film Critics Circle, whose tastes were deemed too similar to those of the Academy and its Oscar Awards. The goal of the National Society was to recognize the year's best films "without distinction of nationality." Indeed, the first movies cited by the National Society were Antonioni's *Blow Up* (1966), two Bergman masterpieces, *Persona* and *Shame* (1967 and 1968, respectively), and Rohmer's *Claire's Knee* (1971). No wonder the Society was accused of snobbery toward Hollywood, of being "too avant-garde" in favoring European art films over commercial American movies.

The publication of Kael's *New Yorker* review of *Bonnie and Clyde* demonstrated the immense power critics could exert on audiences—and on the industry. A new generation of critics began to write for major publications: The *New York Times* appointed Vincent Canby, who formerly wrote for *Variety*, as its chief critic in 1968. In the same year, Sarris's magnum opus, *The American Cinema*, changed the direction of film criticism. Films were no longer evaluated in terms of their stories, but as artworks whose visual style and mise-en-scène were more important than their contents. Writing with fresh viewpoint, witty candor, and heightened perspective, Sarris and Kael introduced new criteria of evaluation. However different their approaches were, they contrasted sharply with the middlebrow "realist" orientation of Bosley Crowther, who was the *New York Times* critic for twenty-five years. Both Sarris and Kael were eager to show their rapport with younger audiences and the New Hollywood, a trend that became clear when Bob Rafelson's *Five Easy Pieces* won Best Picture from the New York Film Critics Circle.

Both Sarris and Kael wrote for powerful publications. It's doubtful that either would have provoked such extreme reactions without the base they shared at their magazines: Kael at the highbrow *New Yorker* and Sarris at the hip downtown weekly, the *Village Voice*. Arguably no American magazine had the clout of the *New Yorker* at its prime, which represented every writer's dream with its minimal editorial interference and high pay. The latitude given by the *New Yorker* to its writers brought out the best in them.

As Louis Menand pointed out, Kael joined the *New Yorker* at a time when movies suddenly caught up with the rest of American culture, when movies seemed to mean a great deal to people. The *New Yorker* made it possible for its readers to feel that antisophistication was the true mark of sophistication. Kael's challenge was to make popular culture respectable for people whose education told them it was not. Kael succeeded in disarming her readers' phobias against both low and high culture. She was also effective in teaching readers how to think critically about movies without the need of special training or academic jargon. For better or for worse, Kael's manner of appreciating movies became the standard of criticism in America.

As for Sarris, it's improbable that his ideas would have spread so quickly had he not become critic for the *Village Voice*. The *New Yorker* and the *Village Voice* implied both mainstream and highbrow acceptance. It was significant that Sarris and Kael were brought from the outside, as Sarris once observed: "Both Pauline and I were outsiders, we were provincial, we were sort of screwballs." This outsiderness gave both of them a large measure of intellectual freedom.

Sarris's and Kael's colleagues, Stanley Kauffman and John Simon, wrote for smaller magazines, the *New Republic* and the *National Review,* respectively. Simon was never taken seriously as a movie critic; he was always considered more of a theater critic. This was a result of the magazine for which he wrote but also of a snobbish style that, while fun to read, didn't illuminate much the movies he discussed. Unlike Kauffman, who considered film to be aesthetically interesting only when it was thematically interesting, Sarris and Kael drew no line between the varieties of film seriousness. They had no inherent prejudice against American movies just because they had mass appeal. Sarris could—and did—endorse a John Wayne western with the same enthusiastic passion as a deconstructive Godard meditation, a Rohmer romantic comedy, or a Truffaut melodrama.

In 1968, Kael published *Kiss Kiss Bang Bang,* whose title was meant to capture in "the briefest statement imaginable" movies' basic appeal. The volume included reviews; essays on Marlon Brando, Orson Welles, and Stanley Kramer; and a piece about the making of Sidney Lumet's *The Group,* which she saw as a paradigm of Hollywood's corrupt moviemaking. In this book, Kael showed her fascination with amateurish sociology, which included tentative projections about the filmmakers' intents as well as efforts to predict audience response to movies in terms of the zeitgeist. Joe Morgenstern singled out in *Newsweek* the ingredients of Kael's approach: "She has a way of mixing together the film, her attitudes toward it, the audience's attitude toward it, and her attitude toward the audience."

Unlike Kael, Sarris emphasized form rather than contents, based on his feeling that humanist–realist critics such as Bosley Crowther and Siegfried Kracauer talked too much about ideas but not enough about style. There was need to redress the balance, to end the prevailing stylistic illiteracy among critics. At the same time, for Sarris, sheer technique never transcended conviction, and visual style was never an end in itself; style cannot be defended except as it relates to directorial sensibility. Any visual style can be reproduced, but without the linkage to directorial vision or personality, the effect is mechanical.

Sarris's aesthetic approach was dominated by two European concepts: montage and mise-en-scène. "Normally, montage is merely a fancy synonym for editing or cutting, but Eisenstein gave montage a mystique by linking it to the philosophical processes of dialectical materialism." For Sarris, montage tends to subordinate ideas to rhythm, to overemphasize the value of editing. He appreciated the montages of Eisenstein and Alain Resnais in *Hiroshima Mon Amour* and *Last Year at Marienbad,* but he also argued that the best moments in *Birth of a Nation* occur when Lillian Gish and Henry B. Walthall reveal the "visual subtleties of screen acting in front of a static, unblinking camera." Sarris pointed out that most movies opted for mise-en-scène, developing a dramatic style of expression to enhance audience identification with star personalities.

Precise definitions of mise-en-scène (and film direction) proved to be more problematic, however. For Sarris, it includes all the means available to a director to express his attitude toward his subject: the camera angle and distance, camera movement, pacing, the guidance of actors and their placement in the frame. Film direction was deemed a contemplative act that reveals the director's emotional attitude toward his material.

Since the term *mise-en-scène* comes from the theater, it "defends the theatricality of the cinema." As developed by Andre Bazin, Alexander Astruc, and Robert Leenhardt, the concept stressed pictorial values instead of the rhythmic flow of images. Through the use of long takes and deep-focus—in which characters are kept in the same frame instead of being shown alternately through cutting—the filmmaker creates a world that's psychologically and spatially coherent.

Sarris wrote: "Mise en scène emphasizes the content of a frame rather than the relationship of one frame to the next. Mise-en-scène believes in a cinema that records something that already exists. Mise-en-scene as an attitude tends to accept the cinema as it is and enjoy it for what it is—a sensuous conglomeration of all the other arts. But mise-en-scène, like montage, has been carried to an extreme. If montage implies the fragmentation of the world, mise-en-scène implies the unity of the world. If extreme uses of montage are too jazzy for the meanings they seek to express, extreme emphases on mise-en-scene result in sheer boredom."

APPROACH TO CRITICISM

Both Sarris and Kael perceived movie criticism as a weird way to make a living. Said Sarris: "Every critic is part show-off: the opportunity to mouth off at someone else's expense and at no risk to themselves. People seldom question the sincerity of a pan, but they are eternally suspicious of raves."

Sarris believed that critics' primary role is to transmit to readers their knowledge of and enthusiasm for movies. This was his reason for approaching criticism intuitively rather than systematically: "American criticism, like American cinema, is eminently pragmatic and anti-theoretical." As for critical priorities, Sarris said: "First, I look for genius, then for talent, then for charm, then for trends. What I do is subordinate myself to the art. The art means more than the artist." The function of film critics is to try to understand what the artist is doing and what he is feeling and how he is conveying it. Sarris understood that film was not a mass art in the way that soap operas or pop music is. Holding that a critic should investigate what worthy efforts are being unjustly neglected, he noted: "I would rather spend my time in search of sleepers regardless of their low costs and unbankable casts," by way of quoting Adlai Stevenson: "I would rather light a small candle than curse the darkness."

Despite different agendas, Kael provided a similar definition: "The role of the critic is to help people see what is in the work, what is in it that shouldn't be, what is not in it that could be. A good critic helps people understand more about the work than they could see for themselves. He is a great critic if by his understanding and feeling for the work, by his passion, he can excite people so that they want to experience more of the art that is there waiting to be seized. He is not necessarily a bad critic if he makes errors in judgment (infallible taste is inconceivable; what could it be measured against?). He is a bad critic if he does not awaken the curiosity, enlarge the interests and understanding of his audience."

Presenting herself as unsophisticated and down-to-earth, Kael cherished a feisty style that aimed at shocking readers. She considered James Agee and Robert Warshow the best American critics because they approached film in a personal way. In her review of *Morgan—A Suitable Case for Treatment,* Kael observed: "It's part of the function of a movie critic to indicate the difference between a bad movie that doesn't matter, because it's so much like other bad movies, and a bad movie that matters (*The Chase, The Wild Angels*), because it affects people strongly in new, different ways. And if it be said that this is sociology, not aesthetics, the answer is that an aesthetician who gave his time to criticism of current movies would have to be an awful fool. Movie criticism to be of any use whatever must go beyond formal analysis—which in movies is generally a disguised form of subjective reaction to meanings and implications anyway."

Sarris's and Kael's contention that "serious" movies should meet the same standards as pulp became widely adopted. Kael rationalized that people may have a hard time deciding whether or not something is art, but they're rarely fooled into thinking they're having a good time when they are not. She therefore devoted a lifetime to according commercial films the status of popular art. But cherishing pop culture didn't mean Kael perceived herself as a consumer guide: "Reviewing the perfect nothing of a movie is rather degrading: It's like giving consumer hints on the latest expensive but worthless gift for the person who has everything."

Kael altered forever the function—and prestige—of movie critics. Positing herself as a player in the filmmaking process, she demanded to be taken seriously. Sarris noted quite rightly that "Pauline makes herself the center of her piece, making it the job of the filmmaker to astonish her." This may explain why Kael's readers could enjoy her reviews for their own sake, without even seeing the films she was writing about.

Kael rejected the view of critics as objective arbiters of taste who judge art according to accepted standards; such an approach would make movies distant and disconnected from life. What mattered most was the immediate, sensory experience of movies, hence her motto: "My initial responses are probably my deepest and most honest ones." Kael showed how audiences could use movies to make sense of the world. A sociological critic, she held that "the most a critic can do is to try to understand the audience responses and maybe enlarge them a teeny bit." As Elliot Fremont-Smith wrote, Kael's method was "relating movies to other experience, to ideas and attitudes, to ambition, books, money, other movies, to politics and the evolving culture, to moods of the audience, to our sense of ourselves—to what movies do to us."

Sarris criticized the sociological approach for its emphasis on contents rather than style, realizing that it takes better critics to do sociological than aesthetic criticism; it was easier to say whether a movie is good or bad than to assess its impact on the audience. Unlike Kael, who tried to integrate the public's view into her criticism, Sarris claimed that critics can never be sure of what specific signals viewers will get from a movie.

Like Kael, Sarris opined that critics need knowledge about areas out-side cinema, such as psychology, sociology, politics. His problem with sociology was not that it should not be done, but that it has been done simplistically. Sociological criticism required a more subtle approach than grouping together a bunch of films, analyzing their plots, and deducing generalizations about their values. Sarris also rejected the obvious formulation of conspiracy theory, according to which Hollywood was "consciously doing things to or against its audience." If some movies have greater impact on audiences than others, it's because certain values that are more convincing or acceptable come to the fore.

Sarris was against theories that stressed film's relation to reality based on the camera's capacity to duplicate fragments of the real world. Auteur criticism was a reaction against sociological criticism, which enthroned the what against the how, ignoring aesthetic concerns. In the 1980s, Sarris himself acknowledged the need for a more complete critical approach that will bring back sociology in a more subtle way.

Kael had no coherent vision, and no consistent criticism emerged from her work. Her approach was materialistic, antipsychological, and antiformalist. Her method was to deconstruct movies into their various components and then reconstruct them again by comparing them with other movies. As John Powers noted, Kael was serious but not earnest, irreverent but not snide, savvy but not stuffy. Kael's antiaesthetic approach derived from her opposition to any theoretical preconceptions. For her, there was no such thing as ideal or pure cinema in the Platonic model; what came first was the experience of movies. Kael's analogy was simple: going to the movies was like having sex—sex can be good or bad.

"She makes movies highly personal events," wrote Martin Knelman in the *Toronto Globe and Mail,* "bringing all her experience to bear on them and channeling everything she knows into them, including a feeling for politics and literature and all the arts, high and low." Indeed, Kael's response to a movie was often more interesting than the movie itself. She introduced a new trend of criticism, one that placed the critic, rather than the movie, at the center of the review.

Kael's preference of the term *movie* over *film* was as much an ideological as an aesthetic statement. Throughout her career, she fought against pretentious, usually European, art films, and preachy, usually American, movies. Allowed by the *New Yorker*'s editor William Shawn to write whatever she wanted at whatever length, Kael developed, as Edward Murray observed, a relaxed, discursive, and chatty style, with salty vocabulary and hip words like *dumb, crummy, crappy,* and *lousy.* Kael's prose had the heat of gossip, a breezy rhythm that pulled in readers. Sarris's style was more formal and elegant; he didn't go out of his way to demonstrate rapport with his young readers. Kael pretended to talk to her readers at their level; Sarris expected them to rise to his.

Kael's flamboyant manner made whatever interested her at the moment—even a trashy film—sound important. She felt no guilt writing about or praising trash. She cited her own experience of movies, reacting in a personal way that often substituted rigorous analysis. Her opponents wished Kael would discipline more her thinking, devote more attention to form than content. They complained about her lack of consistent perspective and visual sensibility and her heavy reliance on cultural references.

Early on, Kael became (in)famous for making outrageous statements, such as the one about Frank Capra: "No one else can balance the ups and downs of wistful sentiment and corny humor the way Capra can. But if anyone else should learn to, kill him." Kael's saving grace was that her opinions were mitigated by wit; a clever slang made it fun to read her reviews. More important than agreeing with Kael was being familiar with her writing. At her prime, "Pauline says" became a conversational opener among the literati; finding out what she thought about a movie was de rigueur. Sarris was just as assertive professionally but much more modest personally.

Kael's *Raising Kane,* first published in the *New Yorker,* later came out as the introduction to an Atlantic–Little Brown edition of the shooting script of *Citizen Kane.* Kael resented that Welles, who starred, directed, and cowrote its screenplay with Herman J. Mankiewicz, was accorded all the credit. She argued that Mankiewicz conceived the film and was responsible for most of its script, whose authenticity was based on his acquaintance with the publisher and his mistress, Marion Davies. Kael's thesis was that less credit should go to Welles and more to the writer. As "proof," she used the fact that after *Citizen Kane* came out, Hearst vented his ire on Mankiewicz, not on Welles. Kael also elevated Gregg Toland's cinematography, which went beyond technical issues to provide much of the visual style and was responsible for introducing elements that were not in the script.

Like her reviews, *Raising Kane* was a mixture of journalism, gossip, and biography written in a bombastic, irresponsible manner. Sarris protested Kael's dethronement of Welles in the *Village Voice,* and so did Peter Bogdanovich in a long rebuttal in *Esquire.* Ultimately, *Raising Kane* was dismissed as serious scholarship or responsible criticism by most reviewers.

In the 1970s, Kael began to overpraise. Hyperbolic abandon was always her signature, equating *Nashville* and the *Godfather* movies with Melville and Whitman. In 1972, Kael caused another stir when she declared Bertolucci's *Last Tango in Paris* the most important movie she had ever reviewed, a "breakthrough" film comparable in its impact to the 1913 premiere of Stravinsky's *Le sacre du printemps.* Once again, her colleagues found her excessive praise unwarranted; *Last Tango* has not held up well. This review might have caused Kael the greatest embarrassment of her career.

Kael's most infamous piece, about Altman's *Nashville,* was published before the movie was even ready. She described the film as "at once a Grand Hotel–style narrative, with twenty-four linked characters; a country-and-Western musical; a documentary essay on Nashville and American life; a meditation on the love affair between performers and audiences; and an Altman party." Infuriated, Vincent Canby devoted a whole column, "On Reviewing Films Before They're Finished," in the *New York Times:* "If one can review a film on the basis of an approximately 3-hour rough-cut, why not review it on the basis of a 5 hour rough-cut? A 10-hour cut? On the basis of the screenplay?"

SUBJECTIVE TASTE OR CREATING A CANON

Kael claimed that she didn't have favorite auteurs whose movies she never panned, that she always went on the basis of individual movies. She told Peter Biskind: "I love about a dozen films of Altman. There are also about a dozen I think are crap. I don't reflect upon *McCabe and Mrs. Miller* and say it wasn't good because I don't think much of *Ready to Wear.*"

But in the 1970s, despite disparagement of auteurism, Kael became an almost indiscriminate devotee of a small clique of favorite directors, using a disguised form of auteurism to evaluate the work of Coppola, Scorsese, Altman, Bertolucci, Peckinpah, De Palma, Demme, and Spielberg, by praising *The Godfather* movies, *Mean Streets, M.A.S.H, McCabe and Mrs. Miller, Chinatown, The Conversation, Nashville, Taxi Driver, Jaws,* and *Close Encounters of the Third Kind.*

Unlike Kael, Sarris had no problems admitting to have made "mistakes," then taking great pains to correct them: "I grossly underrated Billy Wilder, whom I now place in my personal pantheon. I didn't get Stanley Kubrick for the longest time, and though he is still nowhere near the top of my list, I can at last cope with his coldness and artifice." Similarly, Kubrick's pictures were dismissed by Kael as unfeeling and aloof; she was repelled by *A Clockwork Orange* because it argued that human capacity for evil is never exhausted.

In the 1990s, Sarris felt he may have overrated Max Ophuls's *Lola Montes* (1955) when he hailed it as the greatest film of all time in the *Village Voice:* "I still love it, but I realize that Martine Carol presents problems for audiences. I have since substituted Ophuls' *Madame de. . . .* (1953) as my official favorite. Still, I felt a heady exhilaration when I saw a capacity crowd jamming into the Museum of Modern Art auditorium for the 1963 New York Film Festival screening of *Lola Montes,* largely on my say-so. That has always been my biggest thrill: to get people to enjoy movies as much as I do. I have often fallen flat on my face with the effort, but the successes make up for failures."

In the 1992 *Sight and Sound* poll of the Ten Best Films of All Time, Sarris included *Madame de . . ., Rules of the Game, Ugetsu Monogatori, The Searchers, Shadow of a Doubt, Sunrise, The Shop Around the Corner, Sunset Boulevard, Belle de jour,* and the Buster Keaton masterpiece *Steamboat Bill Jr.* Two of his films also appear on Kael's favorites list: *Rules of the Game* and *Steamboat Bill Jr.* Kael's list of great films includes D. W. Griffith's *Intolerance,* Renoir's *Day in the Country* and *La Grande Illusion,* John Huston's *The Maltese Falcon,* and the Marx Brothers' *Duck Soup.*

Kael liked early works of the French New Wave: Truffaut's *Shoot the Piano Player,* Godard's *Breathless* and *Weekend.* She showed appreciation of genre pictures whose forms were inventively opened up, like *The Godfather* movies, gangster pictures with the visual and moral depth of Renoir that made more direct contact with the audience than any other movies. Kael responded intensely to movies that cut to the bone of the American experience, such as *Five Easy Pieces* or *Mean Streets,* movies that urged viewers to change their lives.

Like Sarris, Kael disliked Zinnemann's *High Noon* and George Stevens's *Shane* for their moralism and mythic fakery. Mike Nichols's *The Graduate* was dismissed by her (and Sarris), because it was manipulative while pretending to be sincere. Cassavetes's movies were underappreciated by Kael, because they showed contempt for the audience's desire to be entertained. Kael rejected movies like *Blow Up, Darling,* and *Man for All Seasons* as phony or dull, and she debunked high-minded Hollywood junk like *Ship of Fools.* For Kael, people who claimed to enjoy *2001* more than *The Thomas Crown Affair* were either pretending or puritanical about the pleasures of trash.

One major difference between Kael and Sarris concerned the oeuvre of John Ford, particularly his westerns. Wrote Kael in the *Partisan Review,* in 1963: "If, by now, we dread going to see a 'great' Western, it's because 'great' has come to mean slow and pictorially composed. We'll be lulled to sleep in the 'affectionate,' 'pure,' 'authentic' scenery of the West (in 'epics' like *My Darling Clementine, She Wore a Yellow Ribbon, Fort Apache*)."

Sarris and Kael also had disparate opinions of the westerns of John Wayne and Clint Eastwood. The *Dirty Harry* films were deplored by Kael because they exploited the visceral appeal of blood. She didn't think much of Eastwood as an actor or a director, accusing the press of being "hornswoggled." "I always see Eastwood following the script slavishly," she told *Premiere.* "I never see him taking off as a director. I would have loved to have been around to blast his last couple of pictures that the press has been so excited about. I think people love the idea that a cowboy star actually can speak a sentence."

Judging by both theoretical and empirical impact, Sarris won the battle over auteurism, though there's no doubt that Kael presented some challenges. Inadvertently, Kael contributed more than any other critic to the preeminence of auteurism, first through rejecting it, then through embracing some of its tenets.

END OF AN ERA?

By the early 1980s, as Menand observed, the connection between enjoying a movie and feeling a shock of recognition was severed. In the next decade, adolescents dominated the movie market, making blockbusters out of *Batman, Beverly Hills Cop,* and *The Empire Strikes Back.* The type of American movies with which Kael had made her name had nearly vanished, and the type of foreign films with which Sarris had built his reputation barely got released in the United States.

With few exceptions both Sarris and Kael lost interest in contemporary directors. Kael claimed that she could not face another Oliver Stone work, a bombastic contention that failed to distinguish between a good (*Platoon, Salvador*) and a bad Stone movie. Sarris held that "the great majority of directors are just traffic managers, bums, hacks, they are not worth talking about." In 1989, Sarris left the *Village Voice,* but he has remained an active critic with a column in the *New York Observer.* Kael retired in 1991, after twenty-four years at the *New Yorker* and thirty-eight years as a reviewer. Their departures signaled the end of an era.

As always, the last word belongs to Sarris. At a 1993 forum sponsored by the Film Society of Lincoln Center and the Directors Guild and called "Auteur! Auteur! Thirty Years of the Auteur Theory in America," Sarris said: "And here I am, as always, too much of an academic for the journalists, and too much of a journalist for the academics. Yet it is through a mix of these two disciplines that I seek to recapture the past without foreclosing the future."

Amen!

Circles, Squares, and Pink Triangles: Confessions of a Gay Cultist

Ed Sikov

*K*nifed, beaten, eaten, and choked: the sad and grisly history of gay characters on the screen keeps pointing to the grave. But if the poor wretches who died for our sins were able to have back issues of the *New Yorker* forwarded to Hell, they would find themselves butchered a second time around by the critical meat cleaver of Pauline Kael. The battles over auteurism waged between Kael and Andrew Sarris have long been over. Sarris won. The world takes auteurism so for granted today that nobody even sees it as a theory anymore; the legend has become fact, as it often does. Because of Andrew Sarris, film critics and historians, students and teachers almost always print both the legend of expressive worldviews in the American cinema and the fact of so many great films have blended into a kind of international common sense. Hawks, Ford, Hitchcock, Welles—their work is self-evidently extraordinary, and their personal visions are clear to anyone with eyes, ears, and a soul. As far as the history of American film is concerned, the jury is in, and Kael is out.

But for me, the Sarris–Kael debates of the 1960s take on a personal resonance. I confess I'm an ex-Kaelian. I really thought she was great when I was a teenager. But the more I saw onscreen, the more I loved; the more I read of Kael, the less I liked. As a film lover, it was Andrew Sarris who was my inspiration. Sarris opened my eyes to Hollywood, to the ethos of Howard Hawks, the spirituality of John Ford, the resonant brilliance of Alfred Hitchcock. And as a gay man, after a period of disappointment and necessary rage with my two critical mentors, I now know where I stand with both of them. I'm with Andrew all the way.

The late Stuart Byron, who was a close friend of Sarris, was as militant a gay writer as one could be, but he never lost sight of the cinema. He too inspired me. For Stuart, gay politics and film art were inseparable; they affirmed life, each in their own way. Stuart loved American films, he loved men, and he loved writing about these intertwined aspects of his life. When Kael covertly attacked George Cukor for being gay in her notorious review of *Rich and Famous,* Stuart went on the attack in the pages of *Village Voice.* His essay, written with the mix of passion and intelligence that was typical of his work, didn't just set me to thinking about *Rich and Famous;* I didn't need any encouragement of that score, since I'd seen the film five times in the first three weeks of its release. More significantly for me, Stuart got me going on the subject of Pauline Kael—my original admiration for her writing style, my growing contempt for her taste in films (anybody who didn't love Howard Hawks had to be an idiot—I still believe this, by the way), and my troubled relationship with all straight critics who attempted to talk about homosexuality as if they knew what they were talking about.

Calling Kael's *Rich and Famous* piece "homophobic" really fails to describe the sarcasm, desperation, and overt fag baiting in which Kael dealt there and elsewhere. While she is by no means the only major film critic to fall into this kind of sewer—the ever egregious John Simon once described a Broadway play as "faggot nonsense"—Kael's literary stature, not to mention her clout among acolyte journalists, gave her remarks added weight and smell. Her fans, and they are still legion, labor under the belief that Kael is no mere movie reviewer. Transcending the "Movie Minute" world of hype and cheap opinion, Kael they chant is a diva, a stylist, a mind. All the more intriguing then are those moments when the subject of homosexuality taps directly into the diva's unsettled psyche.

It was thus all the more hilarious when the gay skin magazine *Mandate* published a post *Rich and Famous* interview with none other than La Kael herself. There, tucked comfortably between the cocks, cracks, and lubrication ads, appeared the beaming face of Pauline, who explained away what the interviewer whimperingly called "these awful misunderstandings." "I don't see," Kael emphatically declared, "how anybody who took the trouble to check out what I've actually written about movies with homosexual elements in them could believe that stuff."

Well, Pauline, I did. I had to get you out of my system. So I wrote a long slash-and-burn article for the *New York Native* (from which this essay is drawn). I was coming out as a film critic, in every sense, and I wanted to do it with a bang. What I learned as I went through volume after volume of Kael's old reviews was that "that stuff" is the least of her problems. Kael's easy, nasty opinions turned out to be part and parcel of an approach to films, to art, and to humanity in which hyperbole and gross innuendo take the place of those two elements that are crucial to a good criticism: reason and love. In Kael's work, reason may be lacking at times, but love is often nowhere to be found. And what I'd originally seen as a lively prose style began to look more and more like a series of literary tics.

A case in point: in 1968, in a review of *The Sergeant,* Kael wrote, "There is something ludicrous and at the same time poignant about many stories involving homosexuals. Inside the leather trappings and chains and emblems and Fascist insignia of homosexual 'toughs' there is so often hidden our old acquaintance the high school sissy searching the streets for the man he doesn't believe he is.... Crazier than Don Juan, homosexuals pursue an ideal man, but once they have made a sexual conquest the partner is a homosexual like them, and they go on their self defeating way, endlessly walking and looking, dreaming the impossible dream."

This gem, discountable as criticism and hilarious as prose, is hardly the kind of passage that dissuades one from believing "that stuff." In the first place, the passage precedes her discussion of the film. Typically, Pauline begins by reviewing "homosexuals," not the movie she's paid to discuss. And it goes without saying that she finds us ridiculous and heartbreaking, fundamentally unlike, say, herself. The cozy locution "our old acquaintance," followed as it is by the contemptuous "sissy," is just a cheesy way of asserting her authority. Implicitly having a heap of case histories to draw on, Kael feels fully competent to level judgment. As gay critic Vito Russo put it in his landmark survey *The Celluloid Closet,* "Almost every time Kael reviewed a film with a homosexual theme, she told about a gay friend; after a while it came to be something of a George and Gracie routine."

The quality of *The Sergeant* isn't the issue, frankly; I don't care about *The Sergeant.* But I do care about Alfred Hitchcock, who, bizarrely, ended up getting slammed in the same review. Kael pronounced *The Sergeant* ludicrously poignant, "insufferably tasteful and controlled and careful." (She's enthralled by lists in which the word *and* substitutes for commas.) But this is her conclusion: *The Sergeant* she writes "has less homosexuality in it than many movies have had unconsciously or by the accidents of casting or by carelessness or indifference—*Strangers on a Train* for example." (This time the word *or* makes the poor comma a refugee.)

All the reasons Kael cites for homosexuality in the movies are nefarious mistakes: accident, carelessness, indifference, and of course that great dark pit of sexual mystery and intrigue, unconsciousness. The homosexuality supposedly exuding from these "many movies" insistently points back to some sort of mindlessness on the part of the filmmakers, as if Kael alone knew the score. Smirking with the fallacious self-assurance of a high school guidance counselor from the 1950s, Kael simply couldn't wait to write "latent homosexual" on everybody's Permanent Record Card. But as was also the case in the 1950s, it's the guidance counselor's record that cries out to be reviewed. Hitchcock based *Strangers on a Train* on Patricia Highsmith's novel. The novel contains explicit references to Bruno's attraction to Guy. There is nothing accidental or careless about the homoerotic undercurrent in *Strangers on a Train*. Case closed.

But Kael continues: "And then there was that come-back-to-the-raft-again-Huck-Honey classic of a couple of years ago, *The Fortune Cookie,* with Jack Lemmon leaving his dirty wife for his clean sweet Negro buddy, and with the memorable closing shot of the two of them playing ball together." *The Fortune Cookie,* of course, is Billy Wilder's comedy about a white cameraman (Lemmon) who's knocked down by a black football player while filming a game. The cameraman's wife and shyster lawyer convince him to feign injury in order to reap a tidy profit from the insurance company, but ultimately he renounces the sham and confesses to the player, whom he has wronged. Kael's obnoxious "clean sweet Negro" line is characteristic of her shoot from the hip, aim-at-the-disenfranchised approach to cultural criticism.

I happen to think *The Fortune Cookie* is better than she does, but critical evaluations aside, one can't help but note her contempt for a positive black character. And it's part of a wider pattern. In her equally contemptuous review of *Victim,* as Vito Russo observed, Kael "despaired of the cinematic consequences of treating homosexuals seriously, with sympathy and respect, like negroes and Jews." Oh, for the good old days of rolling eyed train porters and, as Kael herself put it, "bitchy old queens."

If Kael's reviews of *The Sergeant* and *Victim* were just smudges on an otherwise pristine record of fair judgment, their undisguised nastiness would still merit comment. But her antigay swipes are positively inescapable:

On *Sunday Bloody Sunday:* "Murray Head . . . isn't a bitch, but he isn't quite a man either."

On *The Children's Hour:* "I always thought that was why lesbians need sympathy, because there isn't much they can do." (This one's particularly crude, even for Kael.)

On *Rich and Famous:* "It's a hopelessly demented movie. . . . It isn't camp exactly; it's more like a homosexual fantasy."

On *The Damned:* "It seems to be not so much a political movie as a homosexual fantasy. . . . It's really a story about a good boy who loves his wicked mother, and how she emasculates him and makes him decadent—the basic mother-son romance of homoerotic literature dressed up in Nazi drag." On *Triple Echo:* "The brutal beating that the soldier sister gets from the sergeant and his men may make this film some sort of masochistic gay liberation classic." Embarrassingly, some gay men just love this shit. In his rave review in *The Nation* of Kael's *5001 Nights at the Movies* (which covers, by the way, just a little over half that number of films; even the title's a cheat), gay writer Seymour Kleinberg noted that "she is much more reliable when she is contemptuous, which is much of the time." Kleinberg's devotion is so sycophantic that it defies argument. It has religious conviction to it, the ecstasy of a true believer. "The Kael whose prose leaps from the page, whose imagination is so deeply engaged that with every word we sense the vigor of her mind and the deep, passionate engagement characteristic of serious writing" and on and on. So enamored of Kael are some gay writers and readers that they can't even feel the slaps, unless of course they're nodding in agreement of her vision of half-men, Nazi sissy-thugs, and hapless, penis-free lesbians left with nothing to do.

In regard to what lesbians can do, it wouldn't take more than thirty seconds of idle contemplation on a crowded bus to come up with at least five possible sex acts that don't involve a penis. Kael's lack of imagination in this arena is an especially funny deficiency for somebody who made a career out of criticizing art. As for Murray Head "not being quite a man," Kael is faced here with a character who clearly does possess a penis and can therefore find things to do with it, but whose sexual orientation, at least for Kael, negates the organ's he-man function and thus renders the character, painfully no doubt, less than male. Kael's review of *Sunday Bloody Sunday* also contains this fascinating observation: "The Doctor is a competent, intelligent man, more tidy than deep, and he doesn't ask much more from life than the half a loaf he gets from his young friend." Poor Murray Head! First he's not quite a man; then it turns out he got gypped at the bakery.

In regard to *Triple Echo*, one can only stand back and stare, slack-jawed, at Kael's lunatic equation of a violent beating with gay liberation. And once again she sets herself up as the big expert. Her review of *The Damned*, though, is more symptomatic. There she notes that Visconti "lacks the gifts of an F. W. Murnau or a Fritz Lang," a point few would argue. But she never mentions Murnau or Lang again. Nor does she mention Visconti much, except to say that "When you"—meaning strangely Visconti—"don't have a talent for the grotesque but are nevertheless determined to tell the story of a fag-hag mother who turns her son into a dope addicted transvestite . . . it's grotesque, all right."

Having disposed of three major directors without even so much as a nod toward critical analysis, Kael is ready to take on all of gay literature. The emasculation of boys by mothers is, according to Pauline "the basic mother-son romance of homoerotic literature." What the hell is she talking about?

As a critic, Kael is at pains to assert authority; she has the goods on everybody and everything. She knows about Visconti. She knows about Murnau and Lang. She knows about "homoerotic literature." But anybody who might care to learn how Visconti lacks Murnau's gifts or what those gifts are, what is it that Lang does that Visconti doesn't or can't, or which homoerotic literature Kael means (Genet? Gide? Michelangelo? Marbod, the Bishop of Rennes?) is left to play a guessing game. Maybe it's just Kael's taste that runs toward tales of emasculation, but we can't know because she doesn't muck around with specifics.

From the safe distance of the 1990s, it's easy to roar over each peep into the shadowy recesses of a movie reviewer's psyche. Much of Kael's work now reads as pure camp—the best kind, in which the campy queen remains supremely unaware that he or she is being ridiculous and simply plunges on with the spectacle. But the unfortunate fact remains—this is not some second stringer from the *Ozarks Tribune*. This is Pauline Kael, National Book Award winner, mainstay of the *New Yorker*. Gay readers shouldn't feel, though, that they are Kael's targets. According to Pauline Kael, *Fiddler on the Roof* is "the most powerful movie musical ever made." More over Busby! Get out of here Vincente! Fred and Gene, Ginger and Cyd, go take a hike! Norman Jewison's back in town.

"Jewison does not permit the Jewish performers to be too Jewish; that is, to become familiar with the audience with that degrading mixture of self-hatred and self-infatuation that corrupts so much Jewish comedy. Only one of the leads—Molly Picon, as Yente the matchmaker—gets away from him and carries on like a stage Jew, with a comic accent. Why do Jewish performers like Molly Picon have to overdo being Jewish when they play Jews? It is not the Gentiles but the Jews who have created the Jewish stereotypes and not to satisfy any need in Gentiles but to satisfy the mixed up masochism of Jewish audiences."

Or this in regard to *Billy Jack*: "The town's leading citizen and chief bigot, played by beefy Bert Freed, seems to be Jewish and is given a Jewish name; he and his son, the rapist, appear to be the only Jews in town. I would guess that this is an expression not of anti-Semitism but of the frustrations and anger that build up when moviemakers are torn to shreds while trying to make deals with tough movie producers who often physically resemble Bert Freed." In other words, who are Jewish.

Kael, herself born a Jew, is intent on rationalizing: Jews are only good when they aren't "too Jewish." And it's perfectly fine to have a rapist and a creep specifically marked as the town Jews because, well, everybody knows those rich Hollywood Jews are tough to take, and we can all sympathize with the Gentiles' hatred.

Conversely, Jewison's *Fiddler* works for Kael because its director isn't a Jew. Jewison's is a "sensible attitude, full of essential good will, and yet not self-conscious, as a Jewish movie director's attitude might easily have been." Who does she mean here? Lubitsch? Wilder? Ophuls? Arthur Penn? Irving Pichel? Kael's twisted troubles over her own background drive her to distance herself from a roster of phantom "Jews" and yet maintain the patronizing "good will" she lauds in Jewison. The bile aimed at Molly Picon is predictable, since Picon's enormous popularity in the Yiddish theater, frequented as it was by uneducated immigrants who didn't care if they were being "too Jewish" for the Gentiles, makes her a safe target for ridicule and scorn in the pages of the *New Yorker*. But Kael goes further. She indicts "the Jews" for creating their own tradition of entertainment, as if they had no right to do so. Those fools thought they were entertaining themselves, when all the while they should have been pleasing Pauline Kael.

In her glowing review of *Personal Best*, Kael once again applauds a director for not being a member of the group represented by his film. She commends Robert Towne for not being a woman, let alone a lesbian: "Only a man who really loves women could have made *Personal Best*." One might argue that for a film about lesbians this is precisely the problem. Why else would a director turn one of the women straight and leave the other lonely and bitter? Kael is so caught up in this theme that she reiterates it until she runs out of ways of expressing it: "There's an undercurrent of flabbergasted awe."; "Towne's cameras make love to women the way the hero did in *Shampoo*."; "Towne's feelings come through clearly in the steam room scenes."; "He's so entranced by the women's beauty and conviviality." What a man, that Towne! No Murray Head, he!

Through this relentless drumbeat of heterosexual reassurance—and a particularly masculine version of it, to boot—Kael attempts to disarm whatever strength this lesbian relationship might have had. On the brighter side, *Personal Best* may have clued Kael into what lesbians can do, though any nascent understanding she may have had becomes moribund by the middle of the review, when she announces the reason behind Chris's attraction to Tory: "Chris is at that age when you're in a love affair that you don't understand and it's emotionally overwhelming to you." Oh, I get it—Chris is just confused. Like "you" when "you" were at "that age." Never mind that *Personal Best* tells us that Chris and Tory live together for three full years; Kael doesn't bother with that detail. Then again, Kael's critical elision mimics Towne's own failure of imagination, since Towne drastically compresses the women's relationship in screen time in order to get Chris together with a man before we all run out of celluloid. But ideology aside, Kael's review isn't a critique so much as an obsequious rehash; neither Towne nor his publicist could have done a better job.

In terms of compulsive antigay attacks, Kael hit her nadir with *Rich and Famous*. According to Pauline, Candice Bergen is a "big, goosey female impersonator." Jacqueline "Bisset's affairs, with their masochistic overtones are creepy, because they don't seem like what a woman would get into." And the film is "hopelessly demented," all of which turns *Rich and Famous* into, yes, a "homosexual fantasy." It's not a lesbian fantasy, of course, but a fantasy concocted by a sissy half-man of the Murray Head variety. It's the guidance counselor syndrome again. And her target is George Cukor.

Lacking both the courage and the libel insurance to out Cukor while he was alive—and libel would certainly have been an issue, given the expressly malicious tone of the review—Kael still maintains the appearance of being in the know. She smears Cukor without saying what she really means. A frail, elderly director at the sunset of his career was thus treated to snickering innuendo about his personal life in the pages of the most respected magazine in the country. Kael's review of *Rich and Famous* is the ugliest, most underhanded bit of fag baiting I have ever encountered in any film review.

Kael gives no clue to her extreme overreaction to Bisset's "creepy affairs": readers are once again forced into the twilight world of between-the-lines psychodrama. As is often the case, the real subject of Kael's review is Kael herself, though she remains unaware of it. She doesn't describe the sequences she finds offensive, just one shot of Hart Bochner standing in the foreground with Bisset in the background. "She gets a phone call," Kael writes, "and while she's on the phone he stands with his back to the camera, and the focus is held snugly on his bluejeaned rear. (Are we in the audience supposed to be turned on for her?)" In fact, of course, the whole shot is in focus; Bisset, the phone, the room, the rear, and Bochner's entire body is visible. Kael has never been one for critical precision.

Given the opportunity in the *Mandate* interview to extricate herself from this embarrassing gaffe, Kael only dug herself in deeper: "Usually in a movie when we see someone falling for a man or a women, we see from the same point of view as the one who's doing the swooning. . . . We're looking at a voluptuous show of the young man's bluejeaned rear while watching the woman get heated by it but she's facing the wrong way."

One might ask, what about the shots of Bisset and Bochner sitting on the couch? Or the shots of them standing together? Kael loses track of everything but Bochner's "bluejeaned rear," a description of which she's unduly enamored. More absurd is her glib assertion that love scenes are "usually" filmed "from the same point of view as the one who's doing the swooning." Well, Pauline, sometimes there are two people "swooning"; that's why it's handled in a two shot, from neither "point of view." Even when one person has to "get heated," it's rarely handled from that person's point of view. "Usually" the camera is placed in a seemingly neutral position on the swooner's side; the intense subjectivity of a single character's point of view is generally not employed to any great degree in Hollywood filmmaking. A camera, in heat, mimicking a suddenly displaced swooner? This is inane.

Questions of point of view, subjectivity, gender, and that current academic darling, the gaze, are obviously more complicated than Kael can handle. Instead, she fixates on Bochner's ass, then lambastes Cukor for filming her own fixation. In point of fact, Cukor does film the sequence in a way that makes Bochner as much of an erotic spectacle as Bisset. He goes even further in the scene in which Bisset's character picks up a hustler; there; it's the male body that's the object of erotic attention, not Bisset's. Perhaps Cukor finally felt comfortable enough to allow himself to eroticize a man on film; maybe it was his way of coming out. If so, it was a characteristically discreet and elegant way of doing it. Still, Cukor was never one for troweling his personal life onto what he believed was the central point of his films, their stories. Sure, Cukor was gay. But for him, *Rich and Famous* remained the story of two women and their friendship. And it should be no surprise that Cukor considered their erotic lives. Since both women are straight, they desire males. Does that mean they're really closet queers, just like Jack Lemmon and his clean, sweet negro buddy? Scarcely.

Contrast Kael's contempt for *Rich and Famous,* in which a gay director dared to film straight women, with her adoration of *Personal Best,* in which lesbian characters are explicitly applauded for being expressions of their director's essential heterosexuality. Towne gets high marks for making it clear he's straight; Cukor gets slammed in the seamiest terms for making men the objects of desire in a film about heterosexual women, and the directorial choices he made are, in her words, "demented."

When she defends herself, she gets self-congratulatory. "I don't believe," she piously told *Mandate,* "that the overt or honest expression of a homosexual theme has offended me in any way; it's only the covert that I've kidded—and never as a hanging judge." I suspect that Cukor didn't feel especially kidded when he picked up that issue of the *New Yorker.* In any event,

Kael evidently didn't remember her review of *Victor/Victoria,* where it was exactly the openness of the gay theme that enraged her. "Why are homosexual spokesmen celebrating this film? They're hungry to see fantasy versions of themselves on screen, and forced to, they'll accept crumbs." Like Jews and their humor, these unnamed "homosexual spokesman" just don't know what they should like. And anyway, what exactly are homosexual spokesmen? Public relations lackeys from Command Central? Would it have been so onerous for her to have called us "gay critics"?

As for her anti-Jewish attacks, she really hit bottom with *Shoah.* Not surprisingly, the outcry over her shrill, exceptionally mean review of Claude Lanzmann's magnum opus was much more extensive than anything that occurred after *Rich and Famous,* though her response to *Shoah* was certainly no more foolish, spastic, or irrational. But with *Shoah* she picked the wrong target. With a singular lack of forethought, she derided this artistically and culturally resonant film as "full of dead spaces." It had a "deadening weight" for her; the whole thing was just a "long moan." As if *Shoah* wasn't an elegy to 6 million dead Jews. As unpleasant as her review was, however, at least it served to clue a few more readers into Kael's self-aggrandizing misanthropy. For those of us who were stung by the *Rich and Famous* escapade, the *Shoah* piece gave us the chance to say to other *New Yorker* readers, We told you so.

Where does Andrew Sarris fit into this? I don't think I'm alone in seeing parts of Kael's "Circles and Squares" as an underhanded way of attacking the masculinity of film writers like Sarris. I also see a certain sexually defensive quality to some of Andrew's early writing. But one of the things I've long admired about Andrew is his critical introspection, the profound sense that no word is the final word. Kael once boasted that she rarely if ever sees a film more than once; Sarris is quite the opposite, finding revelation in the fifth, sixth, or seventieth viewing of a cherished picture. Andrew knows, as any great critic knows, that he might have missed something along the way. Kael, on the other hand, never lost the absolute certainty of a college sophomore. Kleinberg is right—she's best on stuff she hates at first glance. Sarris, on the other hand, is best when he writes about what he loves. His work is not about himself; it is about the thousandS and thousandS of movies on which he has set his sights and dreams. It is a talent I envy.

In the cinema, Sarris's early devaluation of *Billy Wilder* was his most significant misjudgment, and he retracted it. In fact, he's still retracting it with a regularity that borders on compulsion. It really bothers him to have missed Wilder's genius. In human terms, it's Andrew's critical treatment of gay people that nags at his conscience. He hasn't been above an occasional bit of gay baiting himself. We've all said things we regret; the point is to regret them, as

Andrew does. In an extended apology to Parker Tyler, Sarris wrote that he'd treated Tyler "very unfairly and very ungratefully in a critique of his republished essays. Out of all the pieces I have ever published, that is the one piece I wish I had never written." He concluded, "Perhaps one should rethink all one's bigotries with a post Holocaust remorse. My one regret at this juncture is that Parker Tyler is not alive so that I could say to him that I am sorry."

Andrew Sarris never particularly respected Parker Tyler as a film critic; he has better taste than that. But he came to respect Tyler's humanity in a way he hadn't before, and I suspect that knowing Stuart Byron as well as he did helped him to see it. But Sarris always respected George Cukor, and it was in his review of Cukor's biography *A Double Life* that he most fully came to terms with the ways in which being gay matters to an individual as well as to an art. His review of that book stands as a refreshing antidote to Kael's sour spit but, for me, it also serves as a kind of personal benediction. Andrew has always seen the cinema as a place of redemption; I do, too. Knowing that there is a place for me onscreen, however vicarious and distant that place may be, is crucial. I'm heartened and grateful that my former professor now understands why.

It should come as no surprise that it took a great director to show Andrew Sarris something essential about his world. Characteristically warmhearted, respectful, and kind, Sarris's review is a loving tribute from one generous spirit to another: "In the end, Cukor gave more in sentimental devotion and thoughtfulness than he ever received. Out of sheer admiration, he visited the sickbeds of D. W. Griffith, John Ford, and even his archrival Cole Porter. In his will, he asked to be buried next to Frances Howard (Mrs. Samuel Goldwyn), whom he had known as a young actress in Rochester and on whom he had a lifelong crush. He was a real man, and like F. W. Murnau and Sergei Eisenstein, one of the covertly gay masters of the cinema."

Auteur Theory and Independent Cinema

Geoffrey Gilmore

$\mathcal{T}$hirty-six years after its introduction, Andrew Sarris's scheme for reconsidering the American cinema still stirs controversy, misunderstanding, and debate. The "auteur" theory, as it's popularly known, is too often simplistically understood as a system for prioritizing and privileging the contributions of directors to filmmaking. While on at least one level this is partially true, it misses the real significance and point of Sarris's work. Written as a polemic to literally invite debate as to the nature and existence of cinema and what constituted aesthetic quality, it has sparked contentious discussion that did indeed rehabilitate the reputations of certain Hollywood filmmakers and broaden the definitions and standards as to what constituted great film and/or film art. By focusing on the central coherence of directorial authorship, in opposition to the dominance of a producer working inside of a Hollywood system that imposed its constricting determinants of commerce and bureaucracy, Sarris hoped to resuscitate the classic American film from the dustbin to which snobbish and sometimes high-minded critics had consigned it. Whether he succeeded in the quest or whether more insightful and substantive critical theories allowed for that discovery is perhaps largely irrelevant.

However, in reexamining the context from which Sarris formulated his critical method, one is struck with the realization that a similar antagonism still predominates discussion and debate. If anything, critics seem even more predisposed to the "forest" and the "trees" duality than they were thirty or forty years ago. Hollywood as a "system" has been more acutely and academically analyzed than it was decades earlier, and the kind of paradigmatic dismissiveness that Sarris was fighting against is as entrenched now as ever.

267

The real issue is that the industry itself has changed significantly, particularly the emergence and development of the independent sector. What are the implications for the auteur theory, if the "forest" has been dramatically reconfigured so that it includes havens or oases that are supportive of creative authorship. And perhaps even more importantly, is this indeed the case? Does the independent universe constitute a dramatically changed "system" for filmmaking?

If the genesis of the auteur theory was in response to the dismissive critique of a film universe that is defined as "Hollywood," then perhaps the film universe that is "independent film" is generically its antithesis, that is, a system that is ostensibly creatively positive, supportive, and sympathetic. In typifying independent filmmaking as personal, artistic, even idiosyncratic and quirky, one seems to be almost defining an ideal "system" for auteurs, one that enables the director to be fully in control, to reflect a personal aesthetic rather than just the effect of a "personality." Is the independent world actually a supportive system? In answering, one would certainly argue that relative to studio filmmaking it is, in that generally financial considerations are less present and less decisive, that is, cast, script, director, and so forth are not all determined only with marketability in mind.

But the independent universe is clearly not a utopia, and in reality, the biggest independent distributors take no more a laissez-faire attitude regarding their productions or the singular desires of their filmmakers than do the studios. That said, the possibilities for making films that defy easy categorization, that are not limited to the boundaries of simplistic genre, and that depend on storytelling that is compelling because of the quality of its writing, its personal nature, and its visual style is now largely the province of the independent sphere.

It could be argued that it's only a matter of degree and that the freedom of the independent depends on the attributes of a specific production and the budgetary strings that are attached to it, but although independent cinema is not monolithic, part of its definition implies exactly a lack of certain constraints. So in this sense the import of the auteur theory in assessing the independent world is very different from that of classic Hollywood. One is not examining the qualities of filmmakers who managed to overcome the limitations of an onerous system. Instead, one might be attempting to determine which filmmakers have actually taken advantage of the freedoms or expansive boundaries of independent filmmaking. It's often been argued by art historians that truly great art is more frequently produced when it's in conflict with its environment, and it could be said that independent filmmaking, while it has produced a lot of provocative even groundbreaking work, has yet to generate films of great importance or stature for a number of reasons. But more on this later.

Another significant aspect of the auteur theory is dependant on the analysis of a director's opus in its entirety. Concomitant to the establishment of a different "system" for making films is the reality that very few independent filmmakers are particularly prolific, and for that matter, no filmmaker makes as many films as did studio-employed directors of the classic Hollywood era. In fact, it sometimes seems as if certain independents become practically instant auteurs. Based on an output of no more than two or three films, we discuss their oeuvre as if it represented a complex of filmmaking. This might be an issue only because we're analyzing independents at a stage in their history that is both relatively immature and undeveloped. At the very least, the archetypal independent is often presumed to a young, emerging filmmaker and the number of more fully developed independent filmmakers is relatively few. It does seem likely that independent auteurs will never be represented by as broad an output as their predecessors, and it may also be true that it's an aspect to a critical methodology that was relevant to a certain epoch of filmmaking but not to others.

Whether or not the auteur theory remains a significant method depends on to what degree one conceives it as real theory and thus adapts it for use in a different age and era of filmmaking. As to the first point, it's generally acknowledged that the auteur theory is not really a theory as such but a method that was useful for establishing a critical hierarchy in a forty-year period of studio filmmaking. Is a similar ranking possible in assessing the independent filmmaker? The answer is probably not. Too few filmmakers have produced too few films. In a sense, the independent world is not yet a dense enough forest.

Secondly, the "system" itself is dramatically different. The usefulness of the auteur theory as a method was the discovery and legitimization of filmmakers whose personal vision, sensibilities, and artistry distinguished them from their peers and allowed them to flourish in a commercial industry. Few filmmakers would argue that the Hollywood industry is any less commercial or corporate than at that time; in fact, most would argue that the nature of the film business is even more dogmatically formulaic and anticreativity than ever. The emergence of the independent sector might even be conceived of as a response to the rise of corporate culture, not only by film artists but by at least some segment of the audience.

But if the auteur theory has less relevance as a methodology than it once might have had, its value as a concept, which emphasizes the need to evaluate specific artistic and personal vision, still has strength. Given the tendency by journalists and other media analysts to appraise culture and its significance by both generalizing and employing reductive modes of assessment, it is vital that critical theorists who seek a more comprehensive portrait search out the trees and perhaps even build a topology or hierarchy.

In thinking about independent filmmakers, how does one specifically perceive and judge the output of Rick Linklater, Quentin Tarantino, Todd Haynes, Victor Nunez, Allison Anders, Tom DiCillo, Gregg Araki, and so forth? In doing the kind of topology that Sarris's work pioneered, one could better understand and conceptualize what the independent universe actually incorporates, its diversity and its evolution. By utilizing the broadest definition of independent that includes within it non–American filmmakers both English-speaking and not, different generations of filmmakers, mainstream independents alongside avant-gardists and filmmakers whose diverse work and variety of interests move them from the independent arena to studios to television and back, all of which gets grouped together, it's no wonder that many find the concept *independent* to have lost any real meaning.

Sarris's contributions brought a rigor and seriousness to film study that had not previously existed. If the effect of considering the auteur theory vis-à-vis independents begins a ranking of independent filmmakers in the same polemical fashion as Sarris accomplished with classic Hollywood, it would almost assuredly contribute to a better understanding of the range, diversity, and definition of the independent universe. By learning more about the trees, we would understand that much more the forest. I'm not suggesting a simple empiricism, but the importance for both an understanding of the "system" and a method for evaluating its constituent parts. If the auteur theory is less effective as a critical method for evaluating its constituent parts, it still points in the right direction.

In realizing a new critical methodology for the independent, one may very well rescue the term from total relativism. The new scoreboard for assessing a director's stature is too often linked to the Monday morning announcement of a film's box-office performance. Nothing is more irrelevant to the genesis of the independent than this standard of assessment. If auteur theory stimulates a new evaluation of the trees creating an alternate topology and hierarchy, then one can truthfully say that it is alive and well. But what about highlighting individual directors?

Part Eight

Sarris's Impact Overseas

*S*arris's ideas have had global effects, going way beyond the American cinema, its practitioners, and its critics.

In "The International Film Critic," Serge Losique, president and founder of the Montreal World Cinema Festival, places Andrew Sarris in the same league as another citizen of cinema, Henri Langlois. "In film criticism, Andrew is the first one," notes Losique. "Many people in our field recognize his great contributions to film criticism. Sarris's auteur theory contributed to the creation of a new thinking about filmmaking." For Losique, Sarris's importance is also evident in his serving as "a natural bridge between European critics, particularly French, and American ones." Losique writes, "I am sure that future generations of film will study Andrew Sarris's work. The proof of his legacy is this book, *Citizen Sarris,* dedicated to his work. The proof is also the 'Prix Maurice Bessy,' which was established by the Montreal and Cannes festivals to honor great writers on film. Andrew Sarris was the first to receive this honor on North American soil."

Toronto Festival director, Piers Handling, in "Auteurism in Canada," recalls how he skipped "classes in philosophy to hang around the first film department in the country (Robin Wood and Peter Harcourt were professors . . .)." One of Handling's friends, who "shared a similar love of film," introduced Handling "to his pantheon—Ford, Hawks, and Hitchcock—and to Andrew Sarris's *The American Cinema,*" already "a well-worn volume." The friend had "underlined the films he'd seen, which made me acutely aware of everything I hadn't seen. Dipping into the book, I came across names I had heard of vaguely or never knew. It was like a road map through the breadth and depth of American cinema. Sarris charted the waters, stocked the galley, set his sails, and embarked for the 'new world.' "

As Handling notes, "The excitement of screening the work of Boetticher or a Hawks was exhilarating. Westerns were works of art? How could films that entertained me in the afternoon matinees be taken seriously? Sarris took what was under our noses, undervalued, and elevated it, forced us to rethink it. We may have disagreed with his 'rankings' (everyone's a critic at the end of the day), but he stimulated discussion and forced us to marshal our own thoughts."

Switching to the Canadian experience, Handling observes how profoundly it was influenced by the National Film Board, which in the 1940s, 1950s, and 1960s was "a collective experience." Handling writes, "Auteurism arrived in Canada when the Antonionis and Bergmans were revered by students on campus. The Cronenbergs and Arcands were waiting in the wings for their opportunity. We also needed our own star system, and filmmakers emerged slowly from the shadows. . . . Despite the auteurs who have worked in the margins of Canadian cinema over the decades . . . , the Canadian cinema attains depth when looked at as a national cinema, not as a group of heroic individuals struggling to make their films. David Cronenberg, Atom Egoyan, and Denys Arcand are true auteurs, but even their films are rewarded when placed next to one another, their work seen as part of a cultural continuum."

New York Festival director Richard Pena, in "Andrew Sarris and Romantic Rebellion," records: "I've always been impressed that the one American film critic that Latin American filmmakers, scholars, and critics will always know is Andrew Sarris. Beginning with his columns in *Film Culture* and later with his articles in the *Village Voice* and his subsequent books, Sarris came to be seen in Latin America as the American iconoclast par excellence, the writer who dared champion the small "B" film or the underdog director while sparing no pity on the inflated so-called masterworks of Hollywood cinema." Pena remembers how "during a research trip to several countries . . . copies of *The American Cinema*—usually looking as dog-eared and thumbed-through as mine back home—were prominently displayed on the bookshelves of people I interviewed."

According to Pena, "For many Latin Americans, Sarris and 'auteurism' were synonymous, yet the notion of the auteur was perceived perhaps somewhat differently there. . . . The early history of Latin American cinema traces the various attempts to transform what was generally sporadic . . . film production into genuine film industries, complete with solid financial and industrial bases, government support, and possibilities for export. In truth, only

Mexico was annually producing more films than the rest of Latin America put together. Other nations tried to emulate Mexico's success; in Brazil, there were two major initiatives aimed at creating Hollywood-style industries— Atlantida in the 1940s in Rio, and Vera Cruz in Sao Paulo in the 1950s. Both were conceived around a concept of studio-bound cinema."

Pena holds that "Auteurism quickly became the cinematic version of the romantic myth of the artist, alone and set against a hostile, uncaring world. . . . The role of the film artist within politics and culture continues to be an important theme in Latin American cinema. . . . Meanwhile, the notion of the 'auteur' will continue to haunt film studies; despite decades of 'anti-auteurism' from political, semiological, psychoanalytic, and structuralist positions, the idea that films at least occasionally are created by people who really are trying to say something to us continues to exert a powerful fascination. For this, and for so much else, we have Andrew Sarris to thank."

ilyn Monroe, Bette Davis, Greta Garbo, and Marlene Dietrich were elbowed out of the way by the Scorseses, Coppolas, Spielbergs, and Peckinpahs.

The auteur theory, as a theory went, had certainly worked in other disciplines: art, literature, music. It established a canon, and eventually even a countercanon, of those who had not been admitted to the sacred halls. In cinema, it acted (and still does) as a way of approaching the creative act. There is no question that virtually anyone seriously involved in the cinema follows the work of certain filmmakers, even if they are an anti-auteurist. It is a way of sorting, cataloging.

Inevitably, the reaction set in—as well it should. Valuable work on national cinemas and genres was rapidly followed by those cultural critics who looked to linguistics, women studies, the gay movement, in the many various attempts to decipher the signs and meanings embedded in film. *Screen* and the semiologists rose to the fore. Even *Cahiers* changed its spots. For a decade or so, the edifice of the auteur theory seemed rather fragile and in danger of crumbling. Always alert to the moment, Godard subsumed his identity in that of a group at one point in his career to emphasize how far he had traveled from his own auteurist beginnings.

The auteur theory, made famous and propagated by a group of critics, was a celebration of the individual. When the *Cahiers* critics started to make films, they were collectively embraced as a movement: the New Wave. That this rapidly fragmented once they became famous was inevitable. But, it did speak to something deeply rooted in the Hollywood system—the notion of collaboration, the subsuming of the individual artist into the collective, a studio. Filmmakers are lost without their collaborators. The great film movements—the French New Wave, Italian Neo-Realism, German Expressionism, British Free Cinema, Brazilian Cinema Novo—are often more famous than the individuals who constituted these groups.

The Canadian experience, so profoundly influenced by the National Film Board, was initially—in the forties, fifties, and even into the late sixties—a collective experience. The film units at the Board were teams. The documentary project lent itself to this approach. Documentary filmmakers were rarely stars. In the early years of the Film Board, individual credits did not appear. When they did, it was still apparent that collaboration was at the heart of their project; the names rarely changed on the films.

Auteurism arrived in Canada when the Antonionis and Bergmans were revered by students on campus. The Cronenbergs and Arcands were waiting in the wings for their opportunity. We also needed our own star system, and filmmakers emerged slowly from the shadows. Ironically, so many of them have been forgotten. Perhaps that is the destiny of the auteur system; if you're not in the Pantheon, you disappear from view.

Despite the auteurs who have worked in the margins of Canadian cinema over the decades (names largely unknown except to devotees of Canadian cinema: Jean Pierre Lefebvre, Larry Kent, Gilles Carle, Don Shebib, Allan King, Pierre Perrault), the Canadian cinema attains depth when looked at as a national cinema, not as a group of heroic individuals struggling to make their films. David Cronenberg, Atom Egoyan, and Denys Arcand are true auteurs, but even their films are rewarded when placed next to one another, their work seen as part of a cultural continuum. Despite his fascination with horror and science fiction, Cronenberg is a profoundly Canadian artist. Egoyan cites Cronenberg and Lefebvre as important influences. Arcand's early work owes a debt to Lefebvre (whose production company financed his first two features) and embodies a great deal of Quebec and its cinematic past. The threads all form part of the tapestry that is Canadian cinema.

Cahiers and Sarris seized one historic moment. They left a profound and deep impression not just on the way critics and academics viewed film but on the way mass culture looked at the movies. The director, hitherto largely an anonymous figure, ascended into the heavens to join the film stars already there. Auteurism pushed the boundaries (to the chagrin of many producers!) and in so doing created a debate that has continued to the present. It has informed all of our work. What greater tribute could be paid?

Andrew Sarris and Romantic Rebellion

Richard Pena

I've always been impressed that the one American film critic that Latin American filmmakers, scholars, and critics will always know is Andrew Sarris. Beginning with his columns in *Film Culture* and later with his articles in the *Village Voice* and his subsequent books, Sarris came to be seen in Latin America as the American iconoclast par excellence, the writer who dared champion the small "B" film or the underdog director while sparing no pity on the inflated so-called masterworks of Hollywood cinema. During a research trip to several countries in 1974–75, I can remember how often copies of *The American Cinema*—usually looking as dog-eared and thumbed-through as mine back home—were prominently displayed on the bookshelves of people I interviewed.

For many Latin Americans, Sarris and "auteurism" were synonymous, yet the notion of the auteur was perceived perhaps somewhat differently there. So much of the early history of Latin American cinema traces the various attempts to transform what was generally sporadic and haphazard film production into genuine film industries, complete with solid financial and industrial bases, government support, and possibilities for export. In truth, only Mexico was annually producing more films than the rest of Latin America put together. Other nations tried to emulate Mexico's success; in Brazil, for example, there were two major initiatives aimed at creating Hollywood-style film industries—Atlantida in the 1940s in Rio, and Vera Cruz in Sao Paulo in the early 1950s. Both were conceived around a concept of studio-bound cinema, and consequently a great deal of attention was paid to notions of "production values" and seamless technique.

Neither company lasted very long (although Atlantida was the far more successful of the two), and in a way their importance today is at least partially based on their having been a model of filmmaking practice against which the subsequent generation of Brazilian filmmakers—directors such as Glauber Rocha, Nelson Pereira des Santos, Carlos Diegues, and others—would react. These filmmakers, who together with a few others became known as the Cinema Nove, or "New Cinema," took as their motto "a camera in the hand and an idea in the head." Not only would this generation take advantage of the new technologies available then to move their filmmaking out of the studios and onto actual locations, but more importantly these films would be expressions of their creators' individual visions. Earlier, the emphasis in Brazilian cinema had been on the external features of films—how they looked and whether they could match the quality of the much-admired/much-resented Hollywood films; Cinema Novo, echoing Sarris, would emphasize the internal message or meanings through individual works.

As laid out by Glauber Rocha in his book *A Critical Revision of Brazilian Cinema* (1962), the history of cinema was divided between "autores" (Portuguese for "auteurs"), those who used cinema as a means of self-expression, and "artesaos," "artisans" who manipulated the techniques of cinema more or less skillfully yet who failed to endow their work with an inner life. In their dedication to a cinema of ideals, which might be the equal of Brazilian cultural achievements in other media, the young filmmakers (most were in their twenties) saw themselves as "auteurs" even before they had created bodies of work.

Thus, what had been in the work of Sarris and the *Cahiers* critics before him a critical approach to film history was now transformed into a standard for filmmaking practice. Moreover, auteurist criticism, with its emphasis on deeper meanings and ideas that seemed smuggled into seemingly innocent Hollywood productions, offered a portrait of film history in which having a personal artistic vision was in and of itself a kind of subversion in a system that stressed uniformity and clich For Cinema Novo, the creation of a Brazilian "cinema of auteurs" was the appropriate, and politically engaged, response to the history of failed attempts at creating film industries in the shadow of Hollywood.

To a certain extent, one can claim that Cinema Novo succeeded in establishing its vision of filmmaking; for many of us, the Brazilian sixties was a kind of "Golden Age" of Latin American cinema. Yet its victory can at best be called partial, as certain developments would intervene. One was the military coup that toppled the civilian government on April 1, 1964, and would remain in power over the next twenty years; the other was the emergence of a new, vehemently "anti-auteurist" tendency in the films and theoretical writings of the Bolivian Jorge Sanjines (*Blood of the Condor*), the Argentines Fernando Solanas and Octavio Getino (*Hour of the Furnaces*), and others. As they outlined in their classic essay "Towards a Third Cinema," the notion of "auteur cinema" for Solanas and Getino was at best an understandable if somewhat misguided step along the path of development for Latin American and Third World filmmakers. It did represent, within the Latin American context, an attempt to establish the individual voice or presence within a system that saw culture as something imported.

Yet whatever importance this might have had was superseded by the way in which auteurism quickly became the cinematic version of the romantic myth of the artist, alone and set against a hostile, uncaring world. Instead, Solanas and Getino encouraged the filmmaker to take action against the scenario of alienation by becoming one with "the people." In losing oneself in the attempt to express "popular consciousness," they argued, the filmmaker is reborn as something much greater. This attempt to subvert individual artistic vision and control actually led to a number of interesting experiments with "open" cinematic texts; in *Courage of the People,* for example, Jorge Sanjines asked survivors of a massacre to help him re-create the events, allowing them not only to structure the narrative and create the dialogue but even to determine things like camera angles by consensus.

The role of the film artist within politics and culture continues to be an important theme in Latin American cinema; one can even see it in Chilean filmmaker Raul Ruiz's many references in his films to artists who disappear, get cut up, or perhaps never even existed. Meanwhile, the notion of the "auteur" will continue to haunt film studies; despite decades of "anti-auteurism" from political, semiological, psychoanalytic, and structuralist positions, the idea that films at least occasionally are created by people who really are trying to say something to us continues to exert a powerful fascination. For this, and for so much else, we have Andrew Sarris to thank.

Andrew Sarris's Select Bibliography

The Films of Josef von Sternberg. New York: The Museum of Modern Art, 1966.

Interviews with Film Directors. New York: Bobbs–Merrill, 1967.

The Film. New York: Bobbs–Merrill, 1968.

The American Cinema, Directors and Directions, 1929–1968. New York: Dutton, 1969.

Film 68/69. Edited with Hollis Alpert. New York: Simon and Schuster, 1969.

Confessions of a Cultist: On the Cinema 1955–1969. New York: Simon & Schuster, 1970.

The Primal Screen: Essays on Film and Related Subjects. New York: Simon and Schuster, 1973.

The Films of Max Ophuls. Unpublished, 1973.

The John Ford Movie Mystery. Indiana University Press, 1975.

Politics and Cinema. New York: Columbia University Press, 1978.

St. James Film Directors Encyclopedia. Edited by Andrew Sarris. Detroit: Visible Ink Press, 1997.

You Ain't Heard Nothin' Yet: The American Talking Film 1927–1949, History and Memory. New York: Oxford University Press, 1998.

Contributors' Biographies

JEANINE BASINGER

Jeanine Basinger is the Corwin-Fuller Professor of film studies and American Studies at Wesleyan University, where she is also founder and curator of the Wesleyan Cinema Archives and chair of film studies. She is the author of numerous articles and eight film books, including *The World War II Combat Film: Anatomy of a Genre, Anthony Mann: A Critical Study,* and *A Woman's View: How Hollywood Spoke to Women, 1930–1960.* She is a trustee of the American Film Institute and a former member of the board of advisors of the Association of Independent Video and Film Makers and is a nationally recognized expert on various aspects of American film. Basinger's *American Cinema: 100 Years of Filmmaking* was the companion book for the 1995 ten-part PBS television series, for which she was senior consultant. Her latest book, *Silent Film Stars,* was published by Knopf.

JOHN BELTON

A film professor at Rutgers, the State University of New Jersey, John Belton has taught film in various schools, including Columbia University, where he shared offices with Andrew Sarris. Belton has written several film books, including *Cinema Stylists* and *The Hollywood Professionals.*

ROBERT BENTON

Robert Benton began his career as a magazine art director and editor, coauthoring *The IN and OUT Book* (1959), a tongue-in-cheek guide for city sophisticates, and *The Worry Book* (1962). In 1961, he began a fruitful collaboration with David Newman on special pop-culture projects in *Esquire*. They next tackled the movies as cowriters of the script for *Bonnie and Clyde* (1967), one of the most influential American films. Benton then ventured into directing, making his debut with *Bad Company* (1972). In 1979, he scored a huge hit with the family drama *Kramer vs. Kramer*, a box-office hit that won five Oscars (including Best Picture and Best Director) and established him as one of the most sought after director-writers. Benton also directed the thriller *Still of the Night; Places in the Heart,* a depression-era drama for which he won a Best Original Screenplay Oscar; *Nadine; Billy Bathgate;* and *Nobody's Fool.*

BUDD BOETTICHER

Born in Chicago, Budd Boetticher attended Culver Military Academy and Ohio State University, where he excelled in football and boxing. His school chum Hal Roach Jr. got him minor jobs in the film industry, first as technical advisor on the bullfighting film *Blood and Sand* (1941). After an apprenticeship as a messenger and assistant director, he was given a chance to direct several low-budgeters. For producer John Wayne, Boetticher filmed a fictionalization of his own experience in Mexico, *Bullfighter and the Lady* (1951), which was reedited without his approval by John Ford. Boetticher then formed a partnership with actor Randolph Scott, which led to a string of westerns, including *Seven Men from Now* (1956) and *The Tall T* (1957). He directed a gangster film, *The Rise and Fall of Legs Diamond* (1960), before leaving with his wife, actress Debra Paget, for Mexico for a documentary on the matador Carlos Arruza. His travails there, which included near-fatal illness, divorce, jail, hospital, and an asylum, are detailed in his autobiography *When in Disgrace.*

PETER BOGDANOVICH

Peter Bogdanovich studied acting with Stella Adler and appeared with the New York Shakespeare festivals. In the 1960s, he wrote monographs of filmmakers for the Museum of Modern Art, published books on Fritz Lang, John Ford, Alan Dwan, and Orson Welles, and wrote film articles for *Esquire*. In

1968, he directed his first movie, *Targets,* starring Boris Karloff, followed by the documentary *Directed By Ford,* which premiered at the Venice Festival. In 1971, he made a big splash with critics with *The Last Picture Show,* an evocative look at small-town America of the 1950s, which was nominated for the Best Picture Oscar. A string of successes followed with *What's Up Doc?* (1972), which captured the zing of madcap comedies, and *Paper Moon* (1974), for which Tatum O'Neal won the Best Supporting Actress Oscar. Other films include *Daisy Miller* and *At Long Last Love,* starring Cybil Shepherd; *Nickelodeon* (1976); *Saint Jack* (1979); *They All Laughed* (1981); *Mask* (1985), a moving portrait of a disfigured youth; and *Texasville* (1990), a sequel to *The Last Picture Show.*

DAVID BORDWELL

David Bordwell is the Jacques Ledoux Professor of Film Studies in the Department of Communication Arts, University of Wisconsin—Madison. He has taught there since 1973 and has won a Chancellor's Award for Distinguished Teaching. He is the author of several books on film theory and history, including *The Films of Carl-Theodor Dreyer* (1981), *Narration in the Fiction Film* (1985), *Ozu and the Poetics of Cinema* (1988), *Making Meaning: Inference and Rhetoric in the Interpretation of Cinema* (1989), *The Cinema of Eisenstein* (1992), and most recently *On the History of Film Style* (1997). With Noel Carroll he edited *Post-Theory: Reconstructing Film Studies* (1996). With Janet Staiger and Kristin Thompson he wrote *The Classical Hollywood Cinema: Film Style and Mode of Production to 1960* (1985), and with Kristin Thompson he has written two textbooks, *Film Art: An Introduction* (various editions) and *Film History: An Introduction* (1994). In 1997 he was awarded an honorary doctorate in philosophy from the University of Copenhagen. He is currently at work on a book about Hong Kong cinema.

CHARLES CHAMPLIN

Charles Champlin is arts editor and columnist emeritus for the *Los Angeles Times.* From 1967 to 1980 he was also the paper's principal film critic. Champlin's most recent book is *Hollywood's Revolutionary Decade,* an annotated collection of his reviews of the films of the 1970s. His other books include biographies of John Frankenheimer and George Lucas and a study of the impact of television on films, *The Movies Grow Up 1940–1980.* He has taught film criticism at Loyola-Marymount and USC and hosted "Film Odyssey" (PBS), "Champlin on Film" (Bravo), and other television shows. He was awarded the Order of Arts and Letters by the French government for his service to film.

GODFREY CHESHIRE

A native of Raleigh, North Carolina, Godfrey Cheshire attended the University of North Carolina at Chapel Hill. In 1978, he was a founding editor of the Raleigh-based weekly *Spectator Magazine* and has served as its film critic ever since. Following his move to New York in 1991, his criticism has appeared weekly in the *New York Press*. A contributor to *Variety* and *Film Comment,* Cheshire has also written for the *New York Times, Interview, Filmmaker,* and *Film International* (Teheran). In 1995, he helped found the North Carolina Film and Video Festival, the only annual juried competition for filmmakers of one state. He is currently writing a book about the New Iranian Cinema. He is a member of the New York Film Critics Circle (chairman in 1998), the National Society of Film Critics, and the Federation International de la Press Cinematographique (FIPRESCI).

RICHARD CORLISS

Richard Corliss is a film critic for *Time* magazine; the author of *Talking Pictures: Screenwriters in the American Cinema* (1974, with prologue by Andrew Sarris), an attempt to apply Sarris's auteurist approach to screenwriting; and the editor of the anthology *Hollywood Screenwriters.* He earned his B.A. degree at St. Joseph's College and his M.A. in film at Columbia University. Corliss conducted film research at the Museum of Modern Art for two years, after which he became editor-in-chief of *Film Comment.* For a number of years, he was a member of the selection committee of the New York Film Festival.

ROGER EBERT

Roger Ebert is the cohost of the popular, nationally broadcast Siskel & Ebert weekly television show, renamed in 1999 *Ebert & the Movies.* The syndicated film critic of the *Chicago Sun-Times,* Ebert won the 1975 Pulitzer Prize for film criticism. He is the author of *Roger Ebert's Movie Home Companion* and *Two Weeks in Midday Sun: A Cannes Notebook*.

GEOFFREY GILMORE

Geoffrey Gilmore is a codirector (since 1991) of the Sundance Film Festival. He studied film at UCLA and was a programmer for the UCLA Film and Television Archives.

PIERS HANDLING

Piers Handling is the director of the Toronto International Film Festival Group, which consists of the Toronto Film Festival, Cinematheque Ontario, and The Film Reference Library. He has organized numerous programs over the past fifteen years, including major retrospectives of Canadian, Latin, American, Italian, Polish, Portuguese, and Hungarian cinema. He was one of the cofounders of the Perspective Canada Program and has organized retrospectives of Canadian cinema for Havana, London, Washington, and the Sundance Film Festival. Handling has written on Canadian cinema and has been published in numerous film journals. His publications include *The Films of Don Shebib* and *The Shape of Rage: The Films of David Cronenberg*. He taught Canadian cinema at Queen's University in Kingston and Carleton University in Ottawa. He was formerly deputy director at the Canadian Film Institute and was educated at Queens University, Kingston.

CURTIS HANSON

Curtis Hanson recently directed and produced the screwball comedy *Wonder Boys* (1999), starring Michael Douglas. He directed, produced, and cowrote the screenplay for the Oscar-winning film *L.A. Confidential* (1997), for which he received a Best Adapted Screenplay Oscar (with Brian Helgeland), a directorial Oscar nomination, and the director's citation from all the critics groups in the country. Previously, Hanson directed *The River Wild* (1994), with Meryl Streep; *The Hand That Rocks the Cradle* (1992), with Annabella Sciorra and Rebecca De Mornay; and *Bad Influence* (1990), costarring

Rob Lowe and James Spader. He also wrote the screenplay for and directed *The Bedroom Window* (1987). His other screenplay credits include *The Silent Partner, White Dog,* and *Never Cry Wolf.*

MOLLY HASKELL

Molly Haskell, author and critic, was a longtime staff writer for the *Village Voice, New York Magazine,* and *Vogue.* She currently covers film for the feminist quarterly *On the Issues* and does a monthly column for the *Observer.* She has written for many publications, including the *New York Times Book Review, Mirabella, Esquire,* the *Nation* and the *New York Review of Books.* She has served as artistic director of the Sarasota French Film Festival and as adjunct professor of film at Columbia University. Her books include *From Reverence to Rape: The Treatment of Woman in the Movies* (1973; revised and reissued in 1989); a memoir, *Love and Other Infectious Diseases* (1990); and, in 1997, a collection of essays and interviews, *Holding My Own in No Man's Land: Women and Men and Film and Feminists.*

CARYN JAMES

Caryn James is the chief television critic of the *New York Times* and the author of the novel *Glorie* (Penguin Books). For six years, she was a film critic for the *Times,* where she has also been a cultural reporter and an editor at the *Book Review.* As an essayist, James writes frequently about the media, books, and popular culture. She has a Ph.D. in English literature from Brown University.

DAVE KEHR

A graduate of the University of Chicago, Dave Kehr became in 1975 the first staff film critic of the *Chicago Reader,* Chicago's alternative weekly. In 1986, he replaced Gene Siskel as the chief critic of the *Chicago Tribune* and in 1993 was appointed movie critic for the *New York Daily News.* From 1984 to 1987, Kehr was a member of the selection committee of the New York Film Festival and has served as a jury member at several film festivals, including Sundance, Berlin, Toronto, and Cannes. In 1998, he was reappointed to the New York Festival committee for another three-year term. He is a current member (and past chair) of the National Society of Film Critics and a member of the New York Film Critics Circle. In 1999, he was elected a vice president of FIPRESCI, the international federation of film critics.

PETER LEHMAN

Peter Lehman is a professor in the Interdisciplinary Humanities Program and the Hispanic Research Center at Arizona State University. He is author of *Running Scared: Masculinity and the Representation of the Male Body* and editor of *Defining Cinema.* His work on John Ford and authorship includes chapters in *Authorship and Narrative in the Cinema* by William Luhr and Peter Lehman, *Close Viewings,* edited by Peter Lehman, and *The Western Reader,* edited by Jim Kitses and Gregg Rickman. He is coauthor, with William Luhr, of *Blake Edwards* and *Returning to the Scene: Blake Edwards, Vol. 2.* He has served as President of the Society for Cinema Studies, editor of *Wide Angle,* and director of the Ohio University Film Conference.

EMANUEL LEVY

Emanuel Levy is a senior film critic for *Daily Variety* and *Variety* and a two-time president of the Los Angeles Film Critics Association (LAFCA). He received his Ph.D. from Columbia University and has taught at Wellesley College, Columbia, the New School for Social Research, and UCLA. Levy is film professor at Arizona State University, and the recipient of the university's 2000 Faculty Achievement Award for Research, Scholarship, and Creativity. Levy is the author of seven film books, including *John Wayne: Prophet of the American Way of Life* (foreword by Andrew Sarris); *Oscar Fever: History and Politics of the Academy Awards*; *Small-Town America in Film; George Cukor, Master of Elegance,* the acclaimed biography of the Hollywood director; and *Cinema of Outsiders: The Rise of American Independent Film.* He is currently writing the first biography of Vincente Minnelli, to be published by William Morrow in 2003 for the centennial of Minnelli's of birthday.

PHILLIP LOPATE

Phillip Lopate is an essayist, novelist, and poet. His ten books include the personal trilogy *Bachelorhood, Against Joie de Vivre,* and *Portrait of My Body;* the novel *The Rug Merchant;* and the educational memoir *Being With Children.* Lopate has also written extensively on movies for *Film Comment, Film Quarterly,* the *New York Times, Esquire, Vogue,* and *Interview.* A collection of his movie criticism and essays, *Totally, Tenderly, Tragically,* appeared in 1998. He served on the New York Film Festival Selection Committee from 1988 to 1991. He is currently Adams Professor of English at Hofstra University.

SERGE LOSIQUE

Serge Losique is the founder and president of the Montreal World Cinema Festival, one of the major film festivals in the world. Prior to that he was a professor of film and has written extensively on Canadian and other national cinemas.

TODD MCCARTHY

Todd McCarthy is the chief film critic for *Variety* and *Daily Variety* and a recipient of the international prize for film criticism, the Maurice Bessy Award. He is the author of the acclaimed biography *Howard Hawks: The Grey Fox of Hollywood* (1997), and the coeditor (with Charles Flynn) of the anthology *Kings of the Bs: Working Within the Hollywood System* (1975). He also wrote the introduction to the new edition of John Alton's book on cinematography, *Painting with Light* (1997). McCarthy wrote and codirected *Visions of Light: The Art of Cinematography,* which won the 1993 Documentary Award from the New York and National Society of Film Critics. He won an Emmy for writing the American Master Documentary *Preston Sturges: The Rise and Fall of an American Dreamer* (1990), cowrote the documentary *Hollywood Mavericks,* and wrote and directed *Forever Hollywood* for the American Cinematheque.

LEONARD MALTIN

Leonard Maltin is best known for his annual reference guide, *Leonard Maltin's Movie and Video Guide,* which he has edited since 1969. Since 1982 he has been a commentator and interviewer on television's *Entertainment Tonight.* His other books include *Leonard Maltin's Movie Encyclopedia: The Great American Broadcast, Of Mice and Magic: A History of American Animated Cartoons,*

The Great Movie Comedians, The Disney Films, The Art of the Cinematographer, Selected Short Subjects, and (as coauthor) *The Little Rascals: The Life and Times of Our Gang.* His articles have appeared in *Seattle Direct, Modern Maturity,* the *New York Times, Premiere, Smithsonian, TV Guide, Esquire,* the *Village Voice,* and *American Film.* He has served as guest curator at the Museum of Modern Art, was a member of the faculty of the New School for Social Research, and was president of the Los Angeles Film Critics Association in 1995 and 1996. In 1997, he was named to the National Film Preservation Board.

KATHLEEN MURPHY

A woman under the Sarrisean influence, Kathleen Murphy strong-armed the University of Washington's Department of English into approving its first film-dominated doctoral dissertation (*Howard Hawks: An Auteur in the Hemingway Tradition*), then created and headed a cinema studies program, taught film in the women's studies program, and curated numerous film series. A frequent speaker and panelist on such issues as sex and violence in contemporary cinema, women's roles and films, and the role of the film critic, she has also juried awards in film festivals. As a film critic, Murphy has published in *Movietone News, Seattle Weekly,* the *Village Voice,* and *Newsweek/Japan,* and she now writes for *Film Comment, Websites Cinema Online,* and *New York Sidewalk.* At the Film Society of Lincoln Center, where she is writer-in-residence, Murphy curated the first comprehensive look at Irish cinema and the first New York Sam Peckinpah retrospective.

JAMES NAREMORE

James Naremore is Chancellors' Professor of Communication and Culture at Indiana University. He has written several film books, including *Film Guide to Psycho,* a book on Vincente Minnelli's film work. Naremore's most recent book, *More Than Night: Film Noir in its Contexts,* won the Krasna Krausz Moving-Image Book Award for 1999–2000.

GERALD PEARY

Gerald Peary wrote a Ph.D. dissertation, "The Rise of the American Gangster Film, 1907–1930," at the University of Wisconsin, where he was a founding member of The Velvet Light Trap. He was a contributing editor to *American Film* and a film critic for *Flare, Toronto Magazine*, the *Boston Review*, and *The Real* paper. Currently, he is a film critic for the *Boston Phoenix*, where he writes a weekly column called "Film Culture." Peary is a professor of communication and journalism at Suffolk University, Boston, and a film studies lecturer at Boston University. He is the author of six books on cinema, including coediting the anthologies *The Classic American Novel and the Movies; The American Animated Cartoon;* and *Women and the Cinema: A Critical Anthology.* A seventh book, *Quentin Tarantino: Interviews,* will be published by the University Press of Mississippi. Peary is a member of the Boston Society of Film Critics and the National Society of Film Critics. For 1998–99, he was guest curator of the Harvard Film Archive.

RICHARD PENA

Richard Pena is program director of the Film Society of Lincoln Center and the New York Film Festival. He is an assistant professor of film studies at Columbia University.

JOHN SAYLES

Born in Schenectady, New York, John Sayles was educated at Williams College. He has published several novels, including *Pride of the Bimbos* and *Union Dues,* and a short-story anthology, *The Anarchist's Convention.* Sayles joined Roger Corman's stable, penning *Piranha, The Lady in Red,* and *Battle Beyond the Stars.* One of America's best-known independent filmmakers, he exercises total control over his work. *Return of the Secaucus Seven*, his 1980 directorial debut, was shot in four weeks at the low cost of $40,000. It was followed by *Lianna,* a subtle examination of the changes a married woman undergoes when she discovers her lesbianism; *Baby, It's You; The Brother from Another Planet,* a tale of a mute black alien adrift in Harlem; *Matewan,* an exploration of union-making and breaking in the West Virginia coal mines of the 1920s; *Eight Men Out,* an account of the 1919 Black Sox scandal that rocked the baseball world; *City of Hope; Passion Fish; The Secret of Roan Inish; Lone Star; Men with Arms;* and *Limbo.*

JAMES SCHAMUS

James Schamus is an associate professor of film theory, history, and production at Columbia University. He founded Good Machine with Ted Hope in 1991. In 1997, they produced *The Ice Storm,* which Schamus adapted from Rick Moody's novel and for which he won Best Screenplay at Cannes. The film continues Schamus's longstanding collaboration with Ang Lee, which includes coproducing *Sense And Sensibility* (Golden Bear, 1996 Berlin Festival; Golden Globe Award for Best Picture; Oscar for Best Adaptation); cowriting and associate producing *Eat Drink Man Woman* (Oscar nominee for Best Foreign Film, 1994); producing and cowriting *The Wedding Banquet* (Golden Bear, 1993 Berlin Festival and Oscar nominee for Best Foreign Film, 1993); and producing Lee's first feature, *Pushing Hands.* Schamus has been involved in four of Sundance's Grand Jury Prize Winners: Edward Burns's *The Brothers McMullen* (1995); Tom Noonan's *What Happened Was . . .* (1994); Alexandre Rockwell's *In the Soup* (1992); and Todd Haynes's *Poison* (1991).

RICHARD SCHICKEL

A film critic for *Time* magazine for over two decades, Richard Schickel is the author of more than twenty books, mostly about film, the latest of which is *Clint Eastwood: A Biography* (1997). Schickel's other books include the definitive study of Walt Disney, *The Disney Version;* the biography of D. W. Griffith, which won the 1985 British Film Institute Book Prize; a consideration of the celebrity system, *Intimate Strangers;* critical-biographical studies of Douglas Fairbanks Sr., Cary Grant, and James Cagney; a collection of longer film essays, *Schickel on Film;* and a novel, *Another I, Another You.* He is also the author of *Marlon Brando: A Life in Our Times* and *Double Indemnity,* a study of the Billy Wilder film in the British Film Institute Classic Film series. Schickel has four times been nominated for Emmys, has held a Guggenheim Fellowship, and has taught film criticism at Yale and the University of Southern California.

MARTIN SCORSESE

The son of a Sicilian immigrant family, Martin Scorsese was raised in a tenement in Little Italy. In 1968, after earning B.S. and M.A. degrees from

NYU's film school, he directed his first feature, *Who's That Knocking at My Door,* a small-scale, personal film about an Italian-American youth (played by Harvey Keitel). Scorsese worked on the editing of the landmark documentary *Woodstock* (1970) before turning out his second feature, *Boxcar Bertha* (1972). *Mean Streets* (1973), Scorsese's first significant film, was set in Little Italy and starred Keitel and Robert De Niro. It emphasized characterization rather than plot, and visual style marked by restless camera, elements that would find a more striking expression in *Taxi Driver* (1976), which won the Cannes Festival's Palm D'Or. Scorsese has been nominated three times for the directorial Oscar: for *Raging Bull* (1980), a intense psychological study of former middleweight boxing champion Jake La Motta; for *The Last Temptation of Christ* (1988), faithfully adapted from Nikos Kazantzakis's novel; and for *GoodFellas* (1990), which won the Venice Festival's Director Award.

HENRY SHEEHAN

Henry Sheehan is a film critic for the *Orange County Register.* Previously, he reviewed films for the *L.A. Weekly,* the *Hollywood Reporter,* and the *L.A. Reader.*

ED SIKOV

Ed Sikov is the author of *On Sunset Boulevard: The Life and Times of Billy Wilder* and three other books of film history and criticism. He earned his Ph.D. in film studies from Columbia University and is teaching at Haverford and Colorado College.

DANIEL TALBOT

Born in New York City, Daniel Talbot published *Film: An Anthology* in 1959. He was a film critic for the *Progressive,* 1959–60, and operated *New York Theatre* from 1960 to 1974. He has been president of New Yorker Films from 1985 to the present as well as operator of Lincoln Plaza Cinema. Other theaters operated by Talbot have included The Cinema Studio and The Metro on the Upper West Side, both of which are now closed.

DAVID THOMPSON

Based in San Francisco, David Thompson is the author of numerous film books, including the authorized biography *Showman: The Life of David O. Selznick; A Biographical Dictionary of Film* (now in its third edition); *Warren Beatty: A Life and a Story; Suspects; America in the Dark;* and *Wild Excursions: The Life and Fiction of Laurence Stern.*

KENNETH TURAN

Kenneth Turan is the film critic for the *Los Angeles Times* and the director of the Los Angeles Book Prizes. He was a book review editor for the *L.A. Times,* a staff writer for the *Washington Post* and *TV Guide,* and a film critic for National Public Radio's "All Things Considered" and Monitor Radio. A graduate of Swarthmore College and Columbia University's Graduate School of Journalism, he is the coauthor of *Call Me Anna: The Autobiography of Patty Duke.* He is on the board of directors of the National Yiddish Book Center (where he is chairman) and the Jane Austen Society of North America.

ELISABETH WEIS

Elisabeth Weis is professor of film at Brooklyn College and the Graduate Center of City University of New York. She was the first recipient of a doctorate in film from Columbia University and the third recipient of the unlikely titled chair Stern Professor of Humor at Brooklyn College. Her publications include *The Silent Scream: Alfred Hitchcock's Sound Track* and the anthology *Film Sound: Theory and Practice* (coedited with John Belton). As executive director of the National Society of Film Critics since 1974, she has edited two anthologies, *Movie Comedy* (with Stuart Byron) and *The Movie Star.* She reviewed films for the *Village Voice* in the 1970s and has also published in the *New York Times, American Film, Film Comment, Cineaste,* and *Encyclopedia Britannica.* In 1982, she cofounded and has since coedited the journal *Persistence of Vision.* Having never once defeated Sarris at singles tennis, she abandoned the racket for a piano and has since spent most of her spare time playing chamber music.

MICHAEL WILMINGTON

Michael Wilmington is the movie critic of the *Chicago Tribune* and formerly head critic or reviewer at *Isthmus* of Madison, *L.A. Weekly, L.A. Style,* and the *Los Angeles Times.* He has taught at the University of Southern California, UCLA CalArts and, currently, the University of Chicago Continuing Education Program. He is coauthor (along with Joseph McBride) of *John Ford,* which recently went into its third edition.